Uptown Girl

Uptown Girl

A MEMOIR

Christie Brinkley

HARPER
INFLUENCE

An Imprint of HarperCollins*Publishers*

UPTOWN GIRL. Copyright © 2025 by Christie Brinkley. All rights
reserved. Printed in the United States of America. No part of
this book may be used or reproduced in any manner whatsoever
without written permission except in the case of brief quotations
embodied in critical articles and reviews. For information, address
HarperCollins Publishers, 195 Broadway, New York, NY 10007.

HarperCollins books may be purchased for educational, business,
or sales promotional use. For information, please email the
Special Markets Department at SPsales@harpercollins.com.

FIRST EDITION

Designed by Bonni Leon-Berman

Library of Congress Cataloging-in-Publication Data has been applied for.

ISBN 978-0-06-338575-7

25 26 27 28 29 LBC 5 4 3 2 1

They loved each other
With all their might
Then they loved everyone else
In their sight
So I dedicate this book
With gratitude
To my parents for their
Amorous attitude
Donald Alan and Marjorie Marie
Thank you for literally
Setting me free
To try to be all
That I hoped to be
To not fear mistakes
And I made quite a few
And teaching me that's where
The light gets through
So to my dad the writer
And to my mom the homemaker
From your daughter, your "baby"
And sometime risk-taker
Here is the story
Of a few of my days
That contributed to
Your hair turning gray
With love forevermore.

Contents

Contents

Uptown Girl

Prologue

THE BLADES circled slowly at first, then began to turn faster and faster as the helicopter lifted up into the sky, so big and blue and open, the kind of sky that defines the American West. From where I sat inside the helicopter, I could see the San Juans jutting up from under heavy snow and thick carpets of frozen pine, and after we cleared the groomed slopes of the ski area, there was nothing to see other than unbroken wilderness.

So, this is heli-skiing, I thought, as excitement began to overtake the nerves I'd felt all morning, my stomach churning nearly as much as the deafening blades overhead. Steadying myself, I aimed my video camera lower, directly down and out the glass floor of the cockpit, peering at the outside world through my viewfinder. I could feel it, too, a familiar kind of vertigo as we sped higher and higher up alongside the mountains, into the rarefied air.

The trip, the air, my mind, my life in that moment—it all felt as dizzying as the view.

For a moment I thought about my husband, Billy, whom I'd split with again, and hoping this trip to Telluride would wake him up to the reality that he might actually lose me, I had agreed in a moment of derring-do to go heli-skiing, leaping onto a craggy peak to ski untouched powder with a group of friends that included a ruggedly handsome man who may or may not have been in love with me—and who, eventually, would impact my life in unimaginable ways.

The date, I'll never forget, was April 1, 1994—April Fools' Day—and after finishing a required course on the dangers of heli-skiing and then strapping a transponder to my chest in case of an avalanche, I had begun to wonder if I was the one being foolish. The weather report had called for snow that afternoon, and when I asked my friends if we should still go into the backcountry, they promised me it was worth it—that I just had to see the landscape and experience what it was like to make first tracks and that we'd be back before the storm.

They were right about the first promise. The landscape was incredible, and the ride was thrilling, and when we were finally over the spot where we wanted to land, on a small and narrow saddle between two peaks, the pilot swung the helicopter around to make sure the landing was clear, then took us out over the mountains and into a tight turn.

That's when the helicopter suddenly swooped, flipping my stomach the way it can when you drop down the sheer side of a roller coaster. "Is that normal?" I yelled over the racket of the rotor blades.

But I never got an answer, my words becoming the last intelligible ones you can hear on the video recording—which somehow, miraculously, survived the crash.

In the next instant, there was a loud popping, as if something had broken, and the helicopter just dropped, plummeting out of the sky like an elevator whose cables had been cut.

Oh, my god, we're crashing, I thought, as I saw the ground speeding up toward us, the boulders appearing larger and closer by the second. *This is not a special effect—this is* really *happening.*

If I die like this, my parents are going to kill me.

That's when I remembered I had written down my parents as my emergency contacts on the forms we all had to fill out that morning, printing in neat lettering next to their names and phone number the instructions, "Please be gentle and break the news slowly."

I had known. I had had a feeling.

Then I heard Billy's voice ring into my head as clear as a bell, with something he used to say: "I don't want to know when I'm going to die—I want to know *where*. And then I'm never going near the fucking place."

So, this is where I'm going to die. Well, at least it's a glamorous way to go . . .

Although wait—I'm not going anywhere. I can't. I'm a mom. Alexa Ray needs me.

But it was all so terrifying, and as I realized I was going to die, I decided I wanted my last thoughts to be about Alexa Ray, so I began projecting my soul toward hers, hoping to establish some sort of metaphysical or spiritual connection that would last into eternity. In that moment, it became clear to me that the only thing that mattered was that the people in my life knew how much I loved them.

In the end, it all comes down to love.

That's when the helicopter smashed into the rocks with such speed and force that the impact instantly ripped it apart, the pontoons and tail breaking first, with skis, glass, metal, gas, and fumes filling the air, causing a sickening noise and smell. Inside the shattered cabin, we began to bounce violently from the tip of one blade to another, spinning across the saddle and ricocheting back and forth, then side to side, as I repeated Alexa Ray's name over and over like a mantra.

For a second I thought about the actor Vic Morrow, who had been decapitated by helicopter blades in 1982 while filming a scene for the *Twilight Zone* movie, and began to wonder if that was what was going to happen to me.

In an instant, though, something changed, and we had bounced right off the saddle and started rolling down the steepest side of the mountain, tossing us about the wrecked cabin like clothes inside a laundry machine.

Why haven't I fainted? Aren't you supposed to faint when this happens?

But I didn't faint, as my mind kept spinning: *Alexa Ray, Alexa Ray, I love you so much.*

And then, suddenly, I felt light on my face. I opened my eyes, for the first time in what felt like hours. I realized, miraculously, that somehow I had made it outside the wreckage of the helicopter.

For a split second, I thought I was safe. But then I felt something yank my leg and realized with dread that I was being dragged down the mountain by my seat belt, wrapped around my ski boot and still attached to the doomed helicopter, which was now no longer rolling but sliding toward a sheer cliff. In that moment, I decided to channel everything I'd ever believed about the power of magic and the prevalence of miracles.

So, let me tell you about Chimayo.

Two weeks before the crash, when I visited Telluride for the first time, I went to the Santuario de Chimayo, north of Sante Fe, and fell in love with the hope and miracles emanating from that tiny sanctuary tucked into the Sangre de Cristo Mountains, where the Pueblo Indians believe the golden soil inside can protect anyone who touches it. I found the entire idea to be magical and began wearing a small charm of Chimayo dirt as a necklace, scattering some inside the helicopter that morning before we took off.

Days after the crash, after the storm had finally lifted, investigators flew up to the crash site, and after picking through the twisted wreckage, they told the press they were stunned that anyone had made it out alive, calling our survival nothing short of a miracle. That they also found my Chimayo charm amid the snow and wreckage still amazes me.

Was it the miracle of Chimayo that saved me—and all of us—that day? I don't know. But what I do know is that when you believe in magic, magic happens.

And if you want to believe in the magic with me, let the adventure begin.

PART I

Malibu

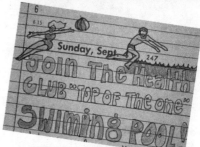

Sunday, Sept. 247

JOiN The HeaLTh
CLUB "ToP of THe oNe"
SWiMiNG POOL!

1

The beginning is like a black-and-white movie, one in which the film keeps breaking up, then picking back up again later, in another time and place.

Flash, click, frame change: Roll the next memory.

LONG BEFORE the camera was on me, I was the camera, my young eyes filming the world around me as I framed and narrated my life, the star of my own movie. "The pavement was hot as she stepped out onto the street. She was forbidden to cross into the cornfield, but now that she knew what was on the other side . . ."

I was born on February 2, 1954, Groundhog Day. Like the eponymous movie about the weatherman who relives the same day over and over again before eventually finding true love, many things in my life have looped and re-looped, reappearing and repeating in ways I would never have imagined: the good and the bad, the marriages and, most of all, the magic.

The first time I felt the magic was in the cornfield across from my childhood home in Canoga Park, a neighborhood just northeast of

Los Angeles, sunken into the San Fernando Valley. I wasn't born in Canoga Park but in Monroe, Michigan, a small town outside Detroit, on the western lick of Lake Erie. But because my parents moved from Monroe to Los Angeles when I was just six months old, I've always considered myself a California girl, a description that followed me throughout my modeling career.

Flash, click, frame change.

Let's edit that last part: It wasn't "my parents" who moved from Monroe, Michigan, when I was an infant. My mom, whom I adored, and my biological dad, a man named Herb Hudson, were the ones who moved. I don't remember how or when my mom met Herb, but they were married for at least a decade until they got divorced, when I was eight. Shortly after, my mom met and married Don Brinkley, whom I've always referred to (and still do) as my father. After her wedding with Don, my mom acted as though her life with Herb—and our lives with him by proxy—had never existed.

I still have memories of those days with Herb, but they come in fits and starts, and all are in black and white, like the photos in the albums my mom kept from those days, where Herb is cut out of every picture, like a body removed from a crime scene.

I remember riding bikes with my brother, Greg, who is eighteen months older than me and so similar looking, with our white-blond hair, ice-blue eyes, and warm bronze skin, that people used to think we were twins. When I was young, I couldn't keep pace with Greg on a bike, but he'd still let me ride with him to the edge of the freeway, where we'd pump our arms up and down as though we were band conductors, trying to get the truckers to blow their horns. When they did, we'd jump and scream "Yay!" in our little, flutelike voices, which were quickly swallowed up by the big horns on the highway.

I didn't hang out only with Greg. I remember posing for party photos with friends in my Prince Valiant pageboy and favorite outfit:

a puffy white party dress with a cropped red vest and patent-leather Mary Janes over thin white ankle socks. And I had a good friend, Deb, who lived across the street, in a house with an ashtray that looked like a real microphone.

One day, I decided to use the ashtray to pretend to be a singer, holding down a button on the handle as I crooned breathlessly into the "microphone" in front of Deb and a throng of imaginary fans. "Thank you so much, ladies and gentlemen," I purred. "Thank you, thank you. You've been a great audience."

As Deb clapped madly, I swayed and blew a kiss to the rest of my make-believe admirers while still holding my microphone . . . which, during my musical number, had heated up because, as it turned out, the microphone was also an electric cigarette lighter. When I took my bow and kissed the microphone in a dramatic finale gesture, my lips singed and stuck to the heated lighter. My mom came rushing to take me home, where for the rest of the night she applied cold compresses to my burned lips. But for what it's worth, you can say I put on a hot show.

Another day, I was showing Deb the two alligators Herb Hudson's parents had sent us from Florida as a gift—yes, you used to be able to keep alligators as pets and even ship them cross-country as souvenirs from Florida. When Deb saw them, she was terrified that they were going to bite me. Oddly enough, I never got nipped by the alligators, but Deb bit my arm so intensely once that she left a small mouth-size scar that makeup artists later tried to hide from the camera. If you look closely enough, you can still see it.

I have other scars from my early childhood, too, ones I haven't talked so openly about. These are emotional scars from Herb Hudson, whom I didn't like. Neither did my mom. He was unhappy, unkind, and oftentimes cruel.

Nearly every night, after Herb came home from work as a milkman for the Carnation Company, he took off his belt and whipped me.

13

Other nights, he'd take me into the bathroom and wash my mouth out with soap, scouring until I tasted lye.

It didn't matter how good or quiet I was: Herb always seemed to find a reason to punish me. Sometimes, he'd order me to the den, where I was to wait to be whipped. Other times, he'd do it immediately, in the kitchen or living room. I'm not sure which was worse: the anticipation of pain or its instant application. Either way, as soon as I saw him reaching for his belt, I knew what was about to happen.

My mom was also frightened of Herb, although I never saw him hit her. She always tried to make everything just so by the time he got home from work, making sure we were already in our pajamas and ready for bed. During the day, she'd spend her time cleaning and organizing, hoping to have things perfect for Herb. Because she was so distracted by trying to protect us from him, I often felt alone when we lived with Herb. But I also learned to develop my own defense mechanisms, which included hiding copies of *Life* magazine in my pajamas so that when Herb whipped me, it wouldn't hurt as much.

In addition to using his belt and the soap, Herb also threatened to send me to an orphanage whenever he perceived I'd done something wrong. As a young girl, I believed this threat was real and lived in fear of the possibility. I had already seen all the Shirley Temple movies, and I knew an orphanage was no place I wanted to be.

THERE WERE some happy occasions during my early childhood, too, like when Greg and I could watch Westerns on TV. I loved Westerns, especially if they starred John Wayne or my favorite Hollywood couple, Roy Rogers and Dale Evans. I also watched *Sky King*, a television series about a cowboy who could fly planes and ride horses. (*Jump cut to the future*: One day, I will meet a real cowboy, or so I will think, who will also fly planes and ride horses. I will marry him. But like the

TV show from my youth, almost everything about this man will also be fiction.)

The primary reason I loved Westerns was for the horses. I had read all the *Black Beauty* books and *National Velvet*, but in the movies, the horses took on a mythical, almost magical significance for me. I watched in awe as they galloped across a grassy hill or jumped through red rock canyons. And the Wild West! It seemed so much more majestic than what I saw outside our home in Canoga Park. I wanted to go where those horses roamed—where *I* could roam.

But the thing I remember most from those black-and-white years—my most vivid memory of my early childhood—took place in the cornfield across the street from our house, which we'd always been forbidden to enter. Or, really, it took place on the other side of that forbidden cornfield.

The day it happened, I was in trouble. Big trouble. I'm not sure what I had done, or even if I had done anything at all, but Herb had sent me to the den to wait to be whipped.

I hated the den. Everything inside the room was sullen and gray, including the ugly, ash-colored couch, the tired old wingback chair, and walls the same shade as smokestacks. Even the portrait of my mom Herb had painted looked sullen and gray, and my beautiful mom was anything but sullen and gray.

Waiting there to be whipped that day, I thought about how I could escape. Could I hide behind the wingback chair? No, at age six, I was too big not to be noticed. Could I cower inside the cramped coat closet? I walked over to the closet and gripped the doorknob tightly to see if I could.

But then, suddenly, my hand still clutching the doorknob, I felt my feet lift off the ground from under me, as I began to float upward. I don't remember opening a window or how I got out, but just like that, I was out of that awful room and floating over the forbidden cornfield. It was like the scene in *Peter Pan* when Tinker Bell takes

Peter and Wendy flying high above London—one of my favorite movies—except, now, instead of flying over a city like Peter and Wendy, I was soaring above acre upon acre of corn, the stalks neatly lined up and glimmering like gold beneath me.

On and on I floated, for what seemed like quite a while, until I noticed a large ranch house at the corner of the field with a wonderful-looking white horse fence. I turned my body, squinting to get a closer look, when I realized, agog, that penned inside the fence was Trigger, the famous palomino owned by none other than Roy Rogers. From above, I could see the horse's tawny body, glistening like melted caramel in the California sun, as he shook his straw-colored mane across the white blaze of his big, golden face. I was so captivated by the horse that I almost didn't see the woman standing next to Trigger, the one who looked just like Dale Evans, her hair tightly curled under a small cowboy hat.

All of a sudden, I heard heavy footsteps coming down the hall outside the den. *Oh, my god*, I thought. *I'm going to get into so much trouble if he finds me floating above the cornfield!*

But, then, *boom*, my feet were back on the ground, and I was inside the awful den again, my hand still gripping the closet doorknob, as Herb thudded down the hall, the sound of his footsteps coming closer and closer. He slammed open the door, and with his belt in one hand, he grabbed me with the other, spun me around, and started to whip me.

Flash, click, frame change . . . Please.

THE NEXT day, I told all the neighborhood kids to meet me under the big tree on the other side of the cornfield, where our parents couldn't see us.

"Listen," I said in a hushed tone after a dozen or so kids had gathered. "I know where Trigger and Roy Rogers and Dale Evans live, and I'm going to take you there. And we're going to go through the cornfield."

There were a few gasps and a couple of murmurs, as the neighborhood kids looked to one another and then back at me. One by one, though, they nodded in solemn agreement. They would do it. They would cross the forbidden cornfield. They wanted to see Trigger, too.

Like soldiers on a mission, we filed into the field one by one, me leading the troops into unknown territory. I wasn't scared, though: I knew where to go, and despite what our parents had warned us many times about the cornfield, I knew we weren't going to get lost. Besides, I wanted so badly to share with the other kids what I had seen and, moreover, confirm for myself that what I had seen had been real.

We must have walked through that cornfield for at least two hours, at times singing "Happy Trails," the theme song of *The Roy Rogers and Dale Evans Show*, but no one complained. They trusted me, and I felt emboldened by their trust. I didn't want to let them down. And I didn't want to let myself down.

Finally, I spotted a little opening in the field and, framed through the stalks, a sliver of a familiar-looking street. "Okay, we have to turn this way," I announced determinedly, weaving the group out of the maize and toward the opening.

And there it was, just like what I saw when I floated over the day before. It was the same house I had seen, distinguishable by its huge horse fence and the pièce de résistance, Trigger, standing in the front yard in all his glory.

When the neighborhood kids caught sight of the stallion, they started whooping with delight.

"Wow, wow, there's Trigger!" one boy yelled.

"It's really Trigger! Come here, Trigger!" a little girl screeched.

We all rushed to the fence, a few kids hitching themselves up on the lower slat and everyone holding out their hands and clicking their tongues, trying to get Trigger to come.

The sight we must have made! There we were, a gaggle of kids bedraggled by dirt and corn silk, trespassing on someone's front lawn while clambering to touch Hollywood's most famous horse.

In our mania for Trigger, we didn't even notice Dale Evans until she was right in front of us, staring down at us like a vision straight from our TV screens. "Well, look at all of you," she said, chuckling warmly. "What are you kids doing here?"

"I came to introduce them to you!" I blurted out while trying to maintain the polite voice I reserved for nice adults. "You're Dale Evans! And I knew how to find your house."

"That's very kind of you," Dale said, her eyes smiling down at me. "Why don't you all come inside? I've just made some fresh cookies."

What? Dale Evans inviting us inside her home? For fresh cookies? We looked at one another in disbelief. "It's Dale Evans!" the oldest boy whispered to our group. "I'm sure it's okay."

"Yes! Yes! Thank you!" we cried in unison.

Dale opened the horse fence and led us across the corral and into the ranch house she shared with her husband, Roy Rogers. Immediately, I smelled the cozy scent of warm cookies, as the TV star handed each of us one from a big baking sheet. Holding my cookie and taking small nibbles, I looked around in wonder at everything: the paintings, the posters, the cowboy regalia. I was gobsmacked, and the other kids were just as wide-eyed as I was.

Our time inside Dale Evans's home was brief, though. Before we could even finish our cookies, she told us she had seen a report on the news that an entire neighborhood of kids had gone missing earlier that day. Were we those children? she wanted to know. She had called the police, an admission that elicited a few gasps from our group. But not to worry: we weren't in any trouble, she said. I didn't care either way. The adventure had been a success.

When the police showed up, Dale thanked us for visiting before we were ushered into the back seats of several police cars, the nice officers promising to let us ride all the way home with the sirens on and lights flashing. I can't remember if I got punished for the escapade, but if I did, it wouldn't have been different from any other day.

What really happened? I can't tell you, but I do believe we were inside Roy Rogers and Dale Evans's home that day.

YEARS LATER, after I was married to Billy Joel and started going on tour with him, I became good friends with his creative director, Steve Cohen, who still does all the lights and production design for Billy's shows. Steve knew I had grown up in Canoga Park and told me that he had, too, and that Roy Rogers and Dale Evans had lived near him. In the *New York Times* archives, you can also find an article about a bus crash that killed Roy and Dale's little girl after their church group from Canoga Park collided with seven other cars on the 101.

There are many things in my life I can't explain, and for that, I feel incredibly fortunate: it's part of the magic and mystery of being alive. And I'd much rather live in the magic than dwell on the misery—any day, any hour. I've had both, that's for sure, but for me, magic wins every time.

2

When I was eight years old, my black-and-white movie suddenly turned Technicolor. It was as though someone had flipped a switch inside my little filmmaker's mind, and I could instantly see in brilliant blues, reds, pinks, purples, golds, and greens. Life was much more vivid and vibrant, and while my problems with Herb Hudson didn't dissipate overnight, it was as though the movie of my life had finally begun in earnest and whatever had happened before was just a monochromic prelude—one that would eventually fade away like photos in an old album.

The fact that the man who brought color into my life also worked in television wasn't lost on me. When my mom met Don Brinkley, he was already an eminent writer who would author hundreds of episodes for series like *Bat Masterson*, *Ben Casey*, *The F.B.I.*, *The Fugitive*, *Ironside*, and *Trapper John, M.D.* For years, I've liked to say that Don made the magic happen, both on-screen and in our lives, and for that, I loved him, as I still do. I've also liked to say that I was the one who introduced my mom to Don, taking credit for what became the most fortuitous meeting of her life—and one of the luckiest of mine, too.

Flash, click, frame change.

I WAS seven when my mother and Herb Hudson separated. This happened in the early 1960s, when not many couples divorced, but my mom was unhappy and, I believe, terrified for herself and for us. So, she moved out of our home in Canoga Park, taking Greg and me with her, and into a cramped apartment on the other side of town that overlooked more alleyways and vacant lots than actual roads and homes. It was all she could afford at the time, and I made the best of it, turning the trash shed outside our building into my own private fort.

My mom had been a housewife while she was married to Herb, but after they separated, she took a job as a switchboard operator, using her lovely, low rumble of a voice, like a contralto, to connect callers. She had a great laugh, too, the kind that made you want to laugh along with her, even if you had no idea what was so funny, and callers loved her, instantly recognizing her by her voice whenever she picked up.

"Oh, hi, it's you! Margie! It's Tom! Can you connect me to Bill?"

"Of course, Tom, honey. Bill's here, and he's fabulous! Stand by."

One day, my mom had to deliver an envelope for her boss to a client across town, and she asked if I wanted to come along. Of course I did: I always wanted to spend as much time with my mom as possible. We hopped into her car and drove together across the Valley.

"Be on the lookout for this address," she said, slowly articulating the number and the name of the street, making me feel as though I were her very important assistant.

I dutifully kept watch, my eyes peeled out the window, and within minutes, I spotted the address. "There it is, Mom! Over there!" I said, pointing to a low-rise office building that looked like a 1960s motel, with a staircase running up the outside and rows of doors that opened onto a parking lot.

"Okay, Christie, this envelope needs to go to 7B," she said after she had parked, handing me the package. "Can you do it?"

"Yes!"

"I'll be able to see you from here and will be watching you the whole time," she said sternly as I jumped out of the car. "Don't go anywhere else, and don't go inside any offices, okay?"

I nodded obediently, pleased and eager to be able to help my overworked mom on her very important mission. Scanning the first row of doors, I realized 7B was on the second floor, so I climbed up, spotted what I thought was the right office, and knocked on the door with my most polite rap.

A man in a white-collared shirt and horn-rimmed glasses stepped out.

"Hi! I'm delivering this envelope to Mr. David Rosen," I said, doing my best imitation of the smart secretaries I had seen on TV.

"Oh, I think you have the wrong office, young lady," the man replied warmly. "Dave's just down the hall." The man stepped outside and pointed to another door while scanning the parking lot, no doubt looking for the adult who must have been accompanying me. "That's your mom down there?" he asked, pointing to my beautiful mom, who was craning her head curiously out the window to see what was happening.

"Yes, that's her!"

The man waved.

My mom fluttered up her hand.

"All right, then, let me take you to Dave's office," he said, steering me down the hall while swiveling his head to make sure my mom could see us the entire time.

When we got to 7B, the nice man knocked on the door. "This lovely young lady has a package for you, Dave," he said after Dave appeared, allowing me to hand the envelope to its rightful recipient.

The nice man then asked if he could escort me back to my mom.

I nodded eagerly, and when we got to the parking lot, my mom's pretty face was already smiling out the window.

"I just wanted to compliment you on your daughter," the man said to my mom. "She knocked on my door by accident, and she was very polite."

As they continued to chat, I walked around to the passenger side of our car, feeling very satisfied with myself for completing this essential task to the admiration of such a nice man with an important enough job to have his own office in the Valley.

That man was Don Brinkley.

Less than a week later, after I got home from school one afternoon, my mom said Don had called to ask her out to dinner that night. I was excited that the nice man was coming for a visit and asked if I could be the one to greet him when he arrived. Later that night, when I heard a tap at the door, I jumped up and threw the door open, and there on the other side was Don, nattily dressed in a blue button-down shirt and khaki pants, holding a pink plastic purse, which he handed to me.

"This is for me?" I asked incredulously, dumbfounded that someone I barely knew would give me a gift.

Don nodded and smiled.

After thanking him profusely, I went to play with my present, thrilled to find inside the pink pretend purse, a pair of pink plastic heels, a little makeup mirror, and a tube of play lipstick. I was in heaven—it was the best gift anyone had ever given me. For weeks, I clomped around in my little plastic heels while carrying my purse and pretending to apply lipstick in its mirror.

My mom's relationship with Don progressed quickly, as they started spending more and more time together. But it also unfolded respectfully: my mom was still legally married to Herb, and in the 1960s, divorcees were viewed as somewhat scandalous. Despite this,

Don was there for Greg and me in ways we had never experienced with Herb. On their third date, for example, when he came over to pick up my mom, I saw him eyeing our sad, meager Charlie Brown Christmas tree with nothing underneath it. The next day, he arrived with an armful of presents and placed them beneath the tree. This was a new phenomenon for me: Herb rarely gave Greg or me a Christmas gift, letting our mom do all the holiday shopping with whatever she managed to save from the grocery money he gave her.

I still saw Herb after he and my mom separated, at least for the first few months. He had weekly visitation days, always on the weekends, when he'd pick us up on Sundays and drive us through the canyons to Zuma Beach, the big public stretch of shore in Malibu. I loved weaving through the canyons and was always excited to get to the beach, but once there, Herb would pay us no attention. On a few occasions, he even brought along a girlfriend we either didn't know or didn't like. The only time he was attentive to us was when it was time to leave, and he'd get so furious because we were too wet and sandy to get back into his car, or so he thought, toweling us off so forcefully that our skin would be raw and red with abrasions. After my first beach trip with Herb, I pleaded with my mom never to make us go again, but those outings were his legal right—at least for the time being.

By comparison, Don acted as though he couldn't wait to spend time with us and seemed genuinely interested in whatever we were interested in, even our most puerile hobbies. For example, as a kid, I loved to play with the water that ran from the rain gutters or the shower heads at the beach, redirecting it through the dirt or sand to create mini moated villages. With Herb, this hobby was strongly discouraged, as it likely meant getting dirty or sandy. But with Don he picked up his army shovel and hopped right into the sand next to me.

From the beginning, Don was also always willing to help us with our homework, putting aside whatever writer's deadline he had to do so. Oftentimes, after we went to bed, I would hear him tapping away at his typewriter late into the night, catching up on the work he'd ignored for our sake. I came to find the sound of his typewriter so soothing because with it, I knew he was there, right outside my door, and that we were safe with him.

Don and my mom didn't live together at first: he lived in Malibu, in a great apartment in a building perched on pilings that spiraled down into the sand of the beach. After they'd been dating for several months, though, Don decided he wanted my mom to live closer, so he rented us a tiny house on Old Malibu Road, at the bottom of Puerco Canyon, which slices through the mountains above Malibu. I loved that house. The front yard was completely covered in ice plant—if you like to garden, as I do, you know that ice plants are hardy succulents with pretty, daisy-like flowers—and the house itself was directly across the street from the beach. I was over the moon, spending time at the ocean whenever I could and sledding down the hill outside the house on the ice plant, its juicy little leaves as slippery as snow for a kid with a cardboard box. Also, the house was on a dead-end street quiet enough that my mom let us skateboard right on the road outside. The best part, though, were the two reefs that jutted out into the ocean from our beach, one we called Pier Rock and the other Volcano Rock, which each had tide pools full of sea anemone and, underwater, abalone that lined the craggy slopes. These two rocks were my most cherished playground, and whenever I visit Malibu today, I make a special trip just to see them.

The day we moved into our new home, however, was horrible. My mom, Greg, and I were at the old house in Canoga Park, the one we had lived in with Herb, who was there at the same time, too. Greg and I lay sprawled on the floor of the living room, watching TV, while our mom packed up the last of our things. That's when we heard a knock at the front door: it was Don, there to help us bring boxes to the new house in Puerco Canyon.

But when Don walked in, before he could even say anything, Herb came rushing in from another room and starting punching him in the face, blow after blow. Don tried to shield his face, imploring Herb to stop hitting him, but Herb wouldn't stop. The two then tumbled into the TV room, where Herb grabbed a coat hanger from a closet, bent it, and, as we kids watched in horror, stabbed it through Don's cheek. Blood started to gush, my mom started to scream, and Herb slinked out the front door.

I was shocked. I had never witnessed anything so violent, not even from Herb, and couldn't fathom why he would do such a thing to Don, who was so kind and gentle. I hated Herb in that moment, and like my mom, I began to tremble and cry.

Seeing me upset, Don walked over, enfolded me in a big bear hug, and started to apologize, even though he had done nothing wrong. "I didn't want that, sweetie," he said softly, as I buried my face in his chest. "You shouldn't have been exposed to that. That kind of violence is never okay."

That fight was one of the last times I ever saw Herb Hudson. The final time was in a Los Angeles County courtroom.

HERE, MY story reverts momentarily back to black and white, like a color movie interrupted abruptly by a splice of old, forgotten footage—a hiccup in the new, happier life I was living. My memories of that day inside a Los Angeles County courtroom are broken and patchy, like my memories of my life with Herb, but I know how his words made me feel and that what happened that day in court has since been repeated, re-looping and reappearing in my life like an ill-fated scene from *Groundhog Day*.

A few weeks before it happened, my mom and Don were married in a small ceremony at the Hotel Bel-Air. I was the flower girl, which I perceived to be a huge honor, but more so, I was ecstatic to see my mom married to Don because she was happier than she'd ever been. She even seemed more beautiful to me after the wedding, looking like a movie star as she sat in a bathing suit on the deck of Don's apartment, with her platinum-blond hair, wraparound sunglasses, and wide smile, balancing a long cigarette holder in one hand and a glass of wine in the other. (This was the 1960s, after all, when *everyone* smoked.)

After their wedding, my mom told Greg and me that we had "grown-up stuff" to take care of and that we needed to go to court to do so. In particular, she said, Herb had decided he didn't have the time to take care of us, and Don was going to be our new dad. She said we were lucky that Herb was so busy and that Don, who was a good person, wanted to be our father.

I was only eight at the time and didn't fully understand what was about to take place, but on the day our mom promised, we went to court, Greg and I sitting with her on the benches facing the judge while Herb and Don sat on either side of him. There were other people in the courtroom that day, too—lots of lawyers and other families and individuals waiting to make their own appearance before the judge. I distinctly remember that we had an audience for what was about to happen.

My mom was nervous and fidgety, especially when the judge turned to Herb and gave him a grave look. "Do you realize that you're about to give up your full parental rights to Christie and Greg?" the judge asked him.

"Yes, I do," Herb replied, as coldly and flatly as if he had been asked to state his full name for the court.

"I need you to understand that you'll no longer be the father of Christie and Greg," the judge said, looking imploringly at Herb.

"I understand," Herb said without a blink, twitch, or any other indication of emotion.

I was stunned. What was happening? Why didn't Herb Hudson want me anymore? Why didn't he love me? Had I done something wrong?

Question after question began to tear through my mind as I stared blankly in front of me. I felt lifeless and numb, as though someone in the courtroom had drawn the blood from my body, leaving me unable to move, think, or feel. I could tell something significant had just taken place, but I didn't know exactly what or how to process it.

At the same time, the proceedings kept going, and the judge was now turning to Don. "Don Brinkley, do you accept full parental responsibilities to be the father of Christie and Greg?" he asked.

"Yes, absolutely," Don said, sending my mom, Greg, and me a sincere look from across the courtroom.

My heart skipped. *Wait, Don wants me? This nice man actually wants to be my father?*

A bit of blood returned to my face, and I started to wonder what life would be like with Don as our dad. I suddenly felt a huge sense of relief, realizing that I would never be whipped, spanked, rubbed raw with towels, or made to gag on soap again.

YEARS LATER, I watched the same scene play out in another courtroom, this time in Manhattan, when my third husband did something similar to our infant son, Jack, relinquishing all parental rights. And I had nearly the same reaction at the time that I had had as an eight-year-old, feeling lifeless and numb, wondering what life would be like for my child without his biological father.

I SAW a psychiatrist only once in my life. It was in 2008, when a court ordered me to do so during my divorce from my fourth husband, Peter Cook. The reason was ridiculous: Peter had already admitted to having an affair with one girl and to communicating with others online, but we were both mandated by the judge to undergo psychiatric evaluation.

Nevertheless, I kept all my appointments with my psychiatrist, even when my last session conflicted with a speech I was scheduled to give at the United Nations on the abolishment of nuclear weapons on the behalf of the Global Security Institute. Because the psychiatrist wouldn't let me reschedule, I met with him only minutes before rushing to the UN to give the address, trying not to appear rattled onstage by what I had just discussed with the doctor.

I told the psychiatrist everything I could about my four marriages during our time together, ending our session by sharing with him what had happened that day with Herb Hudson long ago in the L.A. County courtroom.

After a moment of silence, the psychiatrist cocked his head and looked at me intently. "I don't see how you could ever trust a man again after what you've been through," he said resolutely.

I sat back in my seat, surprised that anyone would draw such a conclusion. "But I believe in love," I said, putting my hand over my heart. "And I believe that if it's the right person and it's really true love, it can outshine all the pain, betrayal, and deception."

I'm still hoping to prove him wrong.

3

C hristie, Christie, wake up."

    I rolled over toward the voice and rubbed sleep from my eyes. I could see the sun peeking in through the curtains and the ocean just beyond, large and listless on a Saturday morning.

"Christie, Christie . . ."

It was my dad. I opened my eyes to see Don sitting on the side of my bed with a sparkle in his eye that meant something wonderful was about to happen.

"Do you want to go to Mexico today?"

"Mexico?" I asked, scooting to sit up and feeling suddenly very awake. "Yes! Yes, I do!"

"Okay," he said, jumping to his feet. "Pack a bag with your swimsuit and something to wear to dinner, and let's go! We're leaving in an hour."

In an hour? On a plane to Mexico? This was so exciting! Nine-year-old me had never been to Mexico . . . or, really, anywhere in the world. And not only were we going, but we were also doing it on a whim, which was something that would happen only to the star of my imaginary movie (which was me). But this time, it was no longer make-believe.

After my parents were married, my world turned Technicolor, meaning life became more vivid, vibrant, and alive. But my world also grew bigger, literally and figuratively, as if someone had finally thought to widen the window of the projector showing the movie of my life—like that weekend my dad spontaneously took us to Puerto Vallarta, Mexico. The very first time I saw Mexico—skipping down on a Saturday and coming back in time for school on Monday—I was mesmerized by how life there spilled out into the streets, people sitting outside their shops weaving straw baskets or carving little wooden ornaments while cats, dogs, and chickens wandered in and out of the homes. My dad knew the best places to get away from the big hotels and resort restaurants, taking us by boat to Yelapa, a village south of Puerto Vallarta, where the homes were rustic and we hiked to a waterfall. Over time, we started going to Tijuana, too, which was an easy drive from Los Angeles and a playland for a kid like me, who loved being on the beach and seeing all the toys and trinkets in the tourist shops that people made by hand. Back then, I was incredibly drawn to Mexico and its food, art, and culture. I still am today.

(*Jump cut*: These early trips undoubtedly influenced what would happen years later, when I would fall in love with a dashing polo player on the coast of Mexico, just south of Yelapa. But that's a story for another time.)

IT WASN'T just Mexico. Another weekend, my dad woke us up to say that we were going for brunch that same day in San Francisco. So, I packed a little to-go bag, and off we went to the airport, making the quick flight up to San Francisco, where my dad was the happy tour guide, taking us on the trolley cars and down the coast to look at the sea otters. He also took us to see the musical *Funny Girl*, starring a young Barbra Streisand. The performance affected me profoundly, sparking a lifelong fascination with musicals and Broadway. Our weekend trips to San Francisco eventually became tradition, and we started spending the night at the Sir Francis Drake, a historic hotel where, for breakfast, my parents ordered cheese blintzes and Ramos gin fizzes, which are elegant cocktails made from orange blossom water and whipped egg white. It felt fancy and fun; moreover, it felt happy. *I* felt happy.

My parents had a way of making life feel fancy and fun without spending a lot of money. They preferred simple things, which included living in my dad's apartment in Malibu, the one perched on pilings over the ocean that became our home, too, after my mom, Greg, and I moved in. While the apartment felt fancy to me—I could wake up every morning and see the ocean or watch the sun set over the Pacific at night—it was still an apartment, not the mega-mansions for the very rich that people often associate with the area. I shared a bedroom with Greg until we got too old, which prompted my parents to move. Our big claim to fame in the apartment was that we lived next door to the Creature from the Black Lagoon—or at least the actor who played it.

Another reason life felt fancy and fun was that my dad was curious and loved to explore, teaching me to adopt the same mentality, which opened the world up to me. Every day was an adventure, even if we never left Los Angeles or the beach right outside our home.

From my dad, I learned that it was up to me—and only me—to create the life I wanted.

"Christie, baby, you write your own script," he always said. "So, go out there and make sure you write a damn good one." He also told me that I could still control my script when life went sideways or things I wanted seemed out of reach. "You just got to figure out how to write yourself out of that corner, honey," he said whenever anything disappointing, unfortunate, or even terrible happened.

I can't tell you how valuable this advice has been over the last sixty years, because I've written myself out of *a lot* of corners.

But as a girl, I knew my script needed to include horses, so, with my dad's help and a part-time job mucking out stalls, I took riding lessons at the White Sun, a dude ranch outside Palm Springs, where we went on vacation. Back then, the desert was less developed, and at the White Sun, I could ride horses like I'd seen in the movies, weaving in and out of cacti, between pale pink walls of sandstone, and up and down the dry ravines that lance the Coachella Valley.

Back in Malibu, my parents had a great group of friends in our building, and we often did things together as a community, like creating an annual contest to see who could build the most seaworthy boat from driftwood and any other treasures we could find on the beach. I couldn't believe how lucky I was to live there, and while the trauma of what had happened with Herb didn't disappear, my dad showed us so much love and affection that it was easy to forget the past. And because my mom didn't talk about Herb, and I didn't miss him, my early life with him began to seem like a poorly scripted pilot that wasn't ready for prime time—at least, not *my* prime time.

After the pall of Herb Hudson went away, my mom's demeanor changed. She became more present and more three-dimensional, wrapping me up in her love and laughter all the time. Her newfound happiness emanated wherever she went, even if it was just up the street to the local service station.

"John, how's it going?" my mom would call out the window as she drove up and John wrangled the gas nozzle into the tank of our car. "Did you ditch that girl yet? She doesn't deserve you—and you know you deserve better."

"Yeah, Mrs. Brinkley. We broke up," John would say, winking through the window at Greg and me in the back seat. "And I met a new girl! She's great and treating me just right."

"Good for you, John!" my mom would say, smacking the steering wheel in enthusiasm. "I'm happy for you! And we'll see you here next week, all right?"

"All right, Mrs. Brinkley! We'll see you next week."

As I grew older, my parents grew with me. When I started to get into music, my dad would sit and listen with me whenever I got a new album, not minding if I put the needle back on the same song three times over just because I thought it was so cool. This was how I introduced him to Joni Mitchell, Bob Dylan, and the Beatles, among others, and in return, he introduced me to American and international artists like Stan Getz, João Gilberto, Astrud Gilberto, Ray Charles, Dinah Washington, Ella Fitzgerald, Billie Holiday, and Edith Piaf. And it was Edith Piaf's songs that eventually became part of the soundtrack to one of my greatest love affairs ever, the one I would have with French language and culture.

I FIRST fell in love with the French language when I saw *Les Parapluies de Cherbourg* (*The Umbrellas of Cherbourg* in English). The musical film, starring a young and charming Catherine Deneuve, is about a girl working in her mother's umbrella shop when she falls head over heels for a garage mechanic. After he's drafted into the Algerian War, the girl, persuaded by her mother, reluctantly marries an affluent jeweler and starts a family with him. Years later, she unexpectedly runs into the mechanic at a service station. He invites her inside, and the two have a conversation before they part wistfully, returning to their disparate lives: she as a wealthy, unhappily married wife and he as the owner of a service station, also unhappily married. The beauty, though, is that each is still madly in love with the other.

(*Jump cut*: This service station scene will play out in a similar way for me much later, when I star in the music video for Billy Joel's hit song "Uptown Girl.")

By the time the movie was over, I was captivated—by the music, the melodious sound of the French language, and the film's pensive storyline of love found and lost. Afterward, my dad, who had taken me to see the film, bought me the soundtrack, which I played on repeat for years. That soundtrack was how I began to learn French, long before I started taking language classes in the seventh grade. I was enchanted by how the words rolled off my tongue, sounding so sophisticated and romantic, even if I was only ordering a croissant or asking for directions to the ladies' room. I even began to think I must have been French in a previous life, especially after I started speaking the language intuitively during an improv exercise in acting class. (Afterward, I began reading books on past lives and convinced myself that if I hadn't been a French actress in a previous life, I surely must have been a French sailor, given my love for the ocean and all things Jacques Cousteau.)

One reason I wanted to speak French was that, by the time I entered junior high, I knew I also wanted to be an artist—and real artists, in my mind, lived in Paris, studied at the École des Beaux-Arts, painted on the Seine, and frequented the city's iconic art salons. I began to dream about moving to Paris one day, where I imagined I would live in a garret, wear a beret, eat feathery croissants, and drink café au laits all day while sketching *en plein air* at a brasserie *terrasse*.

My interest in art had started young. When I was five, I remember being completely absorbed in a school art assignment for Easter, and while my classmates doodled blobs that vaguely resembled eggs or amorphous bunnies, I carefully drew a cartoon chick popping out of an Easter egg, leaving a little hat of broken shell on its head. When the other kids saw it, they gathered around my desk to ooh and ahh over my illustration. Inspired by the attention, I began drawing chickens all the time, then horses and other animals, then flowers, and finally people. By the time I was in junior high, I prioritized art class and trusted my teachers when they told me I had talent. In my other studies, I worked art into my assignments whenever I could, like when we had to outline the countries and continents for geography class, and I tried to make my project look like an antique map, with neat illustrations and a detailed compass.

My parents also encouraged me to draw, framing and hanging whatever I created and curating my art on our walls with such care, you would have thought they worked for the Metropolitan Museum of Art. (I did this as a parent, too, and while they're adults now, you'll still find the artwork of my three children hanging prominently in our Long Island home.) My parents also collected art, which is how they became friends with Rozzell and Roderick Sykes, African American artists who were uncle and nephew and who started St. Elmo Village, a community for Black art and activism that featured so many colorful murals, it looked like a rainbow exploded in that section of the city. When I was sixteen, my parents took me to St. Elmo, and I was blown away by the art and energy. I was also honored when Rozzell Sykes asked me to work as an assistant and help teach art to their youngest students.

In addition to art, I was also involved in activism when I was young. I cared about world issues and truly believed, as I still do, that one person can change the status quo. So, I marched against the Vietnam War, volunteered in the office of Democratic presidential candidate George McGovern, and protested the building of a nuclear power plant (on a fault line no less) only a few miles down the coast from us.

In high school, while other kids were out partying and doing drugs, I often stayed in to work on my art with friends, of which I had a few—more friends than when I lived with Herb Hudson, but not as many as I would have later in life, after I left L.A. Growing up in Southern California in the 1960s and early '70s, I never felt entirely in my element, in part because drug culture was so dominant: nearly every kid I knew smoked pot or did LSD, mescaline, or peyote. I wasn't a Goody Two-shoes by any means: I went to parties, drank alcohol, smoked cigarettes, and even tried pot a few times, including one night when I unknowingly smoked a joint laced with something else and ended up alone inside the Santa Monica Civic Center after it was locked for the evening. My friends had to call a security guard to let me out, and my parents grounded me for days afterward. But by the time I was in high school, I knew I wanted to be a mom, and I was scared that dropping acid or doing other drugs would affect my ability to have healthy children.

What likely helped, too, was that I didn't end up at public high school. Before ninth grade, I learned about a place called Le Lycée Français, a private high school in Los Angeles for French-speaking students, which children of ambassadors and other foreign diplomats attended. Suddenly, I saw a door out of all the drugs and a pathway to punching my ticket for Paris. I started politicking my parents to let me go to the French school, assuring them that this was no teenage fantasy: I was serious about moving to Paris and becoming an artist.

Eventually, I convinced my parents to let me attend the school, and for the next four years, I spoke French and wore a navy-blue beret, a white poplin collared shirt, and a gray pleated skirt that I always rolled at the waist to raise the hemline. (I believed it looked far more fashionable, even though the school administration reprimanded me for it all the time.) The outfit in its entirety made me look like a blond Madeleine, from the classic children's books by Ludwig Bemelmans, and I loved it.

But if you believe in your dream, the rest is just logistics.

Christie, baby, you write your own script.

DURING MY sophomore year, something changed: I fell in love with a boy for the first time.

Before Johnny, I had had plenty of crushes, but they never felt like what I had with him. In grade school, I remember being over the moon about a boy named Lee, who was the older brother of my good friend Hedy, although he never showed me any interest. (Big mistake, Lee.) There was also a "bad boy" who was a senior when I was in eighth grade—I was so obsessed with him that I made myself a bracelet with beads spelling out his name. I also liked Miles, with whom I even went on a "date," going to Bay Theater, a movie house where all the kids hung out, then to a party on the beach, where we drank cheap wine from a jug. When the cops broke the party up, Miles and I ran across the street, leaping over road barriers and running across people's lawns in what felt like a part-comedy, part-frightening, all-the-way-thrilling high-speed chase. The thrill ended, however, when we had to make a pit stop at a gas station bathroom to both throw up.

When I was still in junior high, I went to "second base" with a boy named Randy. I had been at Bay Theater with my girlfriends when we ran into him and his friends, and we all went to a nearby park to hang out. Randy and I eventually drifted off and began to make out, which is when he decided he wanted to feel me up. It was the first time I had ever let a boy touch my breasts, and if it was exciting at all, that excitement quickly soured. The next day at school, Randy told everyone he didn't know if what he'd felt had been my breasts or my stomach fat. I couldn't believe someone would say something so cruel, and while I was more developed than my friends at the time, this was also the age of Twiggy, the skinny supermodel whom every girl wanted to look like. Randy's words cut me to the core, undermining my self-esteem and causing me to go on a diet for the first (but not the last) time.

After I became a model, I was told that I couldn't possibly

understand what it was like to have body image issues, but the truth is, yes, I can. I've always struggled with my weight, and it's fluctuated up and down my entire life.

The only serious boy I dated before Johnny was a tall, handsome surfer named Steve, whose mop of blond hair was always falling into his face like he'd just been blown in by the biggest wave ever. Growing up in Malibu, I had a thing for surfers, with their sun-streaked hair, perpetually tanned skin, and the cool way they'd let their swim trunks slip below their boxers just a little bit. On our first date, Steve picked me up in his car and took me to dinner, which felt very sophisticated and mature. But things with him didn't last long, in part because I met Johnny.

I was fifteen and Johnny was a bit older when we first started dating. He was the brother of my friend Sadie, and it seemed that whenever I was at her house, he would be home, emanating cool from his core. He was an artist and dressed like one too, in a faded-to-perfection tee and a pair of paint-spattered jeans or bell bottoms. He also had long, golden blond hair that flowed down his muscular back and drove a small white Peugeot (a French car!). When I first knew him, he was dating an older girl who made her own clothes from scraps of Chinese silk and other unusual fabrics—and to me, this was the most interesting way to dress. I was so fascinated by her vintage style that I bought a sewing machine and started making my own clothes from whatever material I could find at craft or thrift shops—a skill that proved valuable years later.

After several months, Johnny stopped dating the bohemian dresser, and in a matter of weeks, he and I were boyfriend and girlfriend. Suddenly, he was picking me up in his Peugeot to go hiking and swimming. He knew all the best trails and swimming holes and where to find a cave with boulders so smooth and views of the Pacific so sweeping that you could sit and gaze out at the ocean all day.

My parents liked Johnny and were open-minded, trusting me to make my own decisions with regard to boys and other areas of my life. I also trusted myself and felt safe and comfortable with Johnny. Moreover, I was madly in love, and after we'd dated for a bit, I slept with him, which was my first time. Soon after, he started picking me up in his Peugeot to drive us into the mountains and make love, pulling out the back seat of his car and laying it flat on the ground so we could lie down together.

Spending more and more time with each other, Johnny and I started to take road trips around the state. Our first was to go horseback riding at a ranch near Solvang, a small city in the Santa Ynez Valley that looks more like a European village, with a windmill and old Danish-style architecture. Another time, we went camping in Big Sur, where we pitched a tent together (which felt a little like building a home) and spent the day jumping off a rope swing into an icy pond. We also drove to Sequoia and Yellowstone National Parks, gaping at the wilderness as morning mist lifted off a meadow of wildflowers. It felt magical, as I sat next to Johnny in his car, sticking my hand out the window and letting it fly into the wind while I sang along to my new favorite song, "Hey Jude," on the radio. It was beginning to feel like the movie of my life was turning into a 1970s California romance, not the remake of *Les Parapluies* I had hoped for, albeit with a much happier ending.

Johnny had his own apartment in Venice Beach, and to pay his rent, he worked as a part-time grip on *The Mary Tyler Moore Show* while also studying art at California State University in Northridge. This made him both a working man and a struggling artist—for me, it was the ultimate combination of masculine and mature.

As we grew more and more serious, I started thinking about Johnny all the time. When we weren't together, I wrote him love poems in a journal I kept by my bed. I was deeply in love and believed we would be together forever, a possibility we also discussed openly and often. Whenever we drove up Decker Canyon in Malibu, we'd say about a certain white house up on the mountain that we'd live there one day, painting and creating art.

As a girl, I believed in the romance, as I still do.

By my senior year at Le Lycée Français, I knew I wanted to postpone moving to Paris so that I could be with Johnny. After graduating, I enrolled as an art and anthropology student at California State University in Northridge, where he was also taking classes. Believing we'd soon live together in the white house in Decker Canyon, I started sewing a quilt to keep on our bed there. When I finally finished it, I was so excited for Johnny to see it that I gave it to him as an early Christmas present while also saving my money to buy him something grander, a fancy single-lens reflex camera.

Days before Christmas, with Johnny's camera carefully wrapped and painstakingly ribboned, I went to a holiday party thrown by his sister, my friend Sadie. While all Johnny's friends were there, he wasn't. He had told me earlier in the day that he would come, so I sat eagerly waiting, the gift-wrapped camera on my lap, so that I could see the look of surprise and joy when he opened it.

Minutes turned into hours, and although the party was loud and crowded, nothing could distract me from wondering where Johnny was and imagining how he'd react when he unwrapped his gift. I was near feverish with anticipation when his friend Brian sat down next to me.

"Christie," Brian said in a tone much too serious for a party. "I can't stand it anymore. You don't deserve what's happening to you."

"What?" I said, jolted out of my reverie. "What are you talking about?"

Brian looked down at his hands and started twisting one in the other. "He's cheating on you," he said, still staring at his hands.

"Johnny's cheating on you with one of Mary Tyler Moore's doubles, her stand-in. That's why he's not here."

"What? That can't be true!" I cried.

"Yeah, she's got an apartment off a side street in Santa Monica, near the ocean," Brian said. "You can go see it for yourself. He's practically been living there when he's not with you."

I couldn't move or speak, I was in so much shock. The room started to spin, even though I had had only a little to drink. All I could see in front of me was Johnny with a girl who looked like Mary Tyler Moore, the two of them holding hands, lying down, making love. I forgot all about the party and Brian, until he was standing in front of me again, holding a slip of paper up to my face.

"Here, call this," he said, handing me the slip with a phone number written on it.

I found a phone and dialed the number, shaking slightly as I waited for the wheel on the rotary phone to circle back to the finger stop. Finally, the line was ringing, and a woman answered.

"I'd like to speak with my boyfriend, Johnny, please," I said in a small voice.

Hushed whispers on the other end, then I heard Johnny's voice. "Oh, god, Christie, I'm so sorry," he said.

"How could you do this to me? How could you do this to me, Johnny?" I broke down sobbing, unable to speak, letting the receiver drop from my hand and hit the floor.

Later that night, Brian and I drove to Santa Monica and found Mary Tyler Moore's double's apartment. It was easy to spot because I could see the quilt I had given Johnny, the one I had spent weeks sewing, now cut in half and being used as drapes in the picture window of her apartment. The sight of the quilt gutted me, and sobbing, I went home and straight to my room, which I didn't leave for days. It felt like my movie was over. It was curtains . . . literally.

AFTER THE winter holidays, I didn't go back to California State in Northridge. The university wasn't big enough for Johnny and me—in fact, the entire city of Los Angeles wasn't big enough for the both of us. Now more than ever, I wanted to go to Paris, and I started working different jobs to save money for both a plane ticket and a Eurail pass so I could see the rest of Europe, too.

My first job was scooping ice cream at a Baskin-Robbins next to several big movie theaters in Westwood Village. The films all ended at the same time, at which point customers would come pouring in through the door and I could never scoop cones, cups, and sundaes fast enough. I tended to give out big scoops, too, and after doing so multiple times, an undercover manager ordered a cup from me and weighed it. That same night, I was fired for "over-scooping," which was perfectly fine by me: I'd rather be an over-scooper in life than an under-scooper.

Afterward, I worked selling clothes at a department store in Century City, and then as a waitress at a restaurant right off the Pacific Coast Highway, where they served hamburgers and hot dogs during the day, then spread tablecloths for sit-down dinners in the evening. I worked both shifts, and I was equally bad at both.

One of my last jobs in Los Angeles was at a plant store. My role was to help customers find the perfect plant for their homes while also taking care of the shop's flowers and shrubs. I loved the work—at least, until one day, when I was alone in the back room, pruning a shrub on a planting table. Focused on my work, I didn't even hear my boss, a man in his forties, when he walked up behind me. We'd always been friendly, and he seemed nice enough, so I was horrified when I suddenly felt his hands reach up around me and rest on my breasts. I froze with embarrassment for what felt like one long, insufferable minute before squirming out of his grip.

"Excuse me, I'm sorry," I said, flustered and disgusted. "But your hands! I think you may have touched me by accident."

I hurried past him to the front of the store and avoided him for the rest of the day, leaving the moment my shift was over. After the shop door clanged shut behind me, I knew I'd never be back.

First Johnny, now this. It was time to leave Los Angeles.

In February 1973, at the age of nineteen, I boarded a flight for Paris. *Au revoir, Johnny*, I thought as the plane climbed up over Los Angeles. *Au revoir, creepy plant-store guy. And au revoir to all the drugs and stagnated life below that I didn't want to be my own.*

Christie, baby, you write your own script.

I know I do. So, *bonjour, Paris.*

WHAT I couldn't imagine on that night flight to Charles de Gaulle was that my script wouldn't bring me back to Los Angeles for nearly two years. And the next time I'd see the city, I'd do so with a portfolio of pictures and a rising career as one of the world's top models.

PART II

Paris

les jardins de Paris

CHAPTER

4

MARCH 1973

Dear Mom and Dad,
When we first arrived in Paris, Madam Hormel was at the
airport with her father to greet us. It was raining, and Paris looks
beautiful in the winter, with all the bare trees. As we left Paris,
the trees were just turning pink and green, but all the people
were still bundled up . . .

    Our first week in Paris, Michelle's relatives took turns taking
us to the best French restaurants, private clubs, and jazz places,
showing us all around Paris à nuit while we slept most of the
day. I was exhausted but happy. All her relatives speak French
and little English, and I fell immediately back into it. You'd be so
proud if you heard me! Michelle also helped a lot with my French
when I saw her. But after I met Jean-François the first week, I
didn't see much of Michelle until we went traveling . . .

    I'll send you some photos of Jean-François. I have some good ones, but they're all in Paris. For now, I'll describe him: Jean-François is 24 years old, French, <u>good-looking</u>, and the most fantastic artist I've ever met. I can't even begin to describe his work to you, but I'm so impressed. He's well-known around Paris, having illustrated at least 500 magazine covers and thousands of articles. His drawings are a blend of M. C. Escher, Hieronymus Bosch, and Charles Bragg, with social commentary all rolled into one . . .

Ever since I met Jean-François, I've seen Paris in a new way, through a Parisian's eye. He took me everywhere—places other Americans could have never found, parks I've never even heard of, and small, delicious restaurants. Oh, and you wouldn't believe the foods I eat now! Moules farcies (those are mussels). And escargots! I even filet my own fish, cutting off the head and everything! [By the time I moved to Paris, I had become a vegetarian but still ate some seafood.]

Jean-François is a fantastic cook. He made me my first moules farcies—délicieux. I've acquired such gourmet French taste, but I've lost some weight, too. I don't know how much because I don't have a scale, but my clothes sure are big on me. And I've done so much walking—I bet I outwalk you guys, Mom and Dad! Jean-François lives on the edge of Paris, and we always walk into the main arrondissement, which is the Quartier Latin. He lives in the prettiest, old building at the very top of the stairs on the seventh floor in a room with a balcony and flowers—and, for the last three weeks, me . . .

I've made tons of new friends. A few with Michelle, but most are friends of Jean-François's. With all my new friends and how I know my way around, I really consider Paris my new home. I don't know exactly what I'll do or how I'll do it, but I've decided Europe is where I'm going to live for good. It agrees with me too *well to ever leave. I can't wait until you come to visit and bring the rest of my things. I'll show you the time of your life!*

There's so much I haven't said, but I'll write all the time now that things have fallen into place, once and for all. In case my address in Paris was lost, write to me at: Christie Sasha Mandarin Brinkley, care of Laurent C., 5x Avenue Niel, Paris, Le Dixseptième, France. (Sasha Mandarin is a name I picked up along the way, but I like it. It's pretty, isn't it?)

I really miss you and wonder all the time how you and Greg are. And I worry about the earthquakes there every time the metro passes under me here and shakes my building. I wish you would hurry up and write! What's been happening on All My Children? *Is Phil home from Vietnam? And what's going on in the real soap opera of life back home? Any gossip? If there is, I actually don't want to hear it . . .*

Well, we're going to go out for some nightlife now. Goodnight!

Oh, I want to add that I'm thankful and aware of how lucky I am to be able to do this. I'm taking advantage of every second! But you know I'm never coming back except to visit? Thank you for everything. I love it here.

All my love,
Christie

A fter I moved to Paris, I started writing letters and postcards home as often as I could. I spent hours on these, composing them in careful calligraphy and decorating the margins with postage stamps, dried leaves from Paris parks, or labels I'd peeled off French wine bottles and Camembert cheese. I drew illustrations, too, so that my parents could see what my new life looked like—sometimes accurately so, other times embellished for their sake. Either way, my parents saved most of my letters, and today, I still have many of them, preserved in albums under plastic because I wrote most of them on old airmail paper, which is as delicate as onionskin.

My first letter home—the one in which I told my parents I was never coming back to Los Angeles except to visit (which was mostly true)—I didn't write from Paris. I wrote it in Copenhagen a month after I landed from L.A., when I finally used my Eurail pass to travel through Europe with my friend Michelle, a classmate from Le Lycée Français de Los Angeles who had flown to France with me for the first part of my trip.

Michelle had lots of family in Paris, including an aunt who was a well-known prima ballerina, which sounded very French and appealing to me. From Michelle, I learned that real Parisians buy *les marrons chauds*, or "hot chestnuts," from street vendors in the wintertime so they can stick them in their pockets and warm their hands. To me, nothing could have been more charming, and I was thankful for the tip so that no one would mistake me for a tourist. I never wanted to be a tourist in Paris: from the moment we landed at Charles de Gaulle, I wanted to be *parisienne*.

Michelle and I didn't have a place to stay in Paris, although my dad had gifted us two nights at a nice hotel near the Rue de Rivoli, just so we could get our bearings. Shuttling there in a taxi from the airport through the pouring rain, I remember staring out the window at the city's watery lights, Paris dripping with all the romance I had imagined.

I had been to Paris once before, for only one night, when I was fifteen and a summer school student at the University of Orléans, where I studied French and art for six weeks. On my way to Orléans from Los Angeles through New York, I had made fast friends with four other American girls who were part of the same study-abroad program, and we started doing everything together, so much so that people began to call us "the Fearsome Five." We took side trips together, including one to Switzerland, but our most memorable was an overnight to Paris July 20, 1969. I remember the date because it was the same night the Americans first landed on the moon.

The city was spellbound that evening, as people packed into cafés or huddled on the street around the windows of any bars or shops where they could catch a glimpse of a TV inside, all of which were tuned to the moon landing's live broadcast. Earlier in the day, I had already fallen in love with Paris and its museums, chestnut trees along the avenues, outdoor cafés that spilled into the streets, and all the young girls—many my age—weaving in and out of traffic on their Mobylettes, with baguettes or other groceries peeping out from their panniers. But to experience the city while history was being made, when the whole world was coming together to stare at the evening sky, made Paris seem even more mythical, magical, and otherworldly. I was proud to be an American in Paris that evening, looking up from France at the same moon everyone in the United States and the world was watching, too. Later that night, the five of us ran through the streets yelling, "Les Américains ont marché sur la lune! Les Américains ont marché sur la lune!" and leaping up as though we were trying to touch the same sky in which, somewhere, our American astronauts floated triumphantly in a tiny module.

FOUR YEARS later, after I moved to Paris, nothing had changed: the city was still as mythical, magical, and otherworldly to me. My first morning in Paris, I thew open the casement windows in our hotel room just to see and physically feel the lights and sounds of the city. I was enchanted by those windows, with their huge panes, coiled wrought-iron rods, and curlicued balcony railings. They looked like they belonged in a painting by Matisse, my favorite painter because his artwork is so beautiful, bright, and happy. I felt happy, too, as I looked out the hotel's windows onto the Jardin des Tuileries, where, in February, the magnolia trees were just beginning to bud and small children carried toy sailboats to float in the basin. On the street below, car horns beeped loudly as people clicked by in high heels and dress shoes, the noise carrying up with it the aroma of baked bread and perfume tinged by a hint of cigarette smoke.

In that moment, I wasn't just looking at a Matisse painting; I was *living* in one.

Within days, Michelle and I had a found a more permanent place to stay—with her uncle Laurent, who had offered us his guest room, rent-free. He lived in a less interesting, bourgeois part of the city, but neither of us minded, because it wouldn't cost us a thing. I was on a tight budget, trying to make the money I had saved from my jobs in Los Angeles last as long as possible, until I could find work in Paris after I traveled through Europe.

But during our first month in Paris, we didn't travel outside the city as we had originally planned. One reason was Michelle. Despite being the daughter of one of the most famous food processing magnates in the United States, she never seemed to have any money—though she spent cash faster than she could ask for more. As a result, I kept lending her mine while she waited for more money from her family. Her financial troubles created problems between us and dictated our itinerary when we did travel, and we almost never left a place by choice, but when Michelle ran out of money.

The other reason we didn't travel outside Paris—a far more persuasive factor for me—was Jean-François.

The night I met Jean-François, Michelle and I had gone to La Coupole, an illustrious brasserie in Montparnasse where I had once seen Jean-Paul Sartre and Simone de Beauvoir having dinner together. Dozens of other writers, artists, and intellectuals had also frequented the place, including Ernest Hemingway, Pablo Picasso, Marc Chagall, and, one of my early favorites, Edith Piaf. The brasserie was also celebrated for its art deco design, and sitting in the main dining room was like visting a modernist museum, where you dined surrounded by full-length mirrors, oval banquettes, and thirty-three gilded blue-green columns topped by murals painted by artists, many times in exchange for their food and drink.

The night we went to La Coupole, Michelle and I were having a heart-to-heart over a glass of wine, mostly about her money problems. But we had resolved our issues and were enjoying ourselves when two good-looking men walked in alongside a striking blonde. As they threaded their way toward us, Michelle and I caught each other's eye, then swiveled our heads in unison, like birds on a wire, as we watched the trio take the table in front of ours.

I can still remember what Jean-François was wearing: a white peasant shirt, the kind that French artists wore then, over black jeans tucked into knee-high riding boots. He was tall and thin with broad shoulders and long brown hair that hung over his high cheekbones and square jaw. To me, he looked as though he had just stepped out of a French romance novel.

Me in my Matisse painting, Jean-François in an Émile Zola story.

His friend Antonio was shorter, stockier, and good-looking in a different kind of way, dressed similarly to Jean-François, but in a brooding black sweater. The girl, Mariette, had long, straight blond hair that hung to the waistband of her bohemian skirt, which she wore under a pale blue blouse. Michelle and I were sure she must be a model, a vocation that seemed completely remote and exotic to me at the time.

After they sat down, the three of them started smoking and talking intensely, I presumed about something artsy and intellectual. At one point, Jean-François glanced back at our table, which caused Michelle and me to gush quietly over how handsome he was, and when he walked by us to buy more cigarettes at the bar, I felt a frenetic pull, as though an invisible line of energy connected us across the room. But neither of us spoke to the other, and the night ticked on and on until we heard the chime—*ding, ding, ding, ding*—that meant La Coupole was closing and everyone had to leave

"Oh, my god, Michelle, it's so late!" I said, looking at my watch and jumping up, forgetting about Jean-François for a moment. "The Métro will stop running soon, and we won't be able to get back to Laurent's if we miss it!"

Seconds later, we hurried out onto the street, but we didn't get very far because a dozen or so men had surrounded us—what the French call *les clochards*, "the homeless." I later learned that they did this every night, clustering around the doors of La Coupole at closing to beg for money, but at the time, neither Michelle nor I was prepared for what was about to happen. Maybe they knew we were American or thought we'd be easy targets because we were young girls, but as soon as they saw us, they encircled us and started clawing at our arms, demanding cash.

All of a sudden, I felt a tight grip on my arm. It was Jean-François. "Excusez-moi," he said firmly to the beggars. "Mademoiselle est avec moi. Ne la touchez pas." ("The lady is with me. Don't touch her.")

Immediately, the sea of men parted, and Jean-François steered me to the other side of the street like a gendarme escorting a celebrity out of the crush of paparazzi. No longer frightened, I felt electrified, as the frenetic energy we shared earlier in the evening now coursed from his hands directly into my body.

"I hope you don't mind that I took your arm, but they were pushing you so much," he said softly to me.

"Oh no, thank you, thank you," I murmured, charmed by his eyes as Michelle, Antonio, and Mariette joined us across the street.

"We were noticing the two of you in the café," Jean-François said to Michelle and me. "Where are you from?"

"New York," Michelle said immediately, without glancing at me. She thought New York City was a much more interesting place to call home than Los Angeles, and whenever we spoke with Europeans, she was often right.

"I dream of going there someday," Jean-François said earnestly, staring off with a wistful look before he began speaking again. "Well, we're going to go to a little jazz bar around the corner, if you'd like to join us?"

This time, I was the one who didn't glance at Michelle, promptly nodding yes to his invite. We were going.

Moments later, the five us of us were crowded around a tiny table in the back of a dimly lit jazz club, so thick with cigarette smoke that it didn't seem possible to add any more fumes to the already saturated air. But we smoked anyway, lighting up cigarettes and talking excitedly as a saxophone sighed faintly in the front of the club.

The connection was instant. Jean-François was an artist; I wanted to be an artist. He dreamed of going to New York; I had dreamed of going to Paris. He lived in Paris; I had just visited New York. He loved to explore; I was here, in his city, expressly to explore. We also talked about paints—acrylics, oils, watercolors—and what it was like to brush color onto wood, how he sculpted and how I wanted to learn to sculpt. He explained his work as a political cartoonist, and I told him how much I admired politics. (As an Aquarius, I've always believed one person can change the world.) We waltzed from one topic to another, falling effortlessly through the conversation as though we were dancing—the rhythm easy, the steps organic.

That night, alone with Jean-François while surrounded by dozens of other people, I felt as though I had been struck by lightning—what the French call a *coup de foudre* or what Americans call love at first sight. It was an instant and energizing pull: right away, I knew I had to be with him and that I loved him already. It was something I had never felt before and that I've never felt since. Years later, when I met the race car driver Olivier Chandon de Brailles, I was smitten within seconds. And when I met Billy Joel at a hotel bar in St. Barts, I knew right away that I liked him and wanted to see him again. But of all the men I've met, no one has ever instantly shocked me with love like Jean-François did.

Eventually, though, we had to rejoin Michelle, Antonio, and Mariette, who had been engrossed in their own conversations around the same table while Jean-François and I had orbited above them. That's when I learned that Antonio was from South America and that Mariette, unsurprisingly, was from Sweden. The two of them were madly in love, Antonio said, and lived together in the Latin Quarter under a *vasistas* with a view of the Jardin des Plantes (or "Botanical Gardens").

"What's a *vasistas*?" I asked, enchanted by the sound of it.

The word *vasistas*, Antonio explained, comes from the German phrase *was ist das*, which means "what is that?" The French had co-opted the phrase to describe the funny transom windows that sit on rooftops all over Paris.

Of course! I knew exactly what they were. And hours later, I'd be so glad that I had asked . . .

But in the next second, the music in the club slowed to a stop, the saxophone player packed up his things, and people started to file out. It was closing time . . . again.

"How can I see you?" Jean-François asked. My heart flipped. *He wants to see me again!*

I jotted down my address at Laurent's on a matchbook and passed it to him across the table, our fingers touching before, slowly and cautiously, we let our hands intertwine.

After we left the club, not wanting the night to end, we strolled into some gardens nearby, the trees floating on a sea of low fog that rolled just above the ground, as Jean-François and I walked arm and arm and the others remained caught up in their own conversation. But after rays of sunlight started to slice through the trees, I knew it was time to go.

After Michelle and I said goodbye to Antonio and Mariette, Jean-François walked us to the avenue and hailed us a taxi, handing the driver a few francs. I reluctantly climbed into the cab after Michelle, who handed me a cigarette, hoping it would distract me from the sweet sorrow of parting. Seeing the cigarette between my lips, Jean-François turned around to light it for me with a match, as he'd done all evening. But just then, the taxi started to pull away, and expertly, like a handball player making a fast-moving throw, he tossed the matchbook to me through the open window.

"Did you see that?" I said, turning to Michelle as the taxi sped away. "He's such a gentleman!" But when I opened the matchbook, my heart sank: there, on the inside, was my address, the same one I had written down earlier in the evening in the same matchbook I had given Jean-François. How would he ever find me now? I called to the taxi driver to turn around, and we raced back to the gardens, but Jean-François had disappeared into the misty morning. I was devastated. I had found my soulmate my first week in Paris, and now we were lost to each other in the City of Love.

A few minutes later, though, my total forlornness turned to sudden hope—a recurring theme throughout my life.

"Wait!" I said to Michelle. "Remember how Antonio said they live in the Quartier Latin with a view of the Jardin des Plantes and a *vasistas* on the top floor? If we can find that apartment, we can find Jean-François!"

Later that afternoon, after a brief sleep at Laurent's apartment,

Michelle and I set off for the Latin Quarter, where we began to criss-cross the streets near the Jardin des Plantes, staring up at the sky like religious pilgrims waiting for a cosmic sign from above. Every time we spotted a *vasistas* with a rooftop view of the gardens, we'd climb to the top floor, knock on all the apartment doors there, and ask for Antonio. On our fifth try, Antonio miraculously opened the door. The cosmos had given me my sign.

I explained about Jean-François and the matchbook.

"Oh, my goodness!" Antonio said. "I'm so happy you found me. And yes! Jean-François lives at number thirty-nine rue Pernety, in Montparnasse. You must go see him."

Feeling proud of ourselves, Michelle and I nearly skipped and whistled all the way back to Laurent's. But as she carried on about our great detective skills, doubt began silently to seep into my mind, and I started to wonder if I should, in fact, really show up unannounced at Jean-François's place. Very few Parisian apartments had phones in those days—ours didn't, and neither did his—so I couldn't call. But what if I stopped by and interrupted him while he was busy? Or what if he was with another girl?

I decided that I didn't care: I had to see him again. Once we got to Laurent's, I changed clothes, trying to make myself look as pretty as possible, and jumped the Métro to Montparnasse.

In the 1970s, Montparnasse wasn't the safest neighborhood, just as renowned for its crime as it was for its art scene. But I was charmed by the narrow street on which Jean-François lived, even though his building was a nondescript gray, with a tight, circular staircase that wound all the way to the top floor and his apartment.

As butterflies batted about my stomach, I climbed to the top—a garret apartment!—and knocked on Jean-François's door. When he opened it, he smiled as though he'd been waiting all night for me to arrive.

His apartment was the size of a shoebox, although technically it wasn't an apartment at all, but a *chambre de bonne*, "maid's room"—or what he and I eventually called an atelier, an artist's studio. There was no kitchen, no toilet, no shower in the room—just a sink and a bed and, above the bed, a charming built-in closet for clothes. The place also had a full-length mirror and large French doors that opened onto a wrought-iron railing with window boxes full of flowers. Beyond the railing, you could see the final unfinished floors of the Tour Montparnasse, which, once built, would become the tallest skyscraper in Paris—and all of France—when it was finished in just a few months' time.

That evening, Jean-François made me *moules farcies* on a camping stove he kept beneath the sink. It was the first time I tasted mussels— and the last time I even thought about going back to Laurent's apartment for the night. From that evening on, for the next year and a half, Jean-François and I would live together in his garret in Paris.

Three months later, sometime in June, as I watched fireworks cascading off the finally finished Tour Montparnasse, I realized I was deeply in love.

CHAPTER

5

The wind is in from Africa
Last night I couldn't sleep
Oh, you know, it sure is hard to leave here, Carey . . .

The song kept playing in my head, over and over again, Joni
Mitchell's voice high and sweet as she sang about a man she fell
in love with in Crete. Wherever I went in Greece, I heard "Carey,"
not because Joni's song was always on the radio—it wasn't—but
because it was perpetually in my mind, following me around like
a movie soundtrack, propelling me to go from Corfu to Athens to
Crete so that I could stand "beneath the Matala moon," which looked
just as mystical in person as it sounded when Joni sang the lyric.

I went to Crete alone, even though that had never been our plan. But
days before we were due to depart for Greece together, Jean-François
received a letter from the French military, drafting him to complete
ten months' mandatory service. I was dismayed: three months into
our idyllic love affair, and *mon amour* was being ripped away. Suddenly, I saw reels from *Les Parapluies de Cherbourg* spooling out in

front of me, with images of the movie's mechanic going off to the Algerian War never again to see the beautiful Catherine Deneuve. The same thing couldn't, wouldn't happen to us. Jean-François would find a way to defer his service, we believed: flat feet, a bad back, allergies, whatever it took. In the interim, we agreed, I would go to Greece alone before my Eurail pass expired and find a little flat for us overlooking the ocean on the most beautiful island, and he would join me as soon as he could.

On April 30, 1973, I boarded a Paris sleeper train bound for Brindisi, Italy, where I would catch a ferry to Greece. On the train, I was mesmerized by the scenery and happy to share a cabin with three nice soldiers—an American, a German, and a South American—and in Northern Italy, when the train stopped in the mountains to refuel, the four us got off together to stretch our legs and find a drink.

When it was time to board again, the conductor stopped me with his hand.

"*Mi scusi, signorina,*" he said soberly, holding my Eurail pass to my face. "But, see? Your Eurail pass has expired. You cannot board."

"What? No, that can't be true!" I cried incredulously. "I'm not even at my destination yet!"

"*Mi dispiace*, but you can't get back on this train."

Leaving the soldiers on the platform, I rushed back into the station, found a phone booth, and dialed my parents. *Please pick up, please pick up*, I prayed, without even taking the time to figure out what hour it was in Los Angeles. But the call wouldn't go through. I tried again, as the overhead announcements for the train's departure grew more urgent: it was about to leave. I ran back to the conductor and threw myself on his mercy, and as the train's engines lunged and sputtered to a start, he finally let me slip between the car doors.

Relieved, I chatted with my soldier friends the rest of the way to Brindisi, a port city in the heel of Italy, on the Adriatic Sea, where we all had to deboard before catching the next day's ferries. In Brindisi, I booked a hotel for the night, and worried for my safety, my soldier friends insisted on staying in adjacent rooms, which I thought was sweet but unnecessary. I changed my mind, though, when, in the middle of the night, I heard the doorknob to my room squeak, then turn and twist, as someone without a key tried to force their way in. I screamed, which brought all three soldiers running to my door, scaring off the would-be intruder.

While I didn't realize it at the time, my education in what it was like to be a woman traveling alone had just begun.

The next day, after thanking and saying goodbye to the soldiers, I purchased a flexible ferry ticket to Greece, unsure yet where I would disembark. It was a large ship, and I had booked a seat in steerage, on the lower level—the least expensive ticket and best option for an adventure-seeking girl with a large backpack and a small budget. The following morning, when dawn broke pink and indigo across the Ionian Sea, I looked out a tiny porthole to see something magical: a minuscule island on the periwinkle-hued horizon that grew bigger and bigger and more impressive as we approached. Soon, the captain announced that we were about to dock in Corfu, so I grabbed my backpack with all my worldly possessions and told the purser I wanted off the ship.

When I look back on the experience today, what amazes me most is how fortunate I was to be able to travel with only one backpack and no itinerary. To me, this was and still is the epitome of freedom, and as I've learned through the years, there is no luxury that is more priceless than freedom.

ON CORFU, I rented a moped and drove along the coast, then up the terraced hills into groves and groves of olive trees, their ancient trunks gnarled by age and shrouded with branches weighed down by small white blossoms that would soon turn into tiny pebbles of pale fruit. Wending around crumbling walls and up the island's narrow roads, I could see the ocean at every overlook, and inspired by these endless vistas, I decided to keep driving until I reached the sea again. Eventually, the road dead-ended at a small, crescent-shaped cove with water the color of New Mexican turquoise, encircled by a white-and-pink pebble beach and bounded by rocky cliffs dotted with waifish green trees, which fell over one another like ballet dancers in a pas de deux. *This is where I should wait for Jean-François*, I thought. But I knew I couldn't: it was the first island I'd seen, and while it was enchanting, I wanted to explore more—I loved to explore. So, I stayed one night in a quaint hotel on the beautiful pebble beach, then moved on.

From Corfu, all roads to Greece's other islands went through Athens, so I caught a ferry to the mainland, then took a long, bumpy bus ride to the country's ancient capital. Immediately, Athens intrigued me, and I spent a few days in the city, touring the Acropolis and other ruins and making friends with some young Athenians, who invited me to their home for lunch. While sharing rounds of charred pita and fresh horiatiki, after they learned that I wanted to see the islands, they began drawing up detailed itineraries for me for visits to Paros, Rhodes, Naxos, Mykonos, and other mythical-sounding places. But at that point, all I could hear was Joni whispering about the beauty of standing "beneath the Matala moon," and I knew I had to go where I could do the same.

Matala is a village on the southern coast of Crete where, three years before I traveled to Greece, Joni spent two months. She had gone to Crete to take a break from both her mounting fame and devastating split with singer Graham Nash, who belonged to the trio Crosby, Stills and Nash. What she found there was a new love for a different man and a wellspring of creativity, writing "Carey" in Matala and other songs for her 1971 album, *Blue*.

As a young woman, I adored Joni and her music, as I still do. She's part of the soundtrack to my life, and even before I went to Greece, I knew she had taken this transformative trip to Crete, leaving me with the romantic notion to try to follow in her footsteps. I also thought if I went to Crete, the largest and southernmost island in Greece, it would epitomize all that the other islands had to offer. I thanked my Athenian hosts for their suggestions and hopped the next ferry to Crete.

Ten hours later, when the ferry docked in Heraklion, I felt like I had landed in another country. The island was incredibly dry, feeling more African than European, and the city's ancient Minoan culture and old fortresses and defense walls seemed so foreign to me. But I didn't take the opportunity to explore, not then at least. Matala was on the other side of the island, and I couldn't wait to get there, so I caught a rickety old bus over the mountains and down the other side to the southern coast, where the route ended in a small village named Agia Galini.

The village was still forty minutes northwest of Matala, but I found Agia Galini charming, perched on a steep hill high over a harbor flecked by little white houses that overlooked the Libyan Sea. I also liked that it was exceedingly remote, so much so that the village had just installed its first electric light weeks before I arrived, a single lamp that swung down by the harbor while, at night, the rest of Agia Galini sparkled with candlelight.

Tired from the ferry ride and weighed down by my backpack, I walked the town's main street, peering into shops and little cafés while gazing out on the harbor. At the top of the hill, I spotted a house with an incredible view of the sea and, tacked inside a window, a sign for a room for rent. I asked the old woman who answered the door if I could see the rental, and she brought me up to the rooftop, where there was a single room with a small bed, a table in front of one large window, and a door that opened onto the roof, with an outdoor shower and a lounge bed. The best part, though, was the view, which overlooked the harbor where you could see people playing volleyball and sitting at tables outside the tavernas, as two old wooden boats ferried the day's catch back and forth, back and forth. In the distance, I could also see two islands that, I later learned, were the uninhabited Paximadia islands, nicknamed the Elephantaki because together they looked like a baby elephant lying down in the water, her trunk afloat in front of her.

I told the old woman I'd take it.

FOR THE next month, I lived in my little room in Agia Galini, paint-ing, swimming, and buying from fishermen in the harbor the fresh-est seafood, which the chefs at the tavernas cooked for me for only a few coins. I also spent hours trying to prepare my room for Jean-François's arrival, arranging bouquets of dried flowers in makeshift vases of empty wine bottles, drawing pretty pictures to hang on the walls, and doing whatever else I could on my shoestring budget to make the place feel as homey as possible. In addition to getting to know the villagers, I also made friends with some foreigners, and with my foreign friends, I started exploring other areas of the island. One day, we hiked the entire length of the Samaria Gorge, a long ra-vine so narrow that at one point you have to step over the very creek that carved the gorge when it was still a mighty river.

With my foreign friends, I took the bus often to Heraklion for gro-ceries and other necessities. During one excursion there, the strang-est thing happened, another phenomenon I can't quite explain. (And I love when the unexplained happens.) It took place in the city's main square, a large, humming plaza by the harbor where I shopped for oranges or oil paints or whatever it was I needed that day. The plaza was always clangorous with sellers hawking their wares and shoppers haggling for better prices, but that day, it suddenly fell stock-still, as everyone turned their faces upward. There in the noonday sky, four overpowering lights shone brightly, even in broad daylight, forming a square that pulsed in and out over and over again, as though some ancient god had decided to dazzle the crowd with a New Age aerial show. In between gasps and murmurs in Greek, I understood a gruff string of English letters: "U," "F," "O." Eventually, the four lights tightened together and, in a flash, zoomed off over the mountains behind us.

At the moment, everyone in the plaza just looked at each other—the old Greek women in their black dresses, the tourists with their cameras, the young children who had been brought there by their tired, hardworking parents. Wide-eyed and mouths agape, we had all seen the same thing.

"Oh, my god, we just saw a UFO!" I cried to my friends.

We left the marketplace and caught the next rusty bus back over the dry, dusty roads to Agia Galini, chatting excitedly the entire way about what we had just seen. In the village, shortly after we parted and returned to our respective rooms, I heard a faint shouting and looked out my window to see, in the distance, a man racing down the trail from the mountains as though he were a roadrunner, flapping his arms and kicking up dust behind him. At first, he was just a dot with a tail of dirt behind him, but as he got closer, bigger, and louder, I heard him shouting the same string of English letters—U, F, O—that we had heard in Heraklion, alongside a jumble of frenetic Greek. I rushed back outside and found my friends there, everyone eager to find out what the commotion was about, so we headed down to the harbor to wait for the roadrunner man.

Once he arrived, we got the full story.

"Spaceships! I just saw four spaceships slip into the ocean!" he shouted to the crowd that had gathered at the harbor, one of my friends translating the Greek words so I could understand. "And they didn't *crash* into the sea—it looked like they were *escaping* into it!"

"Yes," another man said very matter-of-factly. "They hide in the ocean when they're on earth!"

My friends and I looked at one another. There was no way the roadrunner man had been to Heraklion—he was a known recluse who lived in a cave on the coast—and there were no telephones or newscasts in those days, so there was no way he could have found out what had happened less than two hours before on the other side of the island. Instead, he had seen what we had seen.

Just then, I remembered Joni's song:

The night is a starry dome
And they're playin' that scratchy rock and roll
Beneath the Matala moon

NOT EVERYTHING that happened in Crete was bewitching or beautiful, though. Quite the opposite, two encounters on the island left me with a disturbing new understanding of what it meant to be a woman on her own.

A few weeks after I'd arrived in Agia Galini, a girlfriend and I decided to hitchhike to Heraklion one morning because the bus wasn't running—few things in Crete operated consistently, I was learning—and we both needed groceries and other goods. The road to Heraklion wasn't well traveled, but about a mile outside Agia Galini, a large truck slowed to a stop next to us, with three men inside the cabin. They waved for us to hop into the back of the truck's trailer, which was enclosed on three sides by tall panels, without any roof. We did, grabbing onto the wooden fencing strung to the front of the trailer, just behind the cab, so we could stand and see out over the cabin, watching the world go by from the back of the truck.

About halfway to Heraklion, the truck suddenly made a sharp turn onto a dirt trail that no bus I had taken had ever traversed. My friend and I exchanged worried glances and, over the blare of the truck's engine and the sound of the rushing wind, tried to come up with possible excuses for the detour. After about a half mile, the trail started to flatten out, and over the cabin, we saw that we were in the middle of nowhere, on land surrounded only by hills, boulders, and dry riverbeds. Then, the truck stopped.

"Oh no," I whispered to my friend as adrenaline began to build at the back of my throat. "These guys are going to do something to us."

Then, as if on cue, all three men climbed out of the cab and began to walk around to the back of the truck.

Without thinking, I whispered to my friend, "Follow me," then climbed the fencing and shimmied across the truck's cabin before sliding down the windshield and off the truck's hood to the ground— just as I heard the giant door to the trailer swing open. Because the trailer was so long and its panels so tall, the men hadn't seen us escape, but I wasn't taking any chances, and we both ran as fast as we could without looking behind us, searching for cover in the flat desert, as I scraped my legs on spiny shrubs and nearly fell as the earth undulated beneath my feet. When I thought I was finally out of eyesight (and certainly out of breath), I jumped into a dry riverbed and lay perfectly flat, my heart pounding against the ground as I began to comprehend what had just happened. I heard the men calling to one another in Greek and, after a few more minutes, the sound of the engine as the truck rattled away.

After what felt like hours, I stood up and scanned the horizon for my friend, who was walking aimlessly a few hundred feet away, looking just as traumatized as I felt. I waved silently to her, and we ran toward each other, hugging and crying while whispering about what to do next. It didn't seem like we had many options, so we ran back to the dirt trail the truck had taken and headed down the hill again, panicked the entire time that the men were hiding somewhere along the way, waiting to ambush us. When we reached the paved road, we felt instantly safer, and when we saw the public bus huffing up the mountain in the distance, we began jumping up and down and flapping our hands like two shipwreck survivors who'd just spotted a rescue plane. After that day, I never hitchhiked again.

But as frightening as the incident was, something even more petrifying happened only days later.

Because it was so wonderfully hot in Crete, I often slept outside on the bed on the terrace, dreaming under the twinkling stars with the whisper of a faint summer breeze, which was my only air-conditioning. I figured I was safe on the open terrace because the town was so small and remote, and because my two new Swiss friends, Reto and Carlos, had rented a room below mine. But as I've learned, few areas are truly safe, no matter how small, quaint, or seemingly remote they may seem.

One night, while asleep on the terrace, I woke to find a man's huge hands on my shoulders, pushing me down on the bed as he mumbled in broken English, "Sorry, Sasha, sorry, Sasha." (While in Greece, I'd been traveling under my nickname, "Sasha Mandarin," because having an alter ego felt more foreign and adventurous.) Terror-stricken, I screamed as loud as I could, and in an instant, Reto and Carlos were running up the exterior staircase to my rescue, shouting in English, German, French, and whatever other languages they knew. Spooked by the commotion and sound of their approaching voices, the hulking man turned and, despite that I had a top-floor terrace, leapt off into the dark night, running off into the shadowy streets as soon as he hit the ground.

After that night, I began sleeping inside, barring the door to the terrace (which didn't lock) by pushing a table against it and then piling a chair, wine bottles, and books on top of it so that if anyone tried to get in, they'd make so much noise, I'd surely wake up. I did this every night except for one: the night I came down with food poisoning.

Maybe it was bad fish from a taverna or spoiled milk in the *staka me agya*, the traditional Cretan dish made from eggs and cream that the old woman served her boarders. Whatever it was, when my landlady saw me looking green and peaked, she gestured with her hands—she spoke no English—that I should spend the rest of the day in bed. I did as I was told, also eating the charcoal she gave me, which she signaled would make me feel better. (This wasn't just an old wives' tale: it's well known today that activated charcoal supplements help block the absorption of toxins.) A few hours later, I fell asleep before I could prepare my barricade, which was unfortunate, because when I woke up, I saw the same hulking man looming in my doorway, his large frame silhouetted by the moonlight that was pouring in through the terrace door and windows.

When the behemoth saw that I was awake, he started walking toward me, stuttering the same "Sorry, Sasha, sorry, Sasha," as I let out the same blood-curdling cry, prompting Reto and Carlos to come shouting up the staircase and the behemoth to fling himself off my terrace and run crashing away. To this day, I have no idea who he was, how he knew my door wasn't barricaded that night, and what he might have done to me if I hadn't screamed so loudly.

After that night, I had had enough: it was time to leave Crete and go back to Paris. I didn't feel safe anymore, and from the letters he sent, it seemed Jean-François wouldn't be able to get a deferment after all. I adored Crete and enjoyed my travels there, but while Joni Mitchell may have found love and creativity on the island, I discovered something else—what it meant to be a woman in the world alone. And as for my love, when I realized that he was about to ship out, I knew it was time for me to do the same.

IN MID-JUNE, I left Crete on the same overnight ferry I had taken to the island, making the long trip back to Athens with Reto and Carlos. After spending the day in the capital with them, I caught a 3 a.m. flight back to Paris, landing the same morning Jean-François turned twenty-five.

When he met me at the airport, I hugged him so long and hard, I thought my body would melt and mold into his. Even though it was his birthday, he had already arranged the atelier with bouquets of flowers, bottles of wine, and a tin of Camembert, my favorite French cheese. Later that evening, we went to the fancy Brasserie Vagenende, in Saint-Germain-des-Prés, to have an elegant birthday dinner with Jean-Francois's brother Jean-Marie and Jean-Marie's boyfriend, Daniel.

Within a day, Jean-François and I were back to the same easy routine we had established before I left for Greece. Every day, something special happened—or, at least, every day felt like something special. Whenever Jean-François wasn't working, we'd spend the day walking through the city, stopping to pick up cheese, mustard, and a baguette along the way as he took me to another hidden park, secret garden, or tiny art museum with an incredible collection and nearly no tourists. We also went to the Petit Palais, the Louvre, and Paris's other grand museums over and over, soaking up the art and allowing ourselves to be moved by what we absorbed, no matter how many times we went.

In the afternoon or evening, we'd picnic on the Seine, meet Antonio and Mariette for dinner, go to a jazz club, or cook at home with whatever we had picked up from the small shops during the day—fish, vegetables, bread. Life together felt so simple, yet so rich.

That spring and summer, we went often to visit Jean-François's mom in Pau, a small city in the South of France, at the base of the Pyrenees. While Jean-François had been born in Morocco, where his father had been a foreign legionnaire, his parents moved back to France when he was young. His father was very proud of having been a legionnaire, and until the day he died, when Jean-François was only a child, he still wore his white kepi, a classic French Foreign Legion hat with a flat top, short visor, and sweeping neck flap. Whenever I saw Jean-François's dad in photos, I always thought he looked so romantic in his kepi, like something from Edith Piaf's song "Mon Legionnaire." Jean-François's mother, whom we all called Mamushka, was a short, pretty woman with sparkling eyes that often glinted with a hint of mischief. She had four sons—Jean-François, Jean-Marie, Jean-Pierre, and Jean-Paul—and one daughter, Marie-Bert, and I adored them all.

When we were in Pau, Jean-François took me to nearby Biarritz to watch pelota, a Basque racket sport played on short courts with small hoops. Back then, only men played the game, and for the occasion, they dressed in the most regal-looking outfits, with white shirts, white pants, red sashes, and red berets. After the game ended, everyone went to a nearby café to drink and sing at the top of their lungs late into the evening. I loved their local café tradition of spontaneous a cappella, and the men in their traditional outfits looked even more handsome under the warm café lights as they toasted everyone at the bar—I even learned a Basque song so I could sing along. Everything about their culture seemed so jolly and joyous to me, and I was grateful to be able to experience it.

WHEN WE were back in Paris, Jean-François was often busy with work, illustrating advertisements for Air France, and together, we'd walk to the air carrier's headquarters in Montparnasse to pick up his assignments. After we got back to the atelier, he'd draw at the table while I painted or drew on the floor, both of us working late into the evening while we listened to French radio. We spent many wonderful nights like this, drawing side by side without speaking, as the voices of Edith Piaf, Serge Gainsbourg, and Jacques Brel filled the atelier and wafted out into the soft evening air through the open windows.

Jean-François earned only an artist's salary for his illustrations, and I was still trying to stretch the money I had saved from my jobs in California, in the hope of enrolling in the fall at the École des Beaux-Arts. But money didn't matter much to us then—we were young and in love, and it was far more interesting to us to live ascetically, going to jazz clubs only when they didn't charge a cover and dropping into gallery openings where we'd fill up on free wine and cheese. I also didn't mind using the shared toilet one flight above our atelier or showering at the public baths several blocks away, as our studio was so small, it didn't even have a bathroom.

Over time, I started to grasp something I had begun to learn from my parents—that money doesn't buy you happiness. Instead, having passions, good health, and love from others does—and if you're lucky enough to have all three, you have all the wealth in the world. After I became successful as a model, I relearned this lesson over and over again, with money often only complicating things for me and rarely ever creating authentic joy. (Then again, there was that time when money did come in handy and, several years ago in Italy, I chartered a gorgeous old wooden sailboat to see the coast with my three children and several close friends, which remains one of the best holidays I've ever taken.)

IN AUGUST that year, our simple, modest life was suddenly upended when Jean-François finally got the letter we were both dreading, the one ordering him to report immediately to Camp de Souge, a military training academy outside Bordeaux. While he packed, I sat on our bed and sobbed. Later that night, I went with him to the Gare du Nord, Europe's busiest train station, so he could catch the three-hour direct line to Bordeaux. By the time he boarded the train, my face was so wet with tears that all I could see were his soft hazel eyes beaming back at me with love from across the platform. I didn't know when I would see him again, but that warmth in his eyes was all I needed to get by.

Before Jean-François left, he insisted on taking me to Air France, asking me to bring along the portfolio of work I had been assembling to apply to the École des Beaux-Arts. When we got to the airline's offices, he explained to his managers that he'd been drafted into the military, then introduced me as his girlfriend and suggested I take over his illustration assignments while he served. His managers flipped through my portfolio, then hired me on the spot, which is how I began drawing for Jumbo, a division of Air France created to market the new 747 jet that was already revolutionizing air travel.

In a matter of weeks, I was working so much for Air France that I didn't have time to apply to Beaux-Arts, which required a rigorous interview process. Instead, I began taking free classes at the Académie de la Grande Chaumière, known for its more laissez-faire attitude toward traditional art "rules," with a similarly impressive roster of former students, including Joan Miró, Marc Chagall, Amedeo Modigliani, and Fernand Léger. I started with figure drawing classes at the Académie at night, bringing my easel to sketch the nude models who posed in the middle of the room, absorbing all the critiques I received from the other artists there, many who were quite talented.

"Oh, that's good, Christie," one would say. "But *peut-être*, you want to try doing it with just a simple line. Just a simple little line here."

Or, "That is *comme ci, comme ça*, but it is lacking something, you know? Focus more on the hands."

Jean-François and I had a big circle of friends in Paris before he left for the military, and after he was drafted, I continued to make more—artists from the Académie, shop owners in Montparnasse, people I saw on the street every day. Over time, Paris began to feel like a small town to me—my town—as I'd bump into friends at a café or hear my name called from across the boulevard. For the first time in my life, I felt I was exactly where I belonged. That year, I came into myself in Paris in many ways, months before the city made me a model.

At the same time, I missed Jean-François terribly. He had three-day leaves every so often, and I lived for these weekends when we fell right back into the same routine, walking through the city, seeing friends, cooking, making art, and making love. On Sunday nights, he'd catch the last possible train back to Camp de Souge, and I always went with him to the station, even though it was always very late. I loved walking hand in hand with him into the Gare du Nord, its arrival hallway gleaming golden in the evening light and immense iron beams framing the exit doors to a dozen different platforms, each leading to a new train bound for another adventure.

Walking out alone, without Jean-François, was an entirely different experience, though, when the station became cold and cavernous, feeling as empty and lonely as the sound of my shoes tapping mournfully across the hard stone floor. As soon as I stepped outside the station doors, it was always raining, the weather continually matching my mood as tears dripped down my face. Hurrying away in the pouring rain, I remembered *Les Parapluies de Cherbourg* every time, and as devastated as I was to watch Jean-François leave, the bittersweet sentimentality of the moment wasn't lost on me as I pulled my trench coat tighter around me and made my way toward the Métro.

Once I got home—and on many other nights without Jean-François—I'd turn on the radio and draw or paint late into the night, just as he and I had always done together. As the weeks went by, I started waiting for one radio show that always came on at midnight sharp, announcing itself with a melancholy whistle before a sultry, canorous female voice began speaking over it: "*Bonsoir, mesdames et messieurs*, we have traffic and weather, but first . . ." The whistling then continued, like a strange melodic vamp during a musical, the sound always quiet and sad. Over time, that whistled tune came to represent everything romantic about midnight in Paris for me, as I drew alone while listening to the hushed sounds of the city below, the streets quiet outside my window except for the occasional honk of a taxicab and the *click-click-click* of a woman's high heels over the pavement.

YEARS LATER, when I was first getting to know Billy Joel and his music, he played "The Stranger" for me one night on the piano in his apartment. I had never heard the song before, and as soon as he began whistling its iconic introduction, I burst out, interrupting his serenade.

"Oh, my god! You're whistling my song from Paris! That's from my radio show," I cried.

"No," he said, "I'm whistling my song."

"No!" I insisted. "It's basically the same whistle from my radio show."

We then both began to whistle the same song, sharing an uncanny but magical moment, as Billy started to sing "The Stranger":

Christie Brinkley

Well, we all have a face
That we hide away forever
And we take them out and show ourselves
When everyone has gone

Hearing the lyrics to his song, I felt that Billy and I must have both found comfort in the same sad whistle and that, just maybe, it captured for each of us what it meant to be alone, even if we had experienced it in different times and places.

On all the nights I heard that whistle in my Paris atelier and during the first few occasions with Billy, I never thought it would be possible to feel more alone with someone else than when you were truly alone. But my life with Billy included that degree of loneliness at times—not at first and not all the time, but some of the time. And for that feeling, I have no bittersweet sentimentality.

CHAPTER

6

April 1. The unofficial start of spring. A day of new beginnings, when everything starts to bud, blossom, and unfold. And of course, April Fools' Day, when people try to create more amusement and mirth in their lives, even if only for a day.

In France, they celebrate April Fools' Day, too, but they call it *poisson d'avril*. It also marks the beginning of "April in Paris," a month so magical that it's the name of both a song from a Broadway musical and a Doris Day movie.

April 1, 1974, was all those things to me and more because it was an April in Paris I'd never forget and a day of new beginnings I couldn't ever have imagined.

It was the day I was discovered as a model.

(*Jump cut*: Twenty years later, on April 1, 1994, I had another unimaginable and memorable day when I nearly died in a helicopter crash.)

I MAY not have been discovered if it hadn't been for my dog, Bianca. Animals have always had a way of influencing my life, beginning with Trigger, the Hollywood horse who helped spur one of my first and most extraordinary memories. Bianca, my little puppy *parisienne*, was no different.

Jean-François and I got her a few days before he left for the military. He thought a dog would keep me company while he was gone, so we went to the pet store together and picked out a pint-size puppy, perfect for our pint-size atelier. Because her coat was the same color as fresh cream, we decided to name her Bianca, which means "white" in Italian.

A few weeks after Jean-François left, Bianca became sick. Or, maybe she had been sick all along, but her symptoms worsened as my weeks alone turned into months. When I took her to the vet, he told me she had distemper and prescribed medicine, hoping it would ease her more serious symptoms. But a week later, I was back in the vet's office, as sick with worry as my dog was with the disease.

Still, I was convinced that, with a good vet and lots of love, we could get through it, so I started taking Bianca to the vet regularly, racking up bills I couldn't afford. While I had been illustrating non-stop for Air France, I was using most of the money I earned to buy train tickets home for Jean-François whenever he had leave, since he was using his small military salary to cover our rent. To save money, I started calling the vet instead of going into his office, using the public pay phone at the post office to do so. I almost always brought Bianca with me when I did, carrying her in my straw basket bag, hoping the constant attention would somehow be curative.

One day, I was so absorbed by Bianca, looking down at her curled up in my bag, which I had slung across my body and cozied up under one arm, that I practically walked right into a tall man standing in front of me outside the entrance to the post office. He was dressed like an artist, in a faded green U.S. Army jacket, dark-wash jeans, and a printed neck scarf. Over his scarf hung a camera, which looked far more expensive than the one I had bought for Johnny that ill-fated Christmas two years before.

"Excuse me," he said with an American accent. "But I've seen you here before. I've been waiting for you to come back to make a call."

The admission tripped a dozen alarm bells in my mind: ever since my solo trip to Greece, I'd become warier of strangers, especially men. But we were surrounded by plenty of people, and there was something about this man—maybe that he looked like an artist or that he was also American—that made me feel comfortable enough to keep listening.

"I'm a photographer," he continued. "And I have a client who's looking for a girl with just your look—a sunny, California girl."

How does he know I'm from California? I thought. *Is this some kind of* poisson d'avril *prank?*

"I am from California," I admitted. "But I'm not a model. Not at all."

"If you're not a model, you should be," he said. "You could earn a lot of money."

Is this really this guy's best line? I nearly rolled my eyes but then caught myself: the idea of making a lot of money was appealing, even if it was likely far-fetched.

"I'd love it if you came by my studio so I could take a few pictures of you," the man continued, jotting down his name and address on a mailing slip and handing it to me.

I thanked him, smiled, and folded the paper inside my bag.

After he left, I rushed inside the post office and hurried over to the public pay phone, but instead of calling the vet, I immediately dialed my friend Stephanie, to tell her about the encounter. When I mentioned the photographer's name, she whooped with surprise.

"Errol Sawyer?!" she said. "Why, Christie, I've definitely seen his name in *Elle*! My friend models for him. She loves working for him!"

She then told me everything she knew about Errol and her model friend, as my attitude slowly shifted from hesitant uncertainty to growing excitement. Why not take a few pictures with this photographer and see what modeling was all about? I had always thought models were interesting and elegant, and growing up, my friends and I had cut their pictures out of magazines and glued them onto paper, stringing the pages together to make our own magazines. But we had always considered ourselves the art directors, never the models. Plus, I didn't think I had what it took to be a model, because for years, kids had teased me about my "chipmunk cheeks," even asking if I hid acorns there. And I thought I was too chubby, a perception reinforced by my mom's constant encouragement that I watch my weight—perhaps her only maternal flaw. Every time she saw me eyeing a dessert, she'd say in a singsong voice, "A minute on the lips, Christie, a lifetime on the hips . . ."

Still, as my dad's daughter, I had an insatiable curiosity and was eager to devour as many new and interesting things as possible—and modeling, even if I did it for only a day, was certainly new and interesting. I decided to go the next afternoon to Errol's studio, which was just a five-minute walk from the atelier.

The next day, when I arrived at his studio, I could see immediately that Stephanie had been right: Errol was the real deal, his studio jammed with cameras, lighting equipment, and fashionable portraits of beautiful models thumbtacked to the walls. His wife, a friendly Frenchwoman, was there too, and after we sat down, Errol explained that he wanted to take test photos of me to show his client and the agency.

"Agency?" I asked.

"Yes," he said. "Agencies represent models—they're the ones who will find you work. If they do, you'll get paid a thousand francs per day for editorial work. That's when you pose for magazines. You'll get paid more if you do advertisements—you know, shoots for catalogues, commercials, and stuff."

A thousand francs per day? At a minimum? My jaw hit the studio floor. That was the equivalent to two hundred U.S. dollars, more than I made in an entire week illustrating for Air France.

"I'd love if you could wear a nice dress and meet me tomorrow at the entrance to the Jardin du Luxembourg," Errol said. "We'll go into the park and take some pictures. How does that sound?"

I agreed and left his studio, excited by everything I had just heard. But as soon as I got home, I began to panic. *A nice dress?* I thought. What on earth would I wear?

I racked my mind. A few weeks ago, I'd seen advertisements on kiosks all over Paris for a clothing company called Cacharel. In many of the pictures, the models wore these shadowy, dreamy dresses that made them appear almost ethereal, and inspired by the look, I bought one, a delicate silk wrap in a pretty floral print with puffy sleeves. It cost more than I could afford, but I was now grateful I made the splurge. *If Cacharel is what all the French girls wear, that's what I'll wear, too,* I thought. I also laid out a knit cloche hat to wear several different ways, to add versatility.

The next morning, I jumped out of bed and rushed to the French doors. I could see the Tour Montparnasse already bathed in sunlight, and the air felt warm and luxurious for early April—an ideal day for a photo shoot. When I arrived at the entrance to the gardens, Errol was already there, and as I walked toward him, he seemed to be pleased with my dress, which pleased me. Once we were inside the park, he began taking pictures, asking me to stand this way, turn that way, keep walking, put on my hat, take it off, or stop and gaze to the left of his lens. I had never deliberately posed for anyone before—only for school photos, which, in my mind, didn't count—and I realized I had no idea what to do with my hands. I kept squirming to ease the awkwardness I felt, and the more I fidgeted, the more Errol complimented me on my poses. He also gave me some targeted pointers, and eventually, I began to relax and have fun. After an hour or two, he stopped shooting and smiled.

"I want to take these to the agency and see what they think, but I believe they're very good," he said.

My heart flipped a bit, pushing out some of the tension I'd been holding in my chest all morning.

"If the agency likes them, I'd like to see if I can get some money to do a real shoot, with other outfits and someone to do your hair and makeup," he continued.

Clothes I don't own? Hair and makeup done by a professional? That sounded even more exciting than our day in the Jardin du Luxembourg had been. I agreed to meet him at his studio the following afternoon, which was when he told me the proposed shoot was a go: the agency had liked my photos and given him money to do more. He asked if I could come back the following day for hair and makeup, after which we'd walk back into the gardens and elsewhere around the city to take more shots.

ON MY fourth consecutive day with Errol since first meeting him at the post office, I became nearly unrecognizable, even to myself, wearing a full, professional face of makeup for the first time and dressed in a white silk shirt and a black tie, with a white A-line skirt and black heels—an outfit that seemed distinctly Chanel to me, even though I had never worn the famed fashion brand. A stylist had also parted my hair off-center and curled it into tight ringlets, transforming me into someone who looked far more sophisticated and chicer than I'd ever thought I'd be.

That afternoon, Errol had a photo assistant with him, and along with the stylist and a friend who had brought the clothing, we went into the Jardin du Luxembourg for several shots, then walked over to Café de Flore, which is an illustrious, old coffeehouse in Saint-Germain-des-Prés. At the café, Errol asked me to sit outside at a table, and feeling more elegant than I ever had in my life, I tried to channel the look I'd seen so often on Parisian women—the ones who sat elegantly at the edge of their seats while cigarette smoke curled around their faces, or the ones who crisscrossed the city on their Mobylettes, their legs folded underneath them while their scarves fluttered behind, caught up in wind-blown wisps of hair.

"That's good," Errol called. "That's very good, Christie!"

Encouraged by his praise, I began to make up little stories in my mind, moving my body as I adopted the starring role in the mental movie in my head—my old childhood trick.

Here I am, waiting for mon petit ami *after we've been apart for months.* I then crossed my legs, brought my hand to my chin, and cocked my head slightly.

Look, someone at the other table is trying to catch my eye. I then shifted in my seat, bent my wrist, and turned toward Errol.

You can't see them, but someone out of frame is very funny. I then laughed, tossed my head, and looked back at the camera.

More from Errol: "Oh, that's great, Christie, that's really great!"

When he finally stopped shooting, I realized a small crowd had gathered around us outside Café de Flore. Dozens of people were stopping to look at us—stopping to look at *me.* What did they see in a big-cheeked blonde amid so many far more fashionable Parisians? The answer didn't matter to me: I was having more fun than I'd ever imagined.

After the shoot, I walked all the way home to Montparnasse, searching for myself in the reflection of every shop window and finding instead only a stylish stranger peering back through smoky eyes, thick lashes, and full, bouncy curls. I smiled at her, and she smiled back: *Enchantée, mademoiselle.* Delighted to meet you.

While I didn't know it at the time, for the next fifty years, I'd meet this made-up stranger over and over again . . .

A FEW days later, Jean-François surprised me by coming home at seven in the morning for a short leave. We spent the entire day together, lying in bed, washing each other's hair in the kitchen sink, and walking hand in hand through Montparnasse. That evening, we went for drinks to our little place, La Coupole, where we had first met. Amid the café's hushed conversation, as people strolled slowly down the boulevard outside, I was telling Jean-François about my whirlwind of a week when, suddenly, we heard thunderous applause, bravos, and cheering.

What on earth was going on? We looked outside and *oh la la*, our first streaker!

Streaking had become a thing worldwide ever since a man raced naked across the stage of the Academy Awards ceremony in Los Angeles earlier that month, flashing a peace sign while wearing only his birthday suit. Apparently, more things than my modeling career were springing up in Paris that year.

For me, the best part of seeing the streaker was how it transformed the restaurant. Suddenly, people were laughing and chatting across tables, as that brief flash of flesh and genitalia broke down social barriers, giving us a shared experience that instantly made us all friends. If streaking had the power to bring people together like this, I wanted to see a whole lot more spontaneous nudity everywhere I went.

Of course, more serious events also took place that month. The day after I was discovered as a model, France's president, Georges Pompidou, died in office, shaking the country to its core. Several days later,

Stephanie and I watched from her apartment windows as his casket somberly floated in a hearse down the boulevard by the Seine, crowds of people lining the street to watch the historic procession. President Richard Nixon attended the funeral, despite the ongoing Watergate scandal, which amazed me. In my letters home, I always asked for news about Watergate, and my dad responded, telling me how Nixon had just been named a co-conspirator in the scandal, which moved him one step closer to either impeachment or resignation.

In my personal life, I had another death to mourn. A few weeks after Pompidou's funeral, I woke up to find Bianca nearly paralyzed with pain on the floor next to our bed. I rushed her to the vet, who gave her several injections, but the drugs didn't work. She died early the next day, at one o'clock in the morning, as I held her tiny body alone in our atelier.

For these reasons, I wasn't thinking much about modeling when I learned from Errol that the agency was intrigued by the test photos he had taken and wanted to meet with me as soon as possible. Days later, I was booked for an interview with Elite Model Management, which was owned by John Casablancas, one of the most notable modeling agents, who would be credited with coming up with the very idea of the supermodel.

When I first met Johnny, as everyone called him, at the agency, he immediately motioned me into his back office, where he picked up a desk phone and dialed several other photographers and bookers (people who assign models to clients), asking them to join us. Instantly, I was surrounded by a throng of people, all of them analyzing how I looked, as though I were a racehorse trotted out for examination before any gamblers placed their bets.

"She's got a baby face, round cheeks, and a womanly body—that's a great combination that we can do so much with," Johnny said to the others, acting as if I wasn't even in the room. "I want her signed."

"She's very California girl sportif," another said. "Very all-American."

"*Vogue* and *Elle* will love her," one of the bookers cooed.

Another chimed in. "I think she'd be great for that German advertiser. Let's get them some of her pictures."

I was thrilled that they were interested in me—but now what? Would I get some kind of model makeover? How would I go from the barefaced, beachy girl who had just walked into their offices to the type of sophisticated, high-gloss, city-chic model I saw in all the magazines?

Johnny asked me to come back later that afternoon, and when I did, his secretary pushed a contract across her desk for me to sign. I read it briefly, then signed it without even thinking to ask to have a lawyer look it over. I was innocent and trusting—two attributes that, over the years, have caused me a lot of heartache. While I would quickly learn how to avoid heartache as a model, I never did as a woman, especially as one who always has and will believe in love.

AFTER I signed with Johnny, I figured I had reason enough to celebrate. Jean-François had a short leave coming up—it wasn't long enough for him to come back to Paris, but plenty long to warrant my taking a train to Pau, where he met me from Camp de Souge and we stayed with his mother.

That trip to Pau was totally calamitous in one way and quite fortuitous in another. Shortly after we met there, Jean-François and I were biking through town one afternoon when, while trying to steer around a parked motorcycle, I popped my bike up onto the sidewalk, which caught my wheel and railroaded my face straight into the parked motorcycle. My bike stopped dead, but I continued moving, flipping head over heels above the handlebars and coming down hard onto the pavement. While I don't remember it, I was rushed to the hospital, where I developed a fever and one of my eyes erupted into a terrifying orb of black, blue, and purple. Even though he had to return to Camp de Souge the following morning, Jean-François stayed by my side the entire night, and after I was released from the hospital, his mom and sister took care of me, gently nursing me until my fever subsided.

But with a big black eye and a raging fever, I ended up staying longer in Pau than I had planned. And because I had a black eye *and* a new modeling contract, I figured I should use the downtime to try to learn something about makeup, which I had never really worn before and didn't quite know how to apply. At a shop in town, I bought bright blue eyeshadow, bubblegum-pink lipstick, jet-black mascara, and an oversize eyelash curler. I had never used an eyelash curler before, and after closing the clamp around the lashes of my healthy eye, I heard a *pop, pop, pop, pop*—the sound of eyelashes being ripped away at the root. I was horrified: Would they ever grow back? I reckoned I should stay longer in Pau to make sure.

As it turned out, my timing was perfect. While I was in Pau, much of Paris and the rest of France was shut down, everyone transfixed on the election of Pompidou's replacement.

But by the time I got back to Paris, I was surprised to see the front door of our *chambre de bonne* completely covered in handwritten messages delivered through the city's pneumatic tubes—how Parisians communicated in those days, before the mass installation of telephones. Because neither Jean-François nor I had been home, the building's concierge had thumbtacked the notes to our door, all of which had been sent by Elite, each message teeming with increasing urgency:

Can you kindly let us know when you're free? A German catalogue AND a German magazine want you ASAP!

Christie, where are you? Elle *wants you for the interior.* Vogue *also wants you for a shoot . . . tomorrow!*

Christie, we have a ton of work for you! Please, please come into the agency immediately.

Apparently, the agency had sent my test shots to dozens of clients, many who had called immediately, asking to book me. But instead of telling these clients, "We have no idea where she is, but we think she's on holiday with her boyfriend," the agents had said that I was already booked and that I was in such high demand that I couldn't possibly find time to do a shoot for *Elle*, *Vogue*, or a high-paying advertiser.

When I called my parents to tell them what had happened, my dad chuckled. "They thought you were negotiating with them," he said.

Whatever I was doing, it worked. When I went into the agency the next day, a booker handed me a long list of "go-sees" all around the city: *Go see this photographer, go see that client.* Within hours, I was dashing off to parts of Paris I'd never been to before, despite having lived in the city for more than a year, which suddenly made modeling seem like an even greater adventure.

After one of my very first go-sees that day, the agency told me that *Parents* magazine wanted me for a cover shoot the following day. *My first modeling shoot is also my first cover?* I thought incredulously. The booker then explained that the shoot would take only two hours, which would give me ample opportunity to go on a few more go-sees the same day.

Welcome to the industry, kid.

While it may seem effortless, modeling is never as easy or as elegant as it looks.

For the *Parents* shoot, I wore another Cacharel dress—this one with tank straps, an apron skirt, a big bow at the waist, and an open back crisscrossed by two thick straps. I also wore a white tee under the dress and pulled my hair back into a ponytail—which, evidently, the photographer liked, because he didn't ask me to change or redo my hair. Then, someone swabbed a bit of makeup on me—not the full glam makeover I had expected—and gave me a bike to ride back and forth in a tight space on the street while the photographer snapped, rotated his camera, and snapped again. At one point, a male model joined us, which was when the photographer asked me to sit on the bike while talking with the man, as though we were having an easy, breezy time, chatting about the weather or our favorite boulangerie for buttery croissants.

"Now we'll go into the studio and do the cover shot," the photographer announced.

Someone then handed me a yellow bikini, and after I changed, the photographer motioned for me to stand in front of a backdrop, and suddenly, I felt out of my element. Being in a bikini wasn't the difficult part of the shoot—growing up in Malibu, I had practically *lived* in a bikini. But it felt different wearing a bikini indoors in a room full of strangers. And I felt even more awkward, because now, without being able to walk, bike, or sit down at a café, I really didn't know what to do with my hands. That awkwardness turned into discomfort when the photographer then asked the male model to stand behind me and kiss my neck and shoulders.

"Pretend you are a young couple with kids," the photographer called out from behind his camera. "A mom and a dad!"

I thought about Jean-François, then countered that thought with the fact that the shoot would likely pay for at least a dozen train tickets home for him. I decided to focus on what the photographer had said, making up a story in my mind as I had done at Café de Flore—only, this time, to distract myself from the strange man nuzzling my neck.

Here I am, a young mom on the Mediterranean Sea, sharing a moment with my husband while our two children play out in the ocean. I smiled and softened my shoulders.

Soon, they'll come bounding out of the water and onto the sand, and we'll all go for ice cream. I bent my knee and moved my hands up to my waist.

The trick worked: *Parents* liked it, choosing one of the images from the shoot for the cover. Although, when I look back at that cover today, I can see that I was holding myself as though I was trying to hug myself, as if to say, *You'll be okay, Christie, you'll be okay.*

Yes, you will.

THERE WAS no time to think about the *Parents* shoot because immediately afterward, I rushed off to a go-see with Uli Rose, a well-known French photographer who booked me the same day for the inside of *Vogue France.* Two days later, I found myself walking under an alley of chestnut trees in the Jardin des Tuileries, doing my first *Vogue France* shoot while wearing a Russian-style coat dress and oversize fur alpaca hat and trying my best to suck in my cheeks and minimize my hips. (My cheeks and hips have always been my "problem" areas, in my mind.)

In a matter of days, my life turned into a succession of go-sees, shoots, commercials, and covers. After the Tuileries shoot, I did a cover shoot for *Votre Beauté*, a major French women's magazine; and another for *Harper's and Queen*, now known as *Harper's Bazaar.* There were also shoots for *Elle France, Marie-Claire*, a hair care company, and other Paris-based magazines and advertisers. One day, I was standing in the middle of a Paris racetrack, then the next day, I was driving two hundred kilometers outside the city to pose near a waterfall, all while getting home in time to have dinner with Jean-François if he was on leave. Another day, a client asked me to lie down on a *péniche*—those flatboat barges you see on the Seine in Paris—while floating down the river, which was incredibly fun. While some people went into an office every day for work, I was more than happy to stretch out on a *péniche* while sunbathing on the Seine.

At one point, the agency asked if I would do an advertisement for a lingerie company. The pay was double the editorial rate—more than two thousand francs a day. *Yes, yes, I would.* The next day, I was standing in a studio wearing nothing up top but a white satin-and-lace bra, feeling more risqué than I had in the yellow bikini. But for twice the price, I was willing to expand my comfort zone.

As different and interesting as all these new experiences were, the thrill didn't compare to the one I had been waiting to feel for nearly a year, which was when Jean-François would finally come home. And in late July, a little more than a month after I began modeling, he did. The French celebrate the beginning of their independence revolution on July 14, Bastille Day, but that year, Jean-François and I had an even bigger independence celebration, on July 27, when he stepped off the train in Gare du Nord for the last time. Finally, he was free from military service, and we were both free to be together forever.

That summer, I started traveling out of France to model, taking the train to Munich frequently to work for a German-based clothing company. Because it was in advertising, the German gig paid exceedingly well, but for me, the best part was staying in a hotel with a real bathroom and bathtub. After living in a studio where the nearest bath was three blocks away, this was a true luxury, made even more lavish by the fact that, every morning, a porter would bring up a basket of bread and muffins, alongside freshly churned butter and strong coffee, which I would eat while soaking in the tub. Following every shoot, I couldn't wait to get back to my room for any leftover bread and butter, which I would take in the bath again. While Johnny had asked me to watch my weight after I signed with Elite, in Germany, all bets were off. Plus, I didn't think I would model long enough for my weight to make any difference.

Germany was a formative experience for me in more ways than one because I also learned there that you always had to keep moving as a model so that your clothes never looked static or wrinkled— there was no retouching in those days—and the photographer could capture your outfit from all angles. During my first trip to Munich, I watched another model on set who was a real pro execute this move where she walked with her purse swinging out behind her before turning suddenly, as though someone had caught her arm. The maneuver created a stunning swirl of motion around her and her clothes, and after I saw it, I knew I had to add it and other moves to my repertoire.

THE MORE I worked, the more I learned. From other models—many who were friendly and helpful, contrary to the catty stereotype—I discovered that blue eyeshadow wasn't my best color. Also, right before another shoot for *Vogue France*, Jean Louis David, one of the country's most eminent hairstylists, chopped my hair into a triangle bob, then permed it, snipping off the hair that didn't curl properly. The hairstyle was inspired by brunette bombshell Dayle Haddon, one of the hottest models and actors in the early 1970s. And while I thought the look was fantastic for about fifteen minutes, when I first washed my hair, I realized I had no idea how to control or style it. Instead, I began tucking it under a beret, continually shifting the hat and always worried about how I looked. What had been a hairdo was quickly turning into a hair don't.

Ironically, though, it was my curly hair that first caught the attention of *Sports Illustrated*, ultimately landing me in the magazine's Swimsuit Issue. That was something else I learned as a model: sometimes, the things you believe are your drawbacks are actually what set you apart and make you stand out and shine. I was never model-skinny, either, which I now know helped launch my career, making me more appealing for swimsuit and lingerie work. The same was true of my early perm, for different reasons. Now, whenever I'm tempted to perceive something as a personal defect, I remind myself, *Go with the flow, Christie.* Because you never know what the flow might bring.

What did the modeling industry see in me that made me so successful right away? I didn't know then, and I still don't know now. During my fifty years as a model, I've always assumed that every job I've ever had would be my last. While some people might call that self-doubt, I say it's the best way to live: When you think every job is your last, you appreciate each one a little more. And when they call you to work again, you're so grateful that you never squander an opportunity or show up feeling bitter or bored.

For every modeling job I've ever had, I've always felt grateful, just like I do for every day I'm alive. And because of that gratitude, when people say, "Smile, Christie," I always can and do.

7

Sometimes, it's all about being in the right place at the right time. And in Hollywood in the 1970s, one of the right places, no matter the time, was the Brown Derby.

If you walked by the restaurant then, you might have never guessed the luminosity of star power circulating inside. Unlike today's celebrity hangouts, the Derby wasn't tucked into some discreet corner of the city or hidden inside a posh hotel lobby behind a curtain of hanging foliage. Instead, the Derby hit like a rest stop eatery off the highway: big and hokey, with anything and everything about it designed to attract the attention of weary drivers—or, in the Derby's case, the attention of bigwig executives and movie stars from the nearby studios. This may have been why the Derby looked more like a movie set, with a sprawling, Spanish Mission–style façade, a half dozen entrances and exits, and several giant signs sticking out of the roof like lawn ornaments, including one for Canadian Club and another in the shape of a derby bearing the restaurant's name.

Once you stepped inside the Derby, though, it was another story, as the mood changed from rest stop eatery into celebrity country club, albeit Hollywood style. Actors, producers, musicians, and other entertainers huddled into large leather booths as gilded chandeliers hung overhead, suspended by long, glittering chains. Covering the walls were black-and-white caricatures of Hollywood's most famous faces, including many who had dined there—Frank Sinatra, Rita Hayworth, Charlie Chaplin, Bing Crosby, and many others. The Derby was where Clark Gable purportedly proposed to Carole Lombard, where the first Hollywood episode of *I Love Lucy* was shot, where the non-alcoholic drink the Shirley Temple was allegedly created so the child star could sip alongside her parents, and where Derby owner Robert Cobb invented the Cobb salad from hastily arranged leftovers for Sid Grauman, owner of the equally famous Chinese Theatre. The Derby was where you went if you wanted to make a deal and where table-side handshakes turned into fully executed contracts, shared martinis became mutual movie agreements, and celebrities and the people who made them came to see and be seen.

When I first went to the Brown Derby, in September 1974, four months into this crazy thing called modeling, I had only heard of the place from my dad, who regaled me with legendary stories of who had been discovered there and what deals he had made inside. But by the time I left the restaurant that day, I had a Derby story of my own, after landing my first three TV commercials ever, all booked and brokered over the course of one lunch of two Cobb salads.

INITIALLY, THE reason I was in Los Angeles that September was to see my family, but while I was there, I agreed to meet with Eileen Ford, who was (and still is, posthumously) a legend in the industry, known for cultivating classic beauties and turning them into household names. While I had never heard of Johnny Casablancas before I first met him in Paris, I had known for years about Eileen and her agency, Ford Models, which she started in the 1940s with her husband, Jerry. By the 1970s, Ford represented all the major models, including Cheryl Tiegs, who I thought so beautiful, especially when she appeared dressed all in white in her CoverGirl commercials.

It wasn't my idea to meet with Eileen. During my initial interview with Johnny, two photographers had joined us in his back office, Mike Reinhardt and Patrick Demarchelier. Both became famous fashion photographers over time—Patrick particularly so, after taking personal portraits of Princess Diana that showed a more intimate side to the royal—and I ended up working with both men many times during the course of my career. When they first saw me in Johnny's office, though, I was a nobody, and they were still just doing test shots for the agency. But they had an eye and called Eileen in New York all the same, telling her a new girl had landed at Elite whom she had to see. That was all that it took to kick the hornet's nest, and once the buzz about me had started, it wasn't going to die down until Eileen laid eyes on the athletic California girl who had started modeling in Paris.

Because I wanted to visit my parents with Jean-François, who had never been to California before, Johnny's office arranged for me to meet with Eileen in Palm Springs, where she had a second home several miles from my parents' vacation house in the desert. Jean-François and I flew together from Paris to Los Angeles, touching down in an entirely different world, one where movie sets, palm trees, and the Pacific defined the city rather than the art museums, cafés, and ornate gardens I had grown to love in the French capital. It was also my first time back in Los Angeles since taking an overnight flight for Paris eighteen months before.

While I had already signed with Elite, Johnny was more than happy to have me meet with Eileen in the States. In 1974, when I flew to L.A., the notorious "model wars" hadn't started yet, marking the era when agents fought viciously over the right to represent models exclusively and when women had to pledge allegiance to one agency over any other. It wasn't until 1977, when Johnny opened an Elite outpost in New York City—Eileen's turf—and sparked a fierce territorial dispute and rivalry, that the model wars began, eventually making the pages of *People* magazine (with a sensational centerfold in which I posed with Johnny and other Elite models).

In the mid-1970s, when I was launching my career, agents still traded models to whoever they thought would make their star rise the fastest—and at the time, Eileen Ford was synonymous with turning modeling stars into supernovas in just a matter of months. She didn't do it alone, of course: she had powerful satellite agents, including Nina Blanchard, who owned her own namesake modeling firm in Los Angeles.

To this day, Nina remains the most candid agent I've ever met, which is saying something, because I've met a lot of agents throughout my career. When she called me at my parents' home in Los Angeles, asking if I would have lunch with her at the Brown Derby the following week, I immediately agreed. While I knew nothing about Nina, I've always believed that when opportunity knocks—or calls, in this instance—you answer. You never know what new or interesting adventure waits on the other end.

THAT WAS how, several days later, I found myself seated with Nina in a booth at the Brown Derby, which, on a Monday afternoon, was packed with well-dressed men and women, all there for the business of show business, as the waiters performed their own show, dancing salads, steaks, and trays of wine and cocktails between tables. Nina and I weren't talking about my modeling career for more than five minutes when a short, older man sidled up to our booth.

"Nina, Nina, why have you been holding out on me?" the man

asked, gesturing toward me and grinning. "Please, you must introduce me to this young lady."

"Ron," Nina said, "this is my new client, Christie Brinkley."

New client? That was news to me.

"Christie, what a pleasure to meet you," Ron said, shaking my hand before turning back to Nina. "We need her for a TV commercial for Yucca-Dew shampoo we're shooting," he told her.

I had never heard of Yucca-Dew shampoo, but it hardly mattered: I had also never done a TV commercial before—or any TV—and I was astonished and excited at the prospect.

"She might be able to do that, but she's only in California for a week, so you'll have to do it soon," Nina countered. "I'll be back in my office in an hour—call me then, and we'll make a deal."

After Ron left, Nina was just beginning to explain to me how her agency worked when a smartly dressed woman approached our booth. "Nina, who is this?" the woman said, eyeing me with a smile.

"This is Christie Brinkley—she's a brand-new client," Nina said. "We brought her over from Paris, but she's originally a California girl."

"Well, she'd be great for Noxzema," the woman said unequivocally. "We want to shoot a new TV commercial, and she's got the perfect look."

"Okay, well, Christie's only here for one week, so you'll have to shoot it soon," Nina said. "I'll be back in my office in an hour—call me then, and we'll make a deal."

By that point, Nina and I had our Cobb salads in front of us, but there hardly seemed time to eat because, within minutes, another person walked up to our booth—this time, a rep from Max Factor who insisted I'd be perfect for a commercial for the brand's new perfume. And as if on script, Nina explained that they'd better shoot it soon and that she'd be back in her office in an hour, which was when the rep should call to make a deal.

After one lunch at the Derby, I had my first three TV commercials ever. But that lunch fast-tracked my career in more ways than one because after doing one commercial for Noxzema, owned then by Noxell, I started working for Noxell's other brand, CoverGirl, which led to a twenty-five year contract—the longest running cosmetics contract for any model to date.

A few days after meeting Nina, I drove with Jean-François and my parents to Palm Springs, where it'd already been arranged that I'd meet with Eileen Ford. From the day I learned that she wanted to see me in the desert, I'd been fretting over what to wear. No one in my family ever dressed up in Palm Springs: we were a tennis family (compared to others in the desert who were golf families), and we wore only tennis clothes and bathing suits when we were there. I couldn't imagine donning a chic suit to see Eileen at her home, so I settled for my most formal sundress and insisted that Jean-François come with me: I was more nervous at the prospect of meeting Eileen than I had been for any other interview of my career.

When Eileen opened the door, I was surprised to see she was dressed more casually than I imagined, wearing only a triangle bikini top, a sarong skirt, and strappy sandals—although she still had a full face of makeup and perfectly coiffed hair, true to her New York heritage. Her husband, Jerry, was dressed similarly, in bathing trunks and a button-down Hawaiian shirt. The two welcomed us, inviting us inside and leading us through their home to a terrace in the back.

"Are you thirsty?" Eileen asked once we were outside on her meticulously manicured lawn, shielded from external view by chic white walls and a row of palm trees. "Jerry, would you mind getting everyone some lemonade?"

Once Jerry was inside, Eileen led us to the patio set on the far side of the terrace, taking my portfolio of pictures with her. After placing it on the table, she began slowly turning the pages, giving a few contemplative murmurs of approval before stopping at one picture. "What is this?" she exclaimed vehemently, gesturing grandly over the photo for emphasis. "This one is terrible! You must get rid of it right away!"

But with that emphatic gesture, one of Eileen's breasts dislodged from her tiny bikini top and popped right out into the open air, where Jean-François and I could see everything. Eileen was oblivious to her wardrobe malfunction, though, and kept chattering away about everything that was wrong with the photo in question while all I could think was, *Panic, panic, panic.* Without even glancing at each other, Jean-François and I both leaned over the photo, staring intently at it—and nothing else—as though trying to fully absorb Eileen's criticism.

"Oh, yes. You're right," I said as naturally as I could. "My hair—it's much too curly there!"

"Eileen?" It was Jerry calling from the entrance to the terrace, wondering where we had disappeared to since he last left us.

Oh no! I locked eyes on the photo in front of me. *We can't let Jerry find us like this, with Eileen's boob hanging out and the two of us pretending not to notice!*

"Darling, we're out here! At the table on the far side of the terrace!" Eileen called, waving her arms in another oversize gesture.

Apparently, Eileen's gesticulations were full-body exercises, because with that gesture, her bathing suit readjusted itself, reclaiming her breast into its small fabric nest, right in time for Jerry to appear with a tray of lemonades. At that point, I didn't care if Eileen liked my pictures—I was just relieved we hadn't been caught with the grand matriarch of modeling and her exposed bosom looking like a cross between a Renaissance Madonna painting and a smutty Slim Aarons outtake.

As it turned out, though, Eileen did like my photos—a lot.

"You've got a look, honey," she said, after she finished paging through my entire portfolio. "You're fresh, you're classic, and you're lovely. I see a big future for you."

My heart flipped harder and higher than it had after my first shoot with Errol. If Eileen Ford saw a future in me, it was the lift I needed as a model (not that I was ready yet to think about anything that needed lifting . . .).

"I'm taking you as a client," Eileen declared. "But I want you in New York City, not Paris. You'll meet with photographers and clients right away, and you'll have plenty of work."

Move from Paris? I thought for a hard second. But as much I had fallen in love with the City of Lights, I knew immediately and instinctively that I had to go to New York for Eileen, at least for a few months. Jean-François and I had already discussed the possibility, and he was excited by the prospect because his dream had always been to draw for the *New York Times*. And while my dream wasn't to model—I still wanted to be an artist—I was intrigued by the plot twists and turns that modeling had written into the movie of my life, and I wanted to see where the storyline took me next.

While I was thinking this, Eileen was still talking, although now she was looking at me a little sternly. "You do have to lose a little weight," she said. "I'm going to recommend that you eat fish—only fish and nothing but fish. You can have as much fish as you want and prepared in any way you like it, but if you're out to eat, you'll push everything else off your plate. If they serve you fish with a potato, don't eat the potato. If they serve you fish with broccoli, don't eat the broccoli. Only fish and water, please."

Wow, this is going to be tough. Not only did I dislike dieting—I was that model, after all, who enjoyed working in Germany expressly for the bread and butter—but also because I had been a vegetarian since age fourteen after reading Norman Mailer's *Miami and the Siege of Chicago*, which includes a graphic scene that takes place in a slaughterhouse. Other than some exploratory *moules* and a few other seafood dishes in France and Greece, I hadn't eaten fish or any other animal protein for years.

But if I had to eat only fish for Eileen Ford, I'd do it.

The following week, I shot my first TV commercial, for Max Factor. They taped it in a Los Angeles studio, where they asked me to swipe solid perfume from a golden compact onto my neck while acting as if it smelled as delicious as blooming citrus trees in California. I hadn't acted since high school, when I played both a cowboy and a Sioux in *Annie Get Your Gun*, and I was concerned that my dramatic skills were sophomoric at best. But I've always believed in doing the things that make you the most nervous: that's when you really know you're alive, whenever you get all the chills and thrills that come with stepping outside your comfort zone. And if I was lousy at TV, so what? Everything about modeling was outside my wheelhouse. At the very least, I would have tried something new, an accomplishment in itself.

After the Max Factor spot, I flew to Arizona to do the Yucca-Dew shoot, then back to Los Angeles for Noxzema. Doing a Noxzema commercial in those days was a fairly big deal—Farrah Fawcett and quarterback Joe Namath had just done one the year before that became instantly iconic, in part due to its undisguised sexual innuendo. While my first commercial for Noxzema was much tamer, the hair and makeup team made me look like I was wearing nothing more than a white spa headband. With my hair stylishly pulled back, my job was to rub Noxzema cream onto my face and then splash it off as though it was the most refreshing and invigorating thing I could do, all while the TV camera spun around me, catching the action from every angle. I loved the feeling of dipping my fingers into the cleansing cream, how it tingled on my skin, and how it smelled so much like eucalyptus, which made it easier to act as though washing my face was the pinnacle of pleasure the client wanted it to seem. But I must have been slightly allergic to the cleanser, because after a few shots, my neck turned bright red, which the director interpreted as excellent acting because I was so exhilarated by the product, it was giving me the ruddy look of blushing youth and beauty.

HOLLYWOOD HAS always been a small town, and within days after my meetings with Nina and Eileen, word shot around that there was a new model on the scene. Because I was more voluptuous than many models at the time, I was an attractive prospect to Jule Campbell, the editor who invented, curated, and produced the *Sports Illustrated* Swimsuit Issue. Once Jule heard about the fresh-faced, full-figured girl "from Paris," she wanted to see me immediately and arranged through Eileen to meet with me at a casting studio in Beverly Hills. The meeting may not have ever happened—or at least gone well—though, if I had taken Eileen's advice and already dieted myself down to her standards.

Sometimes, what you think are your drawbacks are actually what set you apart.

I still remember exactly what I wore to meet Jule: a white cotton tunic over a pair of white flared jeans accented by a bejeweled belt, a chunky orange beaded necklace, oversize sunglasses, and a white beret, under which I tucked my curly hair. I probably looked like I belonged in the Witness Protection Program, but whatever my style was, it evidently worked, because Jule called Eileen the next day to tell her she "had" to have the girl with the curly hair and the white beret. That means my out-of-control perm (and the beret I had used to conceal it) helped land me my very first appearance in *Sports*

Illustrated, ultimately introducing me to the other half of the population (men) and blowing up my career.

After we were back in Paris, Jean-François and I decided to move out of our quaint atelier in Montparnasse and into a larger apartment in Neuilly-sur-Seine, a residential suburb northwest of Paris. Neither of us loved the neighborhood—it was outside the city and a little snooty, with more modern buildings and fewer of the cafés, shops, and markets that made the arrondissements so lively and charming—but we were smitten by the size of the flat, which had a kitchen and a bathroom. (Now that I was making more money as a model, I thought it was time to start washing my hair at home rather than trekking to the public baths to do so.) Plus, the Neuilly apartment had a *jardin d'hiver* (a winter garden), with oversize windows, potted herbs, and other plants, which seemed so European to me. In our *jardin d'hiver*, I dreamed of growing sunflowers that touched the ceiling and vegetables we could cook with, but I never spent enough time in Neuilly to tend to that dream: after our trip to Los Angeles, I was modeling so much and traveling so often that there was little time to do anything other than unpack, kiss Jean-François, then pack again for the next shoot.

IN LATE November, I took my first long trip alone as a model, flying from Paris to Merida, Mexico, for my first shoot for *Sports Illustrated*. After I landed, a car picked me up in the middle of the night to drive me several hours north to Cancún, which didn't have an international airport at the time. In 1974, Cancún was just a quiet fishing village, not the mega tourist destination and resort hot spot it is today. But Jule had seen pictures of the place and thought it ideal for her Swimsuit Issue, which changed locations year to year. Plus, Mexico's then-president, Luis Echeverría, was so intent on developing the area that

111

he agreed to open his private summer home on the ocean for all of us to stay.

In the wee hours of morning, when I finally arrived from Merida at the president's estate, I was terribly nervous. What was I doing there? Who would the other models be? What would a swimsuit shoot be like? Fortunately, an editorial assistant was awake to greet me, whisking me through the house to a spacious room in the back.

"This is where you'll stay, Christie," she said, motioning to the private space. "I think you'll find that you have everything you need, but let me know if you want anything else. The other girls are waking up early tomorrow for a shoot, but Jule wants you to stay here at the beach and work on your tan. Is that okay?"

I nodded, thrilled to have a day to ease into the job. Plus, I was well aware that Paris hadn't exactly done wonders for my sun-kissed California look.

When I woke the next morning, I was delighted to find fishermen had delivered a fresh catch right to Echeverría's door, and after a quick breakfast of tuna—*how proud Eileen would be*, I thought—I headed to the beach outside the president's home, which was a long stretch of powdery, porcelain-white sand with the clearest blue waters I'd ever seen. I couldn't quite believe that my only task for the day was to lie on the beach, dipping in and out of the aquamarine surf whenever I wanted, but I dutifully did as I was told. Hours later, an assistant came to fetch me, explaining that everyone had returned from the shoot and that I was wanted in Jule's room for a fitting for the following day.

Walking into Jule's room that evening was like walking into a swimwear warehouse already ransacked by hordes of tourists searching for the most flattering fit. Piled onto the floor, bed, desk, and every other possible surface were hundreds of suits: bikinis, tankinis, micro-kinis, halter tops, bandeaus, one-pieces, cover-ups, caftans, ponchos, kimonos, and every iteration of beachwear in between. And in the middle of the fabric mountain was Jule, who eyed me up and down as soon as I walked in, mulling over a hundred different factors, including which suit would best fit my body, what color most complemented my skin and hair, which line would flatter the shoot's particular location, and whether she wanted to see me in a wet or dry suit. As I quickly learned, Jule was a real master at matching a model to a suit, location, and shot list—part of why her Swimsuit Issue was so successful.

But for my first fitting, Jule had her work cut out for her: by the time I was standing in her room, my daytime "tan" had turned into a bright-pink burn, as I hadn't realized how intense the sun could be south of the border. Yet, while I was horrified by my scorched skin, Jule remained unfazed.

"Let's go with it!" she said enthusiastically, tossing me a pink bikini bottom and pink shawl. "Try that on. We can tie the shawl in different ways, and it'll look so sexy, like you're wearing nothing on top."

That's because I won't be! I thought. How on earth was I going to pull this off?

That evening, as the sun set in shades of pink as rosy as my skin, I was all nerves as I stood in nothing but a pink shawl and tiny bikini bottom in front of the photographer, Walter Iooss, along with Jule and a handful of assistants. Making matters worse, the shawl was stringy and slippery, stitched from real silk, and I didn't know how to pose in it, so I kept fidgeting, moving my hands up and down my body and constantly rearranging it.

Whatever I was doing, though, worked like a charm.

"Look at her move, Walter," Jule muttered, as the camera's motor drive clicked with the sound of rapid-fire succession. "She's a fabulous mover."

"Smokey!" Walter yelled to me. He was a handsome, easygoing photographer, and while he regularly shot basketball and football players for *Sports Illustrated*, he had just begun to try his hand at the Swimsuit Issue. "You're so smoking that I'm going to start calling you 'Smokey'!"

Well, I guess I must be doing something right, I thought.

I started to relax and intentionally play with the shawl, even giving the camera a few teasing glances from time to time. The more I moved, played, and glanced, the more muttering I heard from Jule, along with cries of "Smokey" from Walter. Suddenly, modeling swimsuits didn't seem so tough.

The next day, however, another mishap occurred—this time, not due to the tropical sun but the tropical water. After I washed my hair for the first time in Mexico, something in the Yucatan water caused my curls to go crazy. I still had my Jean Louis David perm then—and still no idea how to style it—but in new water with a different pH, in addition to all the salt and sun, my curls went wild, coiling up around my face and making me look more like a circus clown than a swimsuit model.

When she first saw me, Jule acted as unfazed by my new look as she had been by my lobster-red tan. "Let's go with it!" she cried. "I think it's charming."

She handed me a white one-piece to wear, and off we went to the day's location, a lagoon, where Walter asked me to lie down in the shallow water. While I didn't realize it at the time, the suit Jule had given me turned transparent when wet, which surprised me when I saw the published pictures: there I was, lying in an inch or two of lagoon, looking innocently off camera while the suit was soaked through to the skin, revealing nearly every detail of my abdomen, breasts, and belly button.

No wonder Walter kept yelling, "Smokey's at it again! She's smoking hot!"

THERE WAS yet another surprise for me when the issue was published several months later, in January 1975. Jean-François and I were still in Paris at the time, preparing to move to New York, when I heard from friends in the States that the Swimsuit Issue had come out with a "scandalous" shot of my behind. I couldn't picture the shot they were talking about, and as my imagination ran wild, Jean-François and I ran all over Paris, scouring newsstands to find a copy. When we did, I was relieved to see the "scandalous" shot in question was just a side angle of me wearing a string bikini as I crouched in the surf. What was so scandalous about that?

Maybe my time in Paris had turned me more European than I realized, with less puritanical ideas about flesh and the human body.

Or maybe, just maybe, I was becoming more of a model than I'd imagined.

To be clear, though, if anyone asked me to pose nude, which they eventually did, I said no. To this day, I have never done a nude shoot—not because I'm a prude, but because I've always wanted to be a mom, and I never wanted my kids to be embarrassed by nude photos of their mother circulating somewhere in magazine world. Plus, I think it's much sexier to suggest than to show it all.

I've refused to do other things as a model, too, most notably when, a few months into my career, a client asked me to fly to the South of France to accompany a group of men on a yacht in the Mediterranean. The job, they said, would be to be nice to everyone on board, because everyone on board could be beneficial to my career. The trip would include an overnight, but in the morning, I could fly back to Paris—no harm, no foul.

I may have been a naïve kid from Malibu, but nothing about the trip sounded right to me. Where, after all, was the modeling part? I heard rumors that other models with more successful careers at the time had taken the same trip and come back with fancy cars, jewelry, and a new magazine cover, but none of that mattered to me. If I was going to get ahead in the industry, I wanted to do it on my own terms, not underneath someone else's.

That proposed trip was the only time in my career I was ever asked, directly or indirectly, for a sexual favor. I know that makes me one of the lucky few, and I like to think that once you declare your worth, no one questions it again, but I know that's not true, either. Instead, you have to declare your worth over and over again, if not in one way, then in another—especially in an industry like modeling, where fame, money, and misconceptions can run wild. But as long as you believe in yourself, it doesn't really matter what other people want or ask you to do.

You write your own script, baby.

And as long I'm writing my own script, I'm also going to call my own shots, no matter which side of the camera I'm on.

PART III

New York City

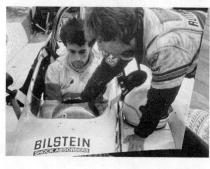

CHAPTER

8

Glamour
CoverGirl
Danskin
Clairol
Hanes
Coty
Woman's Day
Breck
McCall's
Sports Illustrated
Sears
JCPenney
Brides
Max Factor
Kodak . . .

n 1975, after Jean-François and I moved to New York, Eileen made good on her promise: I had a ton of work. My daybook suddenly became crammed with appointments for go-sees and bookings all over Manhattan, as I dashed from one end of the island to the other, quickly learning my way around a big, bustling city that seemed denser and more diverse than Los Angeles and less picturesque than Paris, but still with its own precise charm. One minute, I would be shooting on the Upper East Side in a wood-paneled private club with a grand staircase that flowed into a marble foyer; the next, I would be downtown on Canal Street, doing a commercial inside a gritty studio surrounded by dim sum shops and fish markets. My busy days were almost always capped by meeting Jean-François for dinner or to see a show or a film—the first we saw together was *Jaws*, the movie of the moment, which launched the very trend of the summer blockbuster.

That the blockbuster was created the same year I moved to New York now seems fitting to me, since the concept epitomizes my early years in the city: fast-paced, exhilarating, and wildly successful, without any time to think how the movie of my life was unfolding before me. In New York, my modeling career quickly snowballed, progressing from a flurry of go-sees into a blizzard of shoots around the city, across the country, and, eventually, around the world. Soon enough, as I dashed madly around Manhattan to all my appointments, I started to catch embarrassed glimpses of myself on the covers of magazines, poking out and staring back at me from newsstands I passed.

New York was also new and exciting to me, as Paris had been when I first moved there at age nineteen, and I spent an endless amount of time exploring the city's neighborhoods, streets, and subway lines with their never-ending rotation of restaurants, diners, museums, markets, parks, theaters, shops, and shows. While it wasn't as romantic as Paris, the city had a unique history and its own intrigue, and I loved walking beneath its towering sea of skyscrapers, where powerbrokers wheeled and dealed in the sky, and wandering downtown, where you could still hear millions of immigrant stories whispering through the walls of old tenement buildings. I liked the bright-lights-big-city feel of Broadway and even the urban decay that had crept into New York in the 1970s, bringing with it the angst that helped create punk rock, hip-hop, graffiti art, and disco culture. It seemed that in New York, you could do, be, or find whatever you wanted, whether that was wealth and power or counterculture and cutting edge. When the city finally became my home, I was already enchanted by its urban energy and magic.

New York was different from Paris in other ways, too, especially when it came to modeling. In Paris, the pace of work had been leisurely and the mood fun-loving, where if you were booked for a shoot at nine in the morning, you didn't have to show up before ten. And when you did show up at ten, you didn't start working right away, not before café au lait and croissants, *mais oui,* so everyone would head out to the closest café, where you would have to sit down to eat and drink—otherwise, things would get cold, which would be an insult to French food culture. At the café, you'd discuss politics and world events, because it was fashionable to be informed, and when you finally returned to the shoot at eleven thirty, it was time for hair and makeup, which was another opportunity to talk and learn. *Did you know that this blush works best with your skin?* Or *Mon Dieu, you must try this updo!* . . . All important considerations for a model. Then, at one p.m., it was time for lunch, so everyone would stroll to a nearby bistro, packing into the same booth, with someone inevitably charging the bill to the client. After a long lunch and countless bottles of wine, you finally started shooting, working until seven or eight at night, all while feeling happy and full and having fun.

Compare that to New York City, where, when you were booked for a shoot at eight in the morning, it really meant seven forty-five.

There was no time for café au laits and croissants (or their calories)—instead, you went straight to hair and makeup (or you did your own beforehand, necessitating an even earlier alarm), then worked until one p.m., which didn't mean it was time for lunch but for you to bolt uptown for a shoot in Central Park or a booking in Midtown. Then, it was back downtown for a screen test in the Village until six, when you might have a little time for some fruit and yogurt before going back to work. The only magnanimous thing about modeling in New York was that if you worked past five p.m., you got paid time and a half—extra income, I soon learned, that was necessary just to pay your bar bill, not to mention your rent.

At the same time, the go-sees and shoots in New York were more influential than those in Paris. Shortly after Jean-François and I moved to Manhattan, *Glamour* magazine booked me for a shoot in Sag Harbor, a village in the Hamptons, a hundred miles east of New York City and a place I'd never been before. I was immediately charmed by the town, which seemed quaint and European to me, with its wind-battered wooden fences, thickets of blue hydrangea falling into storm-worn streets, and old sea captain's houses from which you could just make out the ocean from the widow's walks. Although I couldn't have known it at the time, this first-ever *Glamour* shoot introduced me to the place where I'd start two marriages, raise three kids, and spend at least four decades of my life.

That initial *Glamour* shoot also introduced me to something else: the rest of the modeling industry. While I didn't realize it until several months later, when the issue was published, the editors had picked a shot of me for the magazine's September 1975 cover, one of me wearing a cozy maroon sweater with a plaid scarf. In those days, making the cover of *Glamour* was like getting a *Good Housekeeping* seal of approval: you knew you had made it as a model, and so did everyone else in the industry. What's more, advertisers liked to pluck *Glamour* cover girls and drop them directly into their campaigns, hoping to procure the same look the magazine had captured, that of the wholesome, all-American girl. As soon as I got the *Glamour* seal of approval, I also got contracts for all the brands to which that seal was attached.

From September 1975 onward, I appeared on the cover of *Glamour* nearly every other issue, including just two months later, in November 1975, after the magazine flew me out west to do a ski shoot in the Rockies. Traveling from the beach to the mountains, I couldn't quite believe how fortunate I was, and I felt incredibly grateful to be able to experience such beauty and adventure, all for work.

WHILE NEW York lived up to its reputation as the epicenter of the modeling industry, it also adhered to other stereotypes, including the idea that apartment living there wasn't easy. When Jean-François and I first moved to the city, Eileen arranged for us to live in a flat owned by a top Ford model who had gone off to Los Angeles to film a movie, which bought us time to look for our own place while staying in a lovely area, the heart of the Upper East Side. The model's apartment was a beautiful corner penthouse with a solarium over the kitchen, a real step-out terrace, and another terrace off the bedroom. The place was where composer Burt Bacharach had allegedly written "Raindrops Keep Fallin' on My Head," and whenever it stormed, I could see why he might have penned the song there, as I listened to the raindrops pitter-patter above me while sitting at the kitchen table.

But neither the apartment's location nor its history could prevent us from being robbed—or purportedly robbed, an incident that proved both daunting and amusing, all in a New York minute. The morning it happened, I was having one of those days when I couldn't decide what to wear, and I kept trying on one thing after another, hurling the discarded outfits up into the air like a husker shucking corn at a county fair. I didn't have time to hang anything back up, and when Jean-François and I came home that night, we were greeted by a hallway full of police.

"Excuse me, miss, sir," one of the officers said, approaching us with a solemn look. "I'm sorry to inform you, but your apartment has been robbed. All the apartments on this floor have been robbed, in fact."

Jean-François and I looked at each other with alarm.

"We think the thieves climbed in through your terrace, because your front door was still locked when we got here, so we had your super give us the key," the officer explained, pushing open the door with one hand so that we could peer inside. "But I'm afraid they've absolutely ransacked your bedroom, more so than any other apartment on the floor."

After we walked in and saw the "ransacked" room, with dozens of my shirts, skirts, and dresses thrown haphazardly about, I ensured the police that the room was exactly how I had left it.

As it turned out, the thieves hadn't stolen anything from us—we were the only apartment on the floor that wasn't robbed. What spared us, the cops believed, was that I had locked only one of the five bolts on our front door, which confused the thieves when they tried to pick the lock, as nearly everyone who lived in New York City in the 1970s latched each and every bolt on their door, each and every time.

Following our robbery that wasn't really a robbery, we decided to go west, to the new frontier of Manhattan, the Upper West Side. In the 1970s, the Upper West wasn't as fancy or as commercial as it is today, with more of a neighborhood *esprit*, like something from *West Side Story*, which was one of my favorite Broadway musicals growing up, when my dad played the record on repeat. Fire escapes still ran up and down the sides of most buildings, where lovers and loners alike smoked and dreamed under the city sky, while the streets below were almost grungy, lined by Laundromats, bodegas, and cigarette shops. At the same time, no matter where you went on the Upper West Side, you weren't far from the Dakota, the luxury apartment building where John Lennon once lived with Yoko Ono. Before John was shot outside the building in 1980, Jean-François and I often saw the couple walking hand in hand through the neighborhood.

Once we realized we wanted to live on the Upper West, we spent weeks looking for an apartment there, jumping the moment we spotted a promising listing in the paper. But as soon as we saw a place we could afford, it had already been snatched up by someone else. Eventually, though, we found the ideal living situation after Marc, who was the boyfriend of Jean-François's brother Jean-Marie, offered to share his one-bedroom with us in a brownstone, conveniently located on the Upper West Side.

Marc worked as a steward for TWA and wasn't home very often, but when he was, Jean-François and I happily slept in the little lofted bedroom upstairs while Marc preferred the foldout couch below. In those days, we were all on a shoestring budget, but living in Marc's apartment was like flying first class, since he had outfitted the place from top to bottom in TWA swag. All our pillows and blankets were TWA pillows and blankets, and we ate off real china, our plates and bowls bearing the gold insignia and red stripe of the carrier, with airline silverware and thimble-size salt and pepper shakers. When Marc came home, often at odd hours, he would bring with him so much smoked salmon, caviar, and champagne left over from the first-class flight service that we would feast for days. On these occasions, we'd spread a TWA blanket on the floor, light candles, and picnic on our salmon and caviar—ideal for both our budget and my Eileen Ford diet. Years later, when I learned that both Jean-Marie and Marc had died of AIDS, I wept for days.

Marc's brownstone was also a prime study in New York City living, as we could see into dozens of other apartments from the windows, where we had no other choice but to watch the daily lives of strangers unfold before us like a game of *Hollywood Squares*. Immediately across the street from us was an exhibitionist, who would stand in front of his windows completely naked, with only flowerpots hiding his private parts. Whenever he spotted someone he fancied—and we thought he may have been flirting with or at least flashing someone in our building—he'd pick up one of the pots to reveal his own root and bulbs. *Incroyable!* Completing this classic New York City scene was the nosy busybody who lived below the exhibitionist and sat at her window all day, monitoring what was happening across the way and down below. If only she knew what was happening right above!

Despite dining on seafood delicacies all the time at Marc's, eventually I got tired of eating only fish, even if it was the first-class kind. Yet, I still had to lose weight, per Eileen Ford, so I started to cycle through one fad diet after another, many of them published in the same women's magazines for which I modeled. When I look back at my journal entries from my first year in New York (and for several years afterward), they read in part like a registry of self-imposed starvation:

October 12, 1975

BREAKFAST: *One glass milk with protein*
  powder, one protein bar, vitamins.
LUNCH: *One small can V8 juice, two*
  handfuls sunflower seeds.
DINNER: *One spinach salad, one large glass*
  papaya juice, one 0% fat yogurt.

Uptown Girl

October 13, 1975

BREAKFAST: *One glass orange juice with protein powder, handful of raisins.*

LUNCH: *One small orange juice.*

DINNER: *Carrots, one bite Gruyère cheese, one orange, one date.*

October 14, 1975

BREAKFAST: *One sugar-free digestive cookie.*

LUNCH: *One 0% fat yogurt, one orange, one small serving brown rice.*

DINNER: *One bite Gruyère cheese, one 0% fat yogurt.*

A glass of orange juice with protein powder was actually a palatable breakfast? And a bite of cheese with carrots, an orange, and a date was all I ate for dinner? I can't believe that this was my idea of healthy. But at the time, I was so desperate to fit into designer clothes, which came in only one size when I was a young model: runway size, which was impossibly small. Because designer clothing was made first for the runway before the most successful lines went straight to the magazines to be shot for fashion spreads, manufacturers didn't have time to create or distribute a full size run, so I had to squeeze into whatever size they had, usually a zero or a two. The thinner I was, the more likely I would be able to metamorphose into a dress or pantsuit—and the less embarrassed I would likely feel at work. Even so, I did a lot of modeling with the zippers open in the back and with photographers asking me to turn this way or that so the camera wouldn't reveal my jerry-rigged outfit.

In the end, though, I wasn't very good at dieting—or, at least not restrictive dieting. While I've been a vegetarian for years, which is a kind of diet, for most of my career, I refused to starve myself, especially when I traveled for work. In my mind, when I was in a new city or a foreign country, all bets were off, as those modeling adventures were what made the job worthwhile. Plus, I still believed that every modeling trip might be my last, so I figured I might as well enjoy it, with all the piña coladas and banana chips I wanted.

That I refused to constantly diet, though, is one reason I think I had such a long career as a model. Otherwise, I might have dieted my way out of the industry—or, certainly, out of the Swimsuit Issue, lingerie commercials, and other work that favored more voluptuous models. Over time, I also realized that dieting doesn't work—why I started to call it "deny-iting," because you continually have to deny, restrict, and undereat, which isn't a feasible or enjoyable way to live. After years of yo-yo dieting, I finally figured out that the only way to stay fit and healthy is to learn about nutrition so that you can choose to fuel your body with nourishing foods you actually enjoy.

Despite following a very low-calorie regimen at times, I never passed out on the job from starvation, which was (and still is) a common occurrence among models. The only time I ever fainted during a shoot was when I modeled for bridal magazines, which I started to do after Jean-François and I moved to New York. Bridal work was surprisingly difficult because I had to hold the same position for what felt like hours on end, with a veil pinned from my dress to the wall behind me so it would look like the veil was floating up ethereally into the air. If I moved even a millimeter, I would pull the veil from the wall, so I had to stay perfectly still—all while holding a bouquet of flowers and sucking in my stomach so it wouldn't bulge through the dress. During one of these shoots, I simply fainted, dropping to the floor in a pile of lace and silk like the Wicked Witch of the West melting into her cape and hat at the end of *The Wizard of Oz*. Eventually, I told the agencies I didn't want to do any more bridal shoots—one of the few times I've categorically refused work.

Those shoots, however, did prompt me to think about what it would be like to be a bride myself, and while I was being prodded and pinned, I decided that I wanted my wedding with Jean-François to focus more on our love than on any dress or veil. With Jean-François, I didn't need or want the extra trimmings. We were so madly in love that I just wanted us to exchange vows, preferably at the edge of the ocean, with our feet in the water and our hearts in each other's, always and forever.

ON OCTOBER 22, 1975, my journal entry takes a turn. The day began like many other days that year, with what had become de rigueur for me in New York: I did a magazine shoot (that day for *Glamour*) in the morning and then an advertisement in the afternoon (in this instance, I pretended to be a nursemaid, bashfully pushing a baby carriage in front of a colorful backdrop). But when I got home that evening to our little *West Side Story* apartment, there were flickering candles in the living room and a bottle of champagne nesting in a bed of pink and red rose petals. As I walked in, Jean-François dropped to one knee and held out a glistening golden ring with a tiny diamond at its center, sparkling like moonlight on the sea whenever it caught the candlelight.

I didn't hesitate: *Yes*.

We were so excited to be married that we decided to do it right away, one month later, on November 22, 1975. We knew we wanted our wedding to be on the beach and quickly settled on a spot: Kona Village, on the northeastern shore of Hawaii's Big Island. I had vacationed there many times with my parents and described it so often to Jean-François that it was as magical in his imagination as it was in my memory. Hawaii would also be warm, sunny, and tropical—and the timing was ideal: I had already been booked for my second-ever shoot for *Sports Illustrated*, in the Mexican state of Baja California, a relatively short hop, skip, and jump from Hawaii. We didn't want a big ceremony—just my parents, my brother, and his girlfriend, Sue—and because it was too much time and money to ask Jean-François's mom and siblings to come from the Pyrenees, we decided we would fly back to France for the winter holidays so we could celebrate there with them.

But first, I had to do the *Sports Illustrated* shoot, and I loved being in Mexico again, where I could hear happy mariachi music, eat breakfast every morning on a terrace overlooking the ocean, and go out at night with Jule and the rest of the team for margaritas and too many tortilla chips. I also felt more comfortable with the job this time and tried my best when Jule asked me to do an active shoot, in which I had to run in a bikini down a scorching red-dirt road, leaping, twirling, and zigzagging as I tried to keep up with a truck carrying a photographer in its back bed. After the shoot was over, images of me barely made it into the magazine, but I also barely noticed: by the time that Swimsuit Issue came out, in January 1976, I was already a blissful newlywed.

After Mexico, I flew from Baja to the Big Island, then took a car through the island's interior, with its sharply rising volcanoes and deeply cut rainforest ravines, to Kona Village, a little oasis on a blue-water beach lined by palm trees, bright bougainvillea, and pale pink hibiscus. To this day, the resort remains fairly remote, located down a long dirt trail several miles from the nearest public road and at the end of a lava flow, which cooled ages ago into obsidian outcroppings after the hot lava mixed with the cold Pacific. As a child, I used to love scrambling over the black lava, which was jagged and sharp in places but also so nutrient-rich that it made the soil incredibly fertile—why you could plant a coconut in the ground at Kona Village one winter and, by the time you returned the following year, discover it had sprung into a baby palm.

For decades, Kona Village always held a special place for me and my family because it was so beautiful, welcoming, and low-key, with an authentic aloha spirit that drifted among its grass-thatched huts, hammocks, and tennis courts, offering more snorkeling options and arts-and-crafts activities than it did the TVs and fanfare typical to most resorts. There were also several bars on the property, including the Shipwreck Bar, which was once a capsized sailboat before someone pulled it out of the ocean and onto the beach and turned it into a watering hole, quite literally. Over the decades, I've spent a lot of time there with my parents and other family and friends drinking chi chis—piña coladas made with vodka—while laughing hysterically and watching the sun set over Kahuwai Bay. (The Shipwreck was also where the Doors' Jim Morrison, whom I adored so much as a teen that I once snuck out to see him play at the Whisky a Go Go, allegedly set a record for sinking twenty-one mai tais in one night.)

During the week of our wedding, each couple stayed in their own grass hut—my parents, Greg and Sue, and Jean-François and me—and we had so much fun tiptoeing from hut to hut, carving out our own little enclave in the resort's bigger village. Because my parents had been going there for so long and my mom was so smiley and friendly with everyone she met, the people at Kona Village knew us all by name, which made it feel even homier. We often spent our nights socializing and drinking chi chis at sunset while, during the day, we went swimming, played tennis, and fished, a sport Jean-François had recently fallen in love with while visiting my parents in Malibu, where he stood outside their apartment with a pole for hours, happy even if he didn't hook a single fish. It was another reason I loved him so much: despite growing up in the Pyrenees, he was instantly enamored by the Pacific, finding the same tranquility in the ocean that I did and, like me, wanting to spend as much time by the sea as possible.

One afternoon, we went to get our marriage license in Kealakekua, a little town near Kona Village made famous by the singsong tune "My Little Grass Shack in Kealakekua, Hawaii." As a kid, I loved that song and constantly sang its refrain: "I want to go back to my little grass shack in Kealakekua, Hawaii / Where the humuhumunukunukuapuaa goes swimming by." Now, here I was, years later, in Kealakekua, Hawaii, steps away from the bay where the *humuhumunukunukuapuaa*—the Hawaiian word for "reef fish"— notoriously swam, nibbling on unsuspecting tourists' toes as they did. The song I loved as a kid had become my reality, as did many other songs over the years, most famously that one song by Billy Joel. But I was still many years and a full heart away from being anyone's "Uptown Girl."

When our friends who worked at Kona Village learned that Jean-François and I were to be married on the beach at their resort, they trekked up the volcano outside its grounds to gather maile vines, from which they wove us maile leis, traditional Hawaiian garlands used for sacred ceremonies. They also brought us pikake—the "flower of love" in Hawaii, with small white buds and an enchanting scent similar to jasmine—and together, Jean-François and I braided a single strand of flowers into an ivory crown, which I decided to wear instead of the veil that had proved so problematic in my bridal shoots.

The morning of our wedding, the sun rose warm and high over the mountains, with a gentle breeze that carried the fragrance of pikake from the mountains to the water's edge, where we swam in the ocean all day, not fussing over the ceremony or worrying about what would happen. My parents had found a sweet judge to marry us, one of their friends at the resort, and when he arrived just before sunset, Jean-François and I finally rushed out of the water and up to our little grass hut to get ready.

It didn't take us more than a few minutes. I put on a pale pink cotton dress and combed my wet hair back into a ponytail, placing the pikake crown on top. Jean-François wore a simple white button-down shirt and linen drawstring pants, and with our maile leis and pikake necklaces, we walked hand in hand and barefoot down to the beach, where a ukulele player was strumming a soft Hawaiian song upwind of us, so that the music was carried by the breeze to where the judge was waiting. Surrounded by my parents, my brother, and his girlfriend, Jean-François and I were married with our feet in the Pacific, as little wavelets washed the hem of my dress and his pants and the sun dropped behind us into the ocean, sending up bright beams of pink, orange, and purple that framed our faces. We didn't write vows but spoke from our hearts, and afterward, when Jean-François pulled me into him to kiss me, I felt I had all I could ever want.

During the ceremony, we had kept coupes for champagne in the ocean so they would be cold, and after we were married, we took our first sips as husband and wife on the beach, the salt water mixing with the champagne in what tasted to me like the elixir of love. After the toast, we went to the resort's restaurant for a celebratory dinner, then cut into a small white wedding cake frosted with sugar flowers and iced hearts. Not once did I feel any pressure or worry whether we had enough food, if the flowers were right, or who was sitting next to whom. Instead, the day unfolded simply, sweetly, and organically, as if it had always been meant to be, from the moment we first met that spring evening in Paris.

The morning after our wedding, my parents flew back to Los Angeles with Greg and Sue while Jean-François and I stayed behind for a brief honeymoon. The resort was so small that everyone there knew we had just been married, and whenever anyone passed us, they smiled and wished us "much happiness" or "love forever." They also called me "Madame Allaux," using Jean-Francois's last name, and I loved the way the French language mingled with the warm Hawaiian air.

I was now Christie Lee Brinkley Allaux. And I couldn't have been happier.

A FEW weeks before we were married, something upsetting happened. I was shooting for *Glamour* in New York's iconic Carnegie Hall (where other episodes of my life would play out, both inside the building's concert halls and the artist apartments above), and in what had become a nearly ineluctable development, the editors wanted to try for a cover. Back in the day, everything about a potential *Glamour* cover was based on the calculated and careful assessment of various analytics, and for that issue, the editors had already determined that the model's hand should appear on the front. So, I put my hand to my face as they instructed and held it there for the camera to click.

"Love it, Christie," one editor called. "That's great. Stay right there!"

"So good, Christie," the photographer yelled. "Just a little more smile."

"Oh, wait. The ring," the editor said, referring to my engagement ring. "You gotta lose the ring, Christie."

"But I can't take it off," I cried. "I'm going to wear it forever."

"I'm sorry, but you have to," the editor explained. "We can't have an engagement ring on the cover. You understand—it's just part of the job."

I told her I understood and handed her my ring, which she

promised to take care of, slipping it onto her own finger so it wouldn't get lost.

When the photographer announced that the shoot was a wrap, I couldn't wait to wear my ring again. But before I could ask the editor for it back, she walked up with a sober look and explained, slowly, that she had been in the bathroom reaching for tissues above the toilet when the ring had somehow suddenly slipped off her finger and into the bowl, fluttering down to the bottom of the basin like a leaf before being sucked out of sight. And in the time she rushed to get the building's maintenance department to take a look, dozens of other people had used the toilet, flushing my ring farther into the vast underground network of the New York City sewer system.

That night, I walked home slowly, mulling over how I'd break the news to Jean-François. When I told him that our ring was lost forever, he was crushed—not angry, but heartbroken. The ring was more precious to both of us than any Tiffany diamond, a monumental symbol of a whirlwind love affair that had already crossed two continents.

Now, decades later, I know I lost more than my engagement ring too early: I also lost Jean-François years ahead of what might have been.

And, maybe, what should have been.

Marital bliss.
        Incredible modeling trips.

That's the snapshot of my next several years in New York City, where my life became a rotating kaleidoscope of these two prisms, a sliding succession of planes, parties, shoots, homemaking, and love-making . . .

Click, click, click, advance the motor drive.

WHILE JEAN-FRANÇOIS and I never intended to stay so long in New York, my career took off at a dizzying speed in the so-called City of Dreams, where I seemed always to be landing another shoot, cover, or commercial that pushed me farther up the modeling ladder, at a pace as electrifying as the view from the Empire State Building. At the time I began to make New York my home, I also started traveling incessantly for work, packing, unpacking, and repacking all the time, often for far-flung places in the Caribbean, Europe, Africa, and Asia, where not many Americans ventured in the 1970s, when air travel was still largely considered a luxury.

Looking back at my journals, I'm surprised I found the time to do anything else other than work, but apparently I did, spending weeks feathering our new nest—an apartment Jean-François and I had found together on the Upper West Side—while learning my way around New York as I once had Paris, discovering new friends, favorite restaurants, and my own identity in a city overflowing with people, places, and adventure. To that end, I also went on several self-improvement kicks by taking Italian lessons, Pilates classes, and even scuba diving lessons in a grungy cement pool in the middle of Manhattan.

Like mine, Jean-François's career also took off rapidly in New York, and in a matter of months, he was drawing political illustrations for the *New York Times*, which led to work for the *New York Post*, *The New Yorker*, the *Los Angeles Times*, and other publications. That we should stay in the States seemed obvious, and while I still dreamed wistfully of Paris, I was excited and eager to make New York my home. With some bittersweet affection, we moved out of Marc's brownstone, saying goodbye to his world of champagne wishes and caviar dreams, and signed a lease on our own apartment at the corner of Sixty-seventh Street and Columbus Avenue. While we didn't realize it at the time, we had managed to find one of the areas in all of New York known for its artists and art studios, so much so that the block is listed in the National Register of Historic Places as the West 67th Street Artists' Colony.

Our apartment was lovely, bright, and cheery, with double-height frosted artist studio windows to the north and windows to the west with views all the way to the Hudson. The day we picked up our keys, we rushed to Macy's to buy sheets and pillows, even though we didn't own a bed yet, just a futon. But nothing could stop us, and we were tempted by every knick-knack, buying macadamia nuts from the store's exotic foods section so we could celebrate that night with Hawaiian nuts and homemade chi chis. Within days, we had a bed from Gimbels, a stereo and a TV (on which we watched the 1976 Summer Olympics), and two bentwood chairs we found in an antiques store in the Bowery that looked so cute in our kitchen, especially at half the price. Later that month, we had a telephone installed, which, while not as romantic as Paris's pneumatic tube messaging system, was more convenient and also emblematic, because in the white pages, we were "Mr. and Mrs. Jean-François Allaux," at 212-555-2354. The rest of the world would have to reach us together.

We also quickly developed an active social life, making friends in the neighborhood and across the city. Now that we were married, I loved having couple friends even more so, and Jean-François and I started spending some weekends upstate in the Catskills, where one of my model friends owned a home with her husband, the four of us drinking cocktails and cooking together while watching the leaves change color in the fall or burst into bright green buds in the spring. The more I traveled for work, the more friends I made in the industry—other models, in addition to makeup artists, hairstylists, editors, and photographers—and Jean-François and I began having dinner parties at our apartment with theme nights around our recent trips, like margaritas and tacos if we had just been to Mexico, sharing slides of our travel photos. (Slideshows were all the rage in the 1970s.)

My best friend Hops and I used to say we could write a whole movie based on what happened in one single day of work, not to mention a multi-day trip to another country. To this day, I still can't quite believe what occurred on many of my incredible modeling trips—some things strange, crazy, or even dangerous while others were beautiful, breathtaking, or culturally rich. And while he wasn't with me on every trip, what made many of my work forays even more memorable and outrageous was Hops, or Maury Hopson, a hairstylist who was not only my best friend in the business but also my mentor, co-conspirator, and confidant.

I'm not sure where or when I met Hops, but he did hair for many of the major fashion magazines and big-name celebrities like Elizabeth Taylor. After I first worked with him, we were often booked together, which was typical: editors liked to group models, makeup artists, stylists, and other artistic types onto the same teams if they thought they shared good chemistry, in the hope that it would create a better product. Well, with Hops, he and I had chemistry like a house on fire, and whenever we were booked together, it was a guarantee not only of a better product, but also of more laughs and lots of optimism, no matter what happened or went awry. And during our trips together, plenty of things happened or went awry.

My overseas adventures with Hops began in 1976, when we were booked on the same *Glamour* shoot in Harbour Island, a charmer of a Bahamian islet with pastel-painted houses and sand beaches the same color as crushed cherry blossoms. In those days, I traveled a ton for *Glamour*, kicking off the 1976 New Year with a trip to Puerto Rico just days after celebrating our wedding with Jean-François's family in the Pyrenees. From that shoot, the *Glamour* editors picked a shot of me for the May 1976 cover—my fourth one for the magazine since my September 1975 debut—although, this time I'm holding a tennis ball in one hand while resting my chin on a racquet, my wedding band squarely gleaming in place on my ring finger.

I stayed in Puerto Rico after working with *Glamour* to shoot an ad for Coppertone, in which I had to swing on a vine through the jungle wearing only a leafy-green bikini. While some models found this kind of work tiresome or hokey, I felt fortunate that someone actually wanted to pay me to fly across the tops of trees in a rainforest from sunup to sundown. In what other life would I ever get to play Tarzan's Jane?

Later that winter, I found myself in Harbour Island again with Hops, again for *Glamour*, doing a series of shots in which I "had" to sip a fancy tropical drink in front of a real-life backdrop of the turquoise ocean. After we wrapped, we all piled into a golf cart to head back to our hotel—on Harbour Island, there are few cars, only bikes and golf carts, making the island even more idyllic. In those days, though, the only golf-cart rental game in town was operated by a humorless, monolithic Dutchman named Sock, who had very strict rules about what you could and couldn't do with his carts, including that no more than four people could ever ride in one at the same time.

That night, with the precious light waning and one more shoot to do back at the hotel, we loaded up the cart and, determined to get across town as quickly as possible, we realized we would have to violate Sock's sacred rule. So, eight of us piled into the same cart, with Hops behind the wheel, two of us in the passenger seat, and five wedged into the back seat, with arms, legs, and tripods spilling out everywhere into the humid air, making our cart look like an awkward spider lumbering through the tropics.

Sock, who was always monitoring the island for cart violations, spotted us immediately and came zooming monomaniacally toward us in his own cart. This prompted Hops to press the proverbial pedal to the metal, which didn't mean much in a golf cart, but despite our lack of velocity, we suddenly found ourselves in a slow-speed, high-intensity golf-cart chase across the island, with Sock in hot pursuit, madly screaming his head off the entire time. Hops, adamant that the red-haired (and now red-faced) behemoth wouldn't catch us, careened the cart onto someone's front lawn, causing it to tilt like a sailboat heeling against a furious gust of wind. But Hops fought the wheel like a possessed captain, and when we finally bounced up onto the hotel drive, we all leapt off, laughing so hard we could barely walk. But when we realized Sock was still chasing us, our laughter

faded, and we all scattered in different directions. I chose to follow Hops into the hotel lobby, barreling past reception and into the
kitchen, which was empty at that hour. From our hiding place under
a long chef's counter, we could hear Sock thudding into the lobby
before barging into the kitchen, where Hops and I cowered farther
under a cabinet. Thankfully, the angry Dutchman didn't see us and
turned clumsily around like a toy transformer before crashing out to
look for more alleged cart criminals. The next morning, we all caught
the first flight back to New York.

While that wasn't my only high-speed chase with Hops, like your
first love, you never forget your first chase, and Hops, if you're reading now, you and I still have that movie to write.

THAT SUMMER, after several months of nonstop work, I decided
to do something unimaginable for a young model: I "booked out,"
which, in industry terms, means you tell your agency you'll be un-
available to work on certain dates. In my case, though, I told the
agency I didn't want to work for five full months, an absence practically unheard of for a fledgling model. While most young models were only hell-bent on getting ahead, I actually wanted to work
hard—and I did, doing multiple jobs per day, consecutive work trips,
and many late nights in the studio. But I also wanted to live my life,
and I had a lot of other interests, which included adventuring on my
own time with my own husband.

In early July 1976, Jean-François and I flew to Los Angeles to
spend a few weeks with my parents, taking long walks on the beach,
where, one morning, we discovered a huge school of purple ancho-
vies feeding madly in the water, and we eagerly scooped some out
using a spaghetti strainer. We also went backpacking through the
Sierras with my brother, Greg, and his girlfriend, Sue, hiking up to

empty waterfalls and swimming in icy mountain lakes, where we also fished for trout for dinner. At night, we told scary stories around a fire before falling asleep, watching the sparks from the blaze dance with the stars, then woke up early in the morning to do yoga and meditate.

In those days, like many young people, I was into Transcendental Meditation and had even received my mantra as a teenager from the practice's creator, the Maharishi Mahesh Yogi himself, when he came to speak in Los Angeles. While I wasn't a great meditator, I was an opportunistic one, practicing whenever I felt frayed—and always on airplanes, where I've had countless near misses. In fact, after I shared my airplane horror stories on *The Tonight Show* with Johnny Carson, pilots and passengers started sitting down next to me or hovering in the aisle over me to share their own.

THE SAME summer, Jean-François and I took a spontaneous train trip through Mexico, with no destination in mind. From the moment we boarded an "air-conditioned" train—meaning its windows were broken—that accommodated just as many chickens as passengers, to minutes later, when the train squashed an empty truck at the first intersection we crossed, the trip was full of surprises. After several hours, we were both covered in the orange dust that constantly blew in through the broken windows, which made us look like tabby cats after our dripping sweat striped and streaked the dust. For the next eighteen hours, the train must have hissed and chugged through a thousand hot, dusty villages before we finally had enough, jumping off in Guaymas, a port city famous for shrimp, in desperate need of a nice hotel and a cool swim. All we could find at first were closed *posadas* nowhere near the water, but after several margaritas, we finally discovered a deserted hotel on the beach, where we ran into the sea like two lovers in a slow-motion comedy, holding hands as the same hot, orange sand puffed up behind us with every footfall, hitting the water only to have it reach just to our ankles, before tramping out farther through the low-lapping waves so we could dive into the orange surf.

Dusty orange seawater, however, wasn't what we were looking for, so we hopped a two-hour flight south from Guaymas to Guadalajara, where we had dinner at a charming cantina in the city's Mariachi Plaza—a special place for me and my family ever since my dad suggested another spontaneous weekend there when I was young—before flying back to Los Angeles with suitcases full of blankets, cowboy boots, and tortillas, the plane taking off through lightning that flickered around us like snake tongues.

IN NOVEMBER, once we were back in New York and Jimmy Carter had won the 1976 presidential election, I discovered that the only thing my five-month sabbatical from modeling had done was create more demand for me. Suddenly, everyone seemed to want me everywhere. Flying all over the world for shoots, I took my first trip to Japan, where I introduced the modern-day brassiere by appearing in ads for the so-called Foundation, which ran in magazines and on billboards all over the country. In return, Japan introduced me to things I considered much more exciting, like teppanyaki vegetables, elegant tea service, a level of consistent decorum I hadn't experienced in the States, and compact cosmetic kits, used for Kabuki makeup, which organized dozens of tiny palettes of powders, lipsticks, liners, and other products into one orderly box. I was shocked: at the time, I, along with every American model I knew, toted around what amounted to a suitcase full of regular-size products every time we had to do our own makeup. After I brought home an empty Kabuki box from Japan and made my own compact cosmetics kit, I significantly lightened my load as a model. If only I had marketed the concept to American women like I did the bra to the Japanese.

After my inaugural trip to Asia, I went to Africa for the first time, flying across the Atlantic the day before my twenty-third birthday to do two different shoots for American *Vogue*. It wasn't my first time working for the iconic fashion magazine, largely considered the world's most prestigious and the best of the Big Four: American *Vogue*, British *Vogue*, *Vogue France*, and *Vogue Italia*, all of which I had already modeled for. But the trip was one of my most memorable because it launched my long love affair with Africa and also gave me my first opportunity to work with a photographer who often transformed a model's career after a single shoot: Helmut Newton, whose fashion photography was considered more high art than commercial product.

My trip didn't start with modeling for Helmut. First, I flew to Senegal to work with photographer Albert Watson, who did my first headshot in Los Angeles and had become a force in his own right— and who, on that trip, took several legendary photos of me and model Debbie Dickinson, the sister of soon-to-be-supermodel Janice Dickinson. I was instantly mesmerized by Senegal and its colorful marketplaces, where rickety bikes and coughing taxis crisscrossed through throngs of faces—some smiling, some serious—and where thin strips of beach held back the sea and a flotilla of painted wooden fishing skiffs.

One day, Debbie and I took off for the countryside to explore, renting a jeep with a guide who drove us through fields dotted by baobab trees, mud huts, and wild boar to a village where women hid in doorways, old men polished their teeth with twigs, and children reached demurely for the gifts we brought. The *Vogue* photos from Senegal were stunning, too, with one of me, in a candy-red one-piece, laughing while standing in a line of tribesmen, and several more of Debbie and me, sunning ourselves and floating in a pool while wearing such brightly colored bathing suits that our skin looks almost gilded, as if we have been sitting in the hot African sun for weeks, not days.

After we wrapped in Senegal, I had to be in Morocco to work with Helmut, but since there were no direct flights from Dakar, I flew first to León, in Spain, then to Paris, and, after a long layover at Charles de Gaulle, I headed back to Africa, landing in Marrakech. Today, I get exhausted even thinking about that much travel simply for one shoot, but I'd do it all over again as a young model, because, first, it was Morocco, second, it was American *Vogue*, and third, it was Helmut Newton, and that trifecta was about as good as it got for an aspiring model.

While making it into *Glamour* did a lot for a model's career, usually netting her big-brand contracts, the magazine traded in a very clean, fresh look that was distinctly Middle America. *Vogue*, on the other hand, was edgy, sexy, and glamorous, all things Helmut took to the next level by shooting models in erotic, highly stylized, or even shocking poses. Helmut was pure fire, igniting a look so exciting that the outcome for a young model might be a new contract with Gucci, Chanel, or another luxury brand. Given Helmut's reputation as a provocateur, I was pleasantly surprised when I met him in his hotel room in Marrakech, where we did a series of close-up shots: he was kind and funny, setting me at ease for the rest of the trip.

At the same time, it didn't take much for me to feel comfortable in Marrakech, a city I fell so deeply in love with during that first trip that I chose it decades later as one destination to celebrate my fiftieth birthday. From the moment I saw the city's gardens and clay ramparts outside its main medina, I felt at home amid all its dangling bougainvillea (my favorite flower), bright colors that reminded me of Matisse (my favorite painter), and sounds of softly spoken

French (my favorite language) drifting up from the souks. I loved the snake charmers, the beautiful men in turbans, and the city's multiple markets—one for spices, one for baskets, one for lamps, and another for whatever you could think of—every nook and cranny spilling with flowers, tiles, and a sense of mystery. I remember often standing inside the souk and looking in every direction, only to realize that what I was seeing was what others had seen for a thousand years before me—nothing had changed—and when I ran my fingers down a wall's cold clay, it was exactly the same as it had been for centuries.

One unforgettable day, I took a taxi with the other models and magazine crew outside the city ramparts to Villa Taylor, owned then by the Comtesse Madeleine de Breteuil. The house was as historic as it was exotic—Franklin D. Roosevelt and Winston Churchill had once stayed there after trying to plot the fate of World War II at the 1943 Casablanca Conference—and had intricately tiled courtyards full of bubbling fountains, ornate pools, and dozens of orange and olive trees. The entire estate was surrounded by pink clay walls, and in the center was a five-story tower the same color as desert sand from which you could see beyond the minarets of Marrakech, all the way to the Atlas Mountains.

Under this tower, Helmut asked me and top model Dayle Haddon (the same Dayle Haddon who inspired French hairstylist Jean Louis David to bob and perm my hair weeks after I was discovered) to act like we were physically fighting, which we did by jostling and bending backward for hours on end. It was exhausting but also very much in line with Helmut's oeuvre: he often shot women pulling each other's hair or doing other violent or outrageous things. Later that week, we had cocktails with the Comtesse de Breteuil, visited the home of designer Yves Saint Laurent (which was nearly as stunning as Villa Taylor), drank the most delicious mint tea, and watched belly dancers perform at dinner before I somehow ended up dancing on a table myself. Oops . . .

BACK IN New York, I was shopping in Bloomingdale's with my mom one afternoon when I bumped into Sean Byrnes, the boyfriend of American photographer Francesco Scavullo, who, at the time, shot every cover for *Cosmopolitan*—a magazine in which I had yet to appear. I knew Sean because we saw each other at shoots, and determined that Francesco should meet me, he asked me to come by the photographer's studio. Days later, I was booked for a *Cosmo* shoot in New York, where Sean, who doubled as Francesco's stylist, promptly handed me a string of purple fabric.

"Oh, what is this?" I asked naïvely, winding the string of silky material through my fingers.

Sean laughed. "It's a swimsuit!" he said, pointing me toward a tiny toilet where I could change. "Let me know if you have any problems, and I'll help you."

While tiny string bikinis are popular today, they weren't in 1977, and it took me a while to figure out how to put it on, the bottom and top connected to each other by only a single string, which I had to slip into inside a bathroom the size of a London phone booth, where I kept bumping my elbows against the walls. When I finally reemerged, I could feel the crew's eyes swivel to me like a dozen moths to a flame— the suit had that effect.

What made Francesco's photos so incredible in part was that he was a lighting genius—a skill even more valuable in the days before retouching. Using a giant umbrella with a light inside that he tilted in my direction, he asked me to stand in the precise spot where I'd be illuminated perfectly, which he determined by extending a string from the umbrella's shaft to the tip of my nose. While I had felt naked in the bikini in the dressing room, when I stepped into the light at the end of Francesco's string, I felt bathed in gold. And when the shot of me in that itsy-bitsy teeny-weenie purple bikini appeared on the cover (the cover!) of the June 1977 *Cosmo*, the photo caused such a stir that people began stopping me on the street to say things like "Smoking cover, Christie."

That *Cosmo* cover also linked me indefinitely with the bikini's designer, Norma Kamali, whom I would ask to design my wedding dress when I married Billy Joel years later. That wedding dress was the opposite of the teeny purple bikini, with a white lace jacket covering every inch of my torso, but that was also removable, revealing a strapless bustier underneath. Either way, the wedding dress, like the swimsuit, generated a lot of attention after I appeared in it on a magazine cover, in this case, *People*. Similarly, jaws dropped, but for different reasons.

I'll never forget the first time I read an article describing my relationship with Billy as a match between "the beauty and the beast," which shocked and pained me, especially since cruelty and name-calling weren't the commonplace behaviors they've become today. Who would say that and how shallow could they be to judge people they'd never met? How little they actually knew . . .

Click, click, click, advance the motor drive.

THE MORE successful I became, the more I started to merge my worlds of marital bliss and incredible modeling trips, as Jean-François began joining me on some shoots abroad, if not for the entire time, at least for the beginning or tail end. But he was there the whole time I was in Cancún with *Glamour* in 1977, which proved to be unforgettable, not only because it was the first time he was with me wheels up to wheels down for a work trip, but also because our time there didn't disappoint with regard to the craziness that occurred, especially because Hops was in tow.

Things didn't begin auspiciously for adventure, though: the editors had booked us at Club Med Cancún, which had been built since I first visited the area in 1974 with *Sports Illustrated*, back when the land was still undeveloped. And while some may have found the new resort beautiful, all I could see was cement where nature used to be. Plus, the resort was absolutely crammed with tourists, who wanted to take organized exercise classes, play organized games, and eat at organized hours at the resort's gigantic buffet, which seemed to be the club's main draw. I couldn't imagine spending an entire week there, so Hops and I devised a plan in which we would execute the week's shots as quickly as possible by creating an assembly line or human conveyer belt with all the necessary steps: hair, makeup, outfit change, move to the next model, go! Our scheme worked like a charm, too, and we accomplished a week's worth of shots in two days.

The following day, we took off in search of adventure, catching a fifteen-minute ferry to Cozumel, where we all rented mopeds and zipped the island, stopping for a lunch of enchiladas, piña coladas, and tortilla chips.

Later that day, we all went snorkeling together in Cozumel's famous underwater caves, then drove to a remote lighthouse at the very end of a sandy, rutted road to watch the sunset. As the last of the sun's glow faded into darkness, we walked back to our jeep, which was when a group of five drunken men, each with a gun slung across his chest, promptly appeared—apparently, a group of fashion models and their stylists tends to attract attention. This led to another high-speed chase, albeit in a jeep, not a golf cart, but with Hops behind the wheel again, navigating down the bumpy, dark road, our adrenaline pumping, as we alternated between laughter and fear. No matter how many times we pulled over and killed the lights, though, ducking and covering as they zoomed by, we still couldn't shake them. They followed us all the way back to civilization and to the busy parking lot of a nightclub, where, as the song goes, a deejay saved our lives because we were quickly swallowed up by the club's pounding music, pumping heat, and throngs of writhing bodies.

After Cozumel, we all flew back to Club Med Cancún, where the tourists were still comparing their tans at the bar. In good spirits, we joined them for a few piña coladas, then, after saying goodbye to Hops and the others, Jean-François and I caught a ferry to Isla Mujeres, a tiny sliver of an island across the "Bay of Women"—what a name—where we spent a magical several days alone.

Later that week, on our flight back to New York, a female flight attendant's voice came over the intercom. "In a few moments, we'll be passing through the cabin to offer you a drink and something to eat. In the meantime, sit back, relax, and browse our latest in-flight magazine, which you'll find in the seat pocket in front of you. It has some interesting articles about your next travel destination."

Intrigued by new possible travel adventures, I grabbed the magazine. And there, on the cover, was . . . me.

I couldn't believe it—I was even on the front of an airline magazine. My career, very much like the airplane I was on, had not only left the gate but had taken off and was climbing toward an altitude I could never have imagined.

10

The problem was, it all sounded fantastic.

Did I want to go to Tunisia with *Vogue*? Or Las Hadas, Mexico with *Harper's Bazaar*? Or would it be more interesting to go to India with *Woman's Day*? Or maybe I should take a money job in another area of Mexico for a high-paying catalogue.

Decisions, decisions . . . And the best possible kind of "problem" to have.

Oh wait, someone was offering me a week on the French Riviera with two of the most influential names in the industry, Chanel and Helmut Newton?

Evidemment, c'est ça. I'll choose that one.

As my career started to expand in new ways and different directions, the question no longer was whether I'd get booked for a job, but rather which job I wanted, as potential work trips began to multiply and overlap. To my amazement, magazines and advertisers started competing for me, offering me greater and more incentives to entice me to choose one gig over another. Would I take a trip, for example, if they paid for Jean-François to join me? Or if they booked our flights on the Concorde?

Oh la la.

But it wasn't just magazines and advertisers now vying for my time. In 1977, the agencies also started fighting over a short list of top models, on which I was surprised and flattered to find my name, in what became widely and well known as the model wars.

Despite its name, the model wars weren't, as some people like to believe, a bunch of beautiful women wrestling one another for the distinction of "supermodel," a concept that was just starting to emerge in the late 1970s. Instead, the "wars" were between the agents, who began fighting over the right to represent certain models exclusively after Johnny Casablancas expanded Elite to include an office in New York City, stepping directly (and painfully) on the toes of Eileen Ford as he started to court her U.S.-based "girls."

One leafy, sunshiny day in April 1977, Johnny rang me up at our Sixty-seventh Street apartment.

"Hi, Christie, *bonjour, bonjour, c'est Johnny,*" he began cheerfully, taking the time to ask me about my latest projects and making a few obsequious remarks about my most recent *Vogue* spread. Then he cut to the chase.

"Listen, Christie," he said, "I'm opening up an Elite office in New York, and I want to represent you exclusively. I'll take a smaller percentage from you than the other girls because you're a bigger name now, but you started with me, and you need to stay with me."

I was stunned. "But Johnny," I said hesitantly, "we've worked together so seamlessly for three years now—you, me, Eileen, and Nina. It's been like one big happy family. Why can't we stay that way?"

"Christie, I'm the one who launched you," Johnny said matter-of-factly, immediately putting a cap on the conversation. "You need to show me the same loyalty and faith now that I first showed you."

With the phone receiver cold and quiet in my ear, I felt my heart sink into my stomach. I knew he was right. While I didn't want to break things off with Eileen or Nina—and I certainly didn't like how Johnny was wheeling and dealing, offering different percentages to different models, which was true to his reputation as a backdoor-deal kind of guy who also liked to party and sleep with models, according to the rumors—he had seen something in me when I first started that I couldn't even see in myself. He was also an American who had found his way in Paris, and I couldn't blame him now for wanting to come home to expand his career; I had done the same thing.

"Okay, Johnny. I understand," I said softly.

I wanted to break the news to Eileen and Jerry in person because they'd been so kind to me, not to mention they brokered one of my biggest deals ever, my contract with CoverGirl. So, after hanging up with Johnny, I called to make an appointment to see Eileen and Jerry in their New York offices. When I arrived that afternoon, I explained slowly and carefully that while I loved working with them and sincerely wished there was another way, ultimately, I felt like I owed Johnny. They tried to convince me to stay, but they also said they understood my predicament, which was incredibly classy of them. (It was also prescient: Their aboveboard approach ended up winning them back many models, including me. And not once did either Eileen or Jerry ever say, "I told you so.")

Weeks later, *People* magazine ran a story on the model wars, with a photo of Johnny in his newly minted New York office popping champagne with "his girls," which now meant me. The feature caused a buzz, prompting other magazines to run similar stories, and as the wars intensified, so did the media coverage, turning a short list of models into hot commodities. Suddenly, modeling was no longer seen as a side hobby, but as a real profession, one where some women could make big money being photographed in beautiful clothes in fabulous locations. While lots of girls today want to grow up to be CEOs, entrepreneurs, and scientists, in the 1980s, I met many little girls who wanted to become models. The job was not only glamorous but also lucrative.

The model wars also helped us models realize our own value, and as the press coverage ballooned, people all over the country began to know us by name, as we transformed from anonymous clothes racks into actual celebrities. In New York, people started stopping me on the street and even following me into the ladies' room to say, "Wait, you're *that* model."

Yes, I am *that* model.

BUT THE thing about increasing fame is that it often comes with increasing pressure. And when fame hits, it doesn't ever stay in one spot—it takes you (and follows you) all around the world, including to Italy.

That spring, I went to Rome for *Vogue Patterns*, which was an extraordinary trip for many reasons. I already loved Rome, but as a model, I fell head over heels for the ancient city. The job allowed me to see and experience so many things I might never have as a tourist, as I ran all over the city with the team to shoot in luxurious apartments with walls that looked brushed by Michelangelo, atop a working runway of the city's largest airport, in vibrant gardens overspilling with flowers and people, and (once) inside a stately villa with a real, functioning ballet studio—so functioning in fact that we had to stop shooting when the dancers arrived to practice their twirls and leaps.

When I wasn't working, I went shopping with Hops and the other models, stopping for lunch at Harry's Bar, made famous by the 1960 Fellini film *La Dolce Vita* and surrounded by cobblestone streets, grand piazzas, and steep, old limestone steps. In the evenings, we went out to whatever we thought was the latest, chicest restaurant, including one where Hops swore he once saw G. Gordon Liddy and E. Howard Hunt—respectively, the FBI agent and intelligence agent indicted in the Watergate scandal—when they were supposed to be in jail. Most nights, after a leisurely dinner of *insalata caprese* and *vino*, we all went dancing at Jackie O', the hottest discotheque at the time, a place so exclusive, you had to be a celebrity or royalty to get in. (Luckily for us, our photographer, Chris von Wangenheim, was a baron, something he had never told anyone except on the nights we needed a name to get into the club.)

One evening, instead of having a leisurely dinner, we worked until midnight after Chris found a floodlit fountain in the center of the city. There, another model and I sipped champagne in the pouring rain—the editors wanted to see real flutes in the photo—and by the time we got the shot, we were not only soggy but also a little soused, especially after a motorist who stopped to offer his headlights to illuminate the scene also offered us a bottle of whiskey to offset the chill of the rain.

But not everything unfolded like a fairy tale during that trip. While we were in Rome, there was massive social unrest, as students staged protest after protest against the Italian Parliament and the political system. The night we arrived at our hotel, I was unpacking in my room when I heard chanting outside, and looking down from my window, I saw hundreds of students in the street below, marching with arms locked as police with submachine guns lined the boulevard. Several days later, while riding in a van back to the city after doing a shoot by the sea on the Lido di Ostia, we were suddenly surrounded by a swarm of students, all yelling and heaving large signs up into the air. As traffic slowed to a stop, the students began pounding the van's windshield, trying to smash the glass. Cowering in the front passenger seat, I was petrified and quickly began to feel an overriding need to escape before the glass shattered and the students started pounding me. But I was trapped by a metal bulkhead that separated me in the front cabin from the rest of the crew in the back seats, and I certainly couldn't open my door. With nowhere to go, I cracked my window open an inch and started stammering in broken Italian how we supported the students' cause: "Socialismo sì, socialismo sì!"

This seemed to appease the students enough to let us pass, and just as we started slowly moving again, a loud volley of gunfire erupted—*crack! crack! crack!*—as dozens of police mobbed the street, their rifles swinging as they raced toward the students. Instantly, the cries around us deepened and became deafening, as everything turned to chaos and confusion. Somehow, though, our van managed to navigate out of the riot just in time, and it wasn't until days later that we learned a bullet had struck a young woman, killing her on the spot only seconds after we drove away.

After that disaster, the magazine hired a local guide to find safe areas where we could work, and a few days later, when the guide directed us to a beautiful centuries-old bridge just outside the Vatican, on the way to the Roman neighborhood of Trastevere, we assumed we would have an easier day. Boy oh boy, were we wrong.

Earlier that day, we got ready for the shoot in my hotel room, which had become the routine, but that morning, everyone was struggling—models, makeup artist, stylist, hairdresser, photo and art team—to make it through hair and makeup, get everyone dressed and styled, and load the van with our camera gear and garment bags. We were frayed by the unrest and, admittedly, exhausted after a week of working all day and dancing all night at Jackie O'. No amount of cappuccino or espresso was cutting it, so when someone produced a tiny vial of white powder, a volley of "hoorays!" went up around the room.

"I'm so tired," the person said. "I just have to do a little hit."

"Oh, can I have a bump?" someone else asked.

"What are you guys doing?" I asked. "What's in the vial?"

"You've never done coke before, Christie?" someone gushed, incredulous. "Come on! I don't believe you."

Another chimed in: "Oh, my god, Christie, you would love it! It's so much fun. It will wake you! It will keep you going. And you won't get hungry!"

"But it kind of scares me," I said. "Are you sure it can't hurt you? Is it dangerous?"

"Oh, no, no," said the person who had produced the vial. "Einstein used to do it! It just gives you some energy and makes you feel good. And look," he said, holding out a miniature spoon cradling a sprinkle of the white powder, "you can try the tiniest, little amount!"

In that moment, drained and disquieted, I gave in. As they say, when in Rome . . .

Within minutes, I felt more alive and awake, and I loved everything and everyone as we headed to the bridge to do the shoot, the River Tiber flowing serenely under us while the dome of St. Peter's Basilica rose majestically above. The location was sublime for photos, but on that particular spring afternoon, it would turn out to be the most dangerous place in Rome.

Shortly after we began working, a throng of students flooded the bridge from one side, shouting and thrusting signs, just as police in full riot gear—shields, helmets, guns, gas masks—came marching onto the bridge from the other side, looking like a fleet of Stormtroopers from *Star Wars*. And there I was, having taken one hit of cocaine when all hell had broken loose. Making matters worse, we looked like the epitome of the bourgeoisie in appearance alone, with our expensive camera gear and clothing, as the other model and I were dressed in narrow pencil skirts, fancy blouses, chic high heels, and extravagant gold jewelry. Everyone in our crew immediately grabbed the gear and garment bags and, tottering in heels on the cobblestone bridge, I followed the others as we walked toward the students, who looked less intimidating than the Stormtrooper police.

Just then, a single gunshot reverberated across the bridge, cutting through the commotion like a knife, as everyone around me started to scream and run. Terrified, I kicked off my heels and began sprinting as more gunfire erupted, and I started to feel a slight burn—tear gas!—at the corners of my eyes. I was petrified, but there was no time or space to panic, as the bridge became a mob scene, people falling to the ground under the crush of the crowd. I followed Hops and the rest of our group behind a low, dilapidated old stone wall, where we threw ourselves down on the cobblestones so the bullets wouldn't hit us, Hops lobbing a garment bag over my body for protection. In a matter of seconds, dozens of people had done the same, piling around us like soldiers falling into a trench in an old war movie.

Perhaps the taxi driver noticed our ridiculous outfits and giant equipment bags while we were scurrying across the bridge, but by some incredible stroke of luck, a cab appeared out of nowhere, charging from a side street. The driver swerved to a stop, leaned over, and pushed open the passenger door, hollering at us to get inside. Someone in our group heaved one of the garment bags into the car, then I dove in after it, my arms over my head like Superwoman, before several others did the same, flying headfirst into the superhero's taxi. We couldn't all fit into one car, so the driver promised he'd come back for the others after he dropped us off somewhere safe.

Once inside the taxi, I heaved a sigh of relief, but adrenaline still raced through my body as the car hurtled out of the fray, eventually depositing us a few minutes away, on an empty boulevard outside the perimeter of the protest.

As soon as the taxi left to retrieve the others, I heard someone say, "Oh, my god, I need another hit."

"I do, too," someone else said.

Thinking I needed a good PR person more than anything else as I started to picture the potential headlines, I volunteered to watch the gear and garment bags while the others headed into the bushes behind us. I can only imagine what I must have looked like standing there, barefoot in my dirty dress with bags that resembled rifle cases, and within seconds, a police car appeared, and a pair of officers jumped out. The headlines were now flashing before my eyes—"Christie Brinkley Arrested in Rome Riot, High on Cocaine." I could think only about the shame I would bring my family, so I started speaking loudly and deliberately, repeating "O, grazie, polizie, pol-iiii-zie," so the others in the bushes knew things had taken a turn for the worse. Slowly, they reemerged, and I saw someone drop the vial of powder into the nearest open bag, which happened to be mine . . . just as the police demanded to see our luggage!

As the police started rifling through our things, all I could think of was how I'd explain to my parents in my one allotted phone call from a cold, dark Italian prison cell that it really had been my first time ever doing cocaine. But in that moment, the taxi with the others pulled up, and the art director, seeing the police, leaped out and flashed our credentials and permits. The officers looked at our papers, then looked us up and down, scrutinizing our outfits, which, while dirty, were still stylish. Seemingly satisfied that we were there only to do a photo shoot, they sped off, leaving us shaken and in shock. Headlines averted.

Several nights later, we celebrated a hard week of work with another night at Jackie O', and afterward, Hops and I decided to walk back to the hotel through the city's ancient, gnarled streets, which were quiet and calm in the overnight hours after all the unrest of the day. At dawn, we ended up at the Trevi Fountain, which, while closed and idle, looked spectacular in the half light of the early morning, empty and awash in pinks and purples, its stone-white statues quiet in consternation without the gurgle of water beneath their feet, which were forever fixed in rock.

Afterward, we made our way to the Palatine Hill, which overlooks the Roman Forum and the city's oldest ruins, where you can see different layers of civilization, one piled on top of the other, in the ongoing march of time. As the sun began to bathe the crumbling plaza and light up the city below, I started to think about the great expanse of human history and how I was just a tiny speck in its timeline, a glimmering little life without one second to waste. In that moment, I felt grateful to be alive, to be in Rome, and to have experienced everything I had—the good, the bad, the beautiful, and the terrifying—in a week that would go down in modern history as one of the city's most violent. It was a humbling and moving moment, one that, more than forty years later, I've never forgotten, hearing instead Leonard Cohen's visionary words in my head: "There is a crack, there is a crack in everything / That's how the light gets in."

BACK IN New York, I was in the city when a different kind of chaos erupted, this time caused by a massive power outage in what became known as the blackout of 1977, an incident so monumental that it inspired several chart-topping songs and a PBS documentary that aired nearly forty years later. The night New York went black, Jean-François and I were standing side by side in our apartment, looking out our windows, when we saw the city's lights suddenly dim, then cut out completely. Immediately afterward, the Upper West Side looked beautiful, windows everywhere illuminated by flickering candlelight as neighbors sat on fire escapes to flee the one-hundred-degree heat, sharing ice cream and other food from their freezers before it melted. To me, it felt like New Yorkers were coming together for one another, as they always had and would continue to do for decades during other catastrophes, and I remember feeling that one of the biggest cities in the world had suddenly become a small town.

But then Jean-François and I joined a group huddled around a transistor radio, and what had at first seemed quaint became tragic, as news of looting, rioting, and arson became widespread. By the time the blackout was over, thousands of people had been arrested and just as many fires had broken out all over the city, plunging New York into a state of emergency from which it took months to recover. But New Yorkers are resilient, and when the city came back, it did so stronger than ever.

While the city was on the rebound, I was on the outbound, flying all over the world for work, most memorably to the South of France, to shoot a print and TV commercial for Chanel No. 19 perfume with Helmut Newton. The shoot took place in Antibes, at one of the world's most gorgeous resorts, the Caps d'Antibes Beach Hotel, at which I had the privilege only of working, not staying. (At the time, I promised myself I'd come back to stay in the hotel, and I feel very fortunate to have been able to make good on that promise several times over.)

The more TV commercials I did, the more I loved to act, and to this day, that Chanel No. 19 spot remains my favorite because I felt so distinctly French. For the shoot, I wore a pleated white silk Chanel skirt, which fluttered prettily whenever a breeze traveled off the Mediterranean, and a navy-and-white-striped Chanel blouse—I adore anything with a nautical stripe—with my hair parted and pinned to one side, so that it bounced all around me in alluring waves. In the commercial, I had to walk arm and arm with a handsome male model along the Riviera, stopping to pull him in and kiss him in front of a dozen swaying sailboats. When I first saw it air on TV in New York, I loved everything about the commercial: what I wore, where I was. And if you had ever told me when I was a teenager studying French in high school and wearing my little black berets that, one day, I'd be in a Chanel commercial looking like a paragon of French femininity, I wouldn't have believed you for all the croissants in Paris.

But that year, I didn't spend much time watching myself or anyone else on TV. Instead, I was traveling constantly for work and going to many places I hadn't been before, including Brazil, which I visited for the first time with *Sports Illustrated* for the 1978 Swimsuit Issue. Several shots of me ended up in the issue, including one where I'm standing topless in a pool with Brazilian model Maria João, with only a wet towel covering my bare breasts. But what I remember more than the photos was how excited I was to go to Rio de Janeiro, where Antônio Carlos Jobim wrote the music for "The Girl from Ipanema," which was later recorded by three of my favorite childhood musicians, Stan Getz, João Gilberto, and Astrud Gilberto. In my first free moment, I dashed to Ipanema to sit outside at a café and watch all the "tall and tan and young and lovely" people pass by, as the song goes. To my surprise, too, everyone in Rio did seem young and lovely—*and* fit, chasing soccer balls up and down the parks and doing calisthenics on the boardwalk by Copacabana Beach. After we wrapped in Rio, we flew to Bahia, where music wafted out of cafés and where I used the few Portuguese phrases I had learned from Stan Getz and João Gilberto's songs to buy trinkets at tiny storefronts.

By the time the issue came out that winter, I felt as far removed from the balmy climes of Brazil as you could be. That year, 1978, had started as a blur, quite literally, as the Great Blizzard of 1978 buried New York under feet of snow, immobilizing the city and shutting down streets, subways, and airports—so much so that I couldn't fly out to Jamaica with *Harper's Bazaar*. The storm gave everyone in the city a sudden holiday, so Jean-François and I bundled up and headed outside, watching cross-country skiers whoosh down the city streets. In Central Park, we even spotted Salvador Dalí and his signature mustache, under which I detected the slightest smile as he rode in a horse-drawn sled through the park's snowy Narnia with his wife, Gala, the two looking like a mythic snow king and queen. Talk about surreal.

That year, I was in New York only 143 days, spending the rest of the time on the road or on location, and while I took dozens of work trips, one that certainly stands out was when I went to Alaska with *Vogue*. Jean-François joined us because, like me, he was eager to see Alaska; also, the magazine wanted to use him as a male model. Our first day there, we flew in a tiny pontoon plane to an area of the world that seemed untouched by human civilization, landing right in the middle of the tundra, which would become our photo studio for the afternoon. The photographer was Stan Malinowski, whom everyone in the industry knew for his work with Estée Lauder and helping capture the brand's face at the time, model Karen Graham. In the alpine tundra, it was Stan's idea to shoot me standing knee-deep in frigid water while wearing nothing but a leopard print bikini bottom, a white sleeveless vest, and hunter-green fishing waders as the icy wind whipped my bare arms and legs. I was so visibly cold that Stan, in a sign of solidarity, took off his jacket and shirt and stood there bare-chested, shivering along with me, as he shot and rotated his camera.

Another day, we took a helicopter to a glacier, where the pilot landed precariously on the lip of a crevasse—one false move, and we would have plunged to our deaths—all so Stan could capture me at a vertiginous angle from the other side of the rift. Afterward, we flew to the bottom of the glacier, where I kayaked through the arctic water wearing nothing but a red bathing suit, paddling to the very edge of the glacier, where the ice looked even bluer in the water's reflection. The entire experience was exciting and spectacular, so much so that I didn't even feel the cold.

To close out the trip, we did a shoot on top of an immense oil rig stationed in the ocean. To get there, we had to take a helicopter, which careened us over and through massive moose-covered mountains. While we were flying through one canyon, a storm suddenly descended, masking us in a thick fog that took away all visibility, forcing the pilot to hover in place for what felt like an eternity, so that we wouldn't crash into the mountains around us.

Helicopters, airplanes, averted accidents . . .

The thing about all these close encounters, though, is that I've made so many promises to do good if I made it out alive that I'd now give Mother Teresa a run for her sainthood.

NOT ALL my shoots were adventurous or glamorous, though. Once, *Harper's Bazaar* offered to fly me and Jean-Francois to Paris to shoot the "collections," when designers debut their seasonal line and all the magazines vie to shoot the new clothes at the same time. We landed early in the morning, only to wake up two hours later because I had to be at work at five, which wasn't the Parisian way, but all bets were off during collections.

Another reason we started early was American photographer Bill King, whose trademark move was to catch models in action as they flew through the air, causing their clothes to take on dynamic shapes, and working with him was like doing aerobics for twenty-four hours straight. He was always asking us to jump, spin, leap, kick, twirl, or hop so he could get his signature shot, using the strongest, biggest, industrial-size wind machines to make us look windblown. But it was eye-watering, exhausting work, especially because Bill could work all day and all night—this was the 1970s, when many people in our industry were powered by cocaine, which was as ubiquitous as lipstick.

One day, after getting only an hour's sleep, I woke up at 6 in the morning to wash my hair before I had to be in makeup. Our first location was on a bridge over the Seine, where Bill asked me to do the usual Bill routine—leaping, jumping, and twirling—but despite all the heart-pounding activity, I was freezing in the flimsy cocktail dresses, especially after it started to snow. When we finally got the shot, we headed over to the Champs-Élysées to do more, and then to the Arc de Triomphe, where we immediately drew a crowd, which attracted the police who made us stop shooting.

Standing there in the chilly air, I could hear five hundred cameras clicking away, all at me, but not one of them was Bill's, so we grabbed all the gear, jumped back in the van, took one spin around the Arc de Triomphe, then rushed out again to try to quickly grab the shots we needed before the police returned. Overtired, overworked, hungry, and in a rush, everyone started acting frantically, throwing clothes on me, jabbing me with pins, and criticizing my makeup, which had started to run, all while the tourists kept clicking, Bill kept shooting, and our hairstylist, a lovely woman named Ruthie, started to sob.

I wanted to sob, too, because for the first time in my career, I felt like I was just a disposable accessory—or, to be more precise, a pin cushion, as the stylists, under pressure to keep up the pace, started stabbing my skin and scalp with pins, trying to fit another dress on my body and affix a large feather headdress to my head. I suddenly wanted to be anywhere but there, even though I was in the city I loved so much, and after the final pin speared my scalp, I turned and, with a tear flying out of one eye and the camera still clicking, ran out of the frame, through the tourists, and into the arms of Jean-François.

In the end, though, something wonderful came out of my being in Paris at that moment, something that wouldn't have happened if I hadn't done the *Harper's Bazaar* job.

AFTER THE shoot wrapped and the makeup artist flew home with the others, Jean-François and I stayed in Paris, wandering through the city that had originally brought us together, miraculously and inseparably, that first evening at La Coupole. While we'd visited Paris a few times since moving to New York, always wondering if we should move back, on this trip, I knew something had changed. I was still in love with Paris, but now I knew there was no moving back—not for the foreseeable future, at least. New York had more to offer us both, professionally and personally, and I knew Jean-François realized it as much as I did. Sitting in a quiet café on the Seine, amid the din of coffee cups and spoons and the hushed murmur of spoken French, we decided to commit to New York and to chasing our dreams there until we no longer had the same dreams to chase. It felt like a breakthrough, and to celebrate our decision, we got dressed up that evening and went to our favorite restaurant, Brasserie Vagenende. It was the restaurant where we had spent Jean-François's birthday the night I returned from Greece all those years before, when being a model wasn't even a remote possibility or fleeting thought.

Brasserie Vagenende is an old and elegant restaurant from the Belle Époque, and full of art nouveau details—paneled glass walls, mosaic tiles, and rich, dark wood. At one point that evening, a young man with a guitar stood up in one corner of the restaurant and began softly singing old French ballads. As the night wore on and empty wineglasses turned into empty bottles, a group of elderly men and women joined the man, singing with him the songs they had known for decades, songs the rest of us had only ever heard on old records and the radio. Hearing their voices, the tinkling of wineglasses, and the muted laughter of the half-empty restaurant, I felt a lump begin to form at the back of my throat, as tears started to drip down my face. For the last few years, I had always believed I was a Parisienne visiting New York. But now, I was a New Yorker visiting Paris.

"Don't worry," Jean-François said, grasping my hand firmly under the table. "We'll be back here to live one day."

Of course, we never did. Or, maybe more to the point, *I* never did. And he never did, either.

But what I did do was decide that if I was truly going to devote myself to New York, I also had to devote myself to modeling, which meant no longer viewing the job only as a ticket to see the world. Instead, I now had to see what the fashion world could offer me. Sure, I still wanted to have all the adventures models do, but I had to take the job more seriously, I told myself. I had to become the model everyone assumed I already was—which, in my mind, meant dieting and exercising more. A lot more.

My decision to double down on modeling paid off. Several months later, I had made the cover of eleven magazines, all published around the same time, my face splashed across the front of *Mademoiselle*, *Cosmopolitan*, *Redbook*, *Vogue France*, *Vogue Patterns*, Italian *Harper's Bazaar*, American *Harper's Bazaar*, and several different issues of *Glamour*. I also started doing commercials for Black Velvet Whisky, in addition to more ads for Revlon, Breck, Clairol, CoverGirl, Sears, Bloomingdale's, and dozens of other clients.

In his typical wheeler-dealer style, Johnny Casablancas wanted to capitalize on my cover spree by having me do a bunch of magazine interviews and TV shows, and while I agreed to do several, I also decided to book out the summer of '78, when many of my covers were on newsstands, exasperating the agency. But hard work demands balance, and I wanted to live my life, see my parents, and spend quality time with Jean-François, which we did that summer by learning to sail big boats, taking an advanced class so we could charter our own ship, without a captain or crew, and sail to the islands off the California coast. (On one of those trips, my brother and I ended up swimming with a shark bigger than our boat while trying to unhook a pesky anchor.)

That summer in Los Angeles, I also took acting lessons, and when I returned to New York in the fall, I hired a movie agent: I had caught the acting bug, and even if movies weren't in my future, I thought the lessons would sharpen my skills for all the TV commercials I was doing. Within days, while wrapping a shoot for *Vogue Patterns*, I got a call from the movie agent: Would I meet Robert De Niro for a drink in two hours' time? He was doing a movie called *Raging Bull*, the agent explained, and wanted to fill a smaller part. Of course I would. I swiped on some blush and rushed uptown to meet Robert and the film's casting director, Cis Corman, at Cis's apartment. When I walked in, Robert saw me and did a double take—*Is that a good sign?* I wondered—and invited me to sit down. While he looked through my portfolio, we talked about traveling and the trips we'd each taken to various parts of the world. Eventually, Cis joined us, and while they were both lovely, I knew I wasn't going to get the part: they wanted a hardened New Yorker, and while I had determined that the city would be my destiny, I was still a romantic Parisienne at heart, without the acting chops yet to play a tough New Yorker. And I was okay with that.

Eventually, I did do movies, though, along with television series, a major Broadway show, and several music videos, including "Uptown Girl." But the one role I never got to play—the one I always wanted to play—was wife "until death do us part," a wife who looks back with her husband on all their years together, the two reminiscing and reminding each other of a life well lived.

And as 1978 became 1979, I realized I would never play that role with Jean-François.

CHAPTER

11

Lying in the sand at the edge of a never-ending sea, I felt like I was about to fall off the beach and into the night sky. Bird Island was so small—just a speck of rock and sand in the middle of miles of ocean—that it was impossible to tell the difference between the inky water all around me and the inky firmament above. Like a scuba diver who loses orientation in water too deep and dark, I couldn't tell what was up from what was down anymore, and in that moment, the stars looked so close, as if they had tumbled right out of the sky to sit suspended next to me, dazzling and dizzying, on the sandy beach.

Oh starlight, star bright
You've got the lovin' that I like all right . . .

I heard Joni Mitchell singing softly in my head as I breathed in the velvety air of midnight in Seychelles, a string of more than one hundred islands in the middle of the Indian Ocean, so far from cities that the stars seem only inches away, not light-years. When I saw a meteor later that night, I almost ducked for cover, splaying my hands in the pink, powdery sand beneath me.

Of all the locations I went to with *Sports Illustrated*, Seychelles was the most remote. It took me three days just to get there via a caravan of commercial jets and tiny prop planes, but the variety of experiences on the islands was well worth the journey. On one island, we had to crawl through a watery grotto to get to a beach where the photographer wanted to shoot, and while pushing through waist-deep water under rock, I remember trying to look for the light on the other side so we could find the keyhole and slip out onto a beach few people had ever seen. On another island, I spent the night in a hut on the beach where the door to my room didn't reach the floor, and in the morning, from bed, I could see the peddling feet of fishermen as they walked by dragging lobster traps behind them and causing the sand to spray up in glittery white whorls.

The journalist George Plimpton followed us on that trip for a story, and the prestige of having an American magazine *and* a great American writer on the islands attracted the attention of the president of Seychelles, who invited us all to his home for dinner. On our way there, a guide explained how critical it was to eat whatever we were served, per local custom. But when the waiters placed bowls of steaming bat curry in front of everyone, I was so happy to have the excuse that I was a vegetarian, which allowed me to avoid the dish without offending anyone.

Many mornings in Seychelles, I'd go jogging on the beach—I was now exercising daily to try to whittle my figure—running through hundreds of seashells, many of them still fully formed, as though someone had taken them straight out of a souvenir shop and scattered them in the sand. Every day was a different adventure in a new location, and one afternoon, we went by foot to boat to oxcart, the latter of which could be driven only by a local man named Choppy, to get to our shoot on an empty beach that looked as though no human being had ever touched its sand before. On another afternoon, our photo studio was a forest of huge coco de mer ("coconuts of the sea") trees, which make love when the wind blows their enormous palm fronds together. Yet another afternoon, I ran back and forth on a white-sand peninsula while the photographer snapped pictures and a thousand fairy terns screeched and winged around me. *How fitting for Bird Island!* I thought as I smiled for the camera, feeling as though I were in a Hitchcock movie, albeit a happy one with a much better ending.

And that trip did have a fantastic ending because I made the cover of *Sports Illustrated*.

The shot was of me in a high-cut, embellished black one-piece, my hands suggestively holding my hair back from my face, with my full name in type right there on the issue, hugging the curve of my breasts.

At first, I didn't think making the cover of *Sports Illustrated* was such a big deal. I had already appeared on dozens of other covers, and while I was delighted to have one more, along with five of the twelve pages inside that the issue gives to swimsuit models, I didn't realize at the time how much that cover would change my career, especially since it included my full name, introducing me to the other half of the world's population, men, and shooting my celebrity higher into the cosmos.

With the kind of celestial sky in Seychelles, it was easy to thank my lucky stars.

Once the issue came out, the calls started coming in. Would I do this talk show? What about Johnny Carson? My mom also phoned to tell me that my aunt had heard a three-hour radio tribute to me in Michigan. I was stunned. *In Michigan? For three hours? What was there possibly to say?*

That spring, *Sports Illustrated* threw a party for me, presenting me with a cake decorated by a frosted facsimile of me, looking gauzy and gossamer in my black buttercream swimsuit as I melted into a sugary sea of icing. I had already started to receive fan mail, but after the *Sports Illustrated* cover, the letters started pouring in, one from a mother whose son had lost his arm in a bus accident ("He loves you. Could you write him a letter to lift his spirits?") and another from a young girl whose mother had just died ("It would mean the world to me if you could write back"). These letters made me realize that I could use my newfound notoriety to do good, which was an honor I had never imagined.

BUT ALL this success came with a price: a new and growing feeling of anxiety. Beginning in 1979 and lasting for months, I started to feel not unlike that frosted facsimile of me on the *Sports Illustrated* cake— diaphanous and delicate, full of questions and uncertainties, and as though I might blur and melt around the edges at any moment.

The anxiety wasn't constant; it came and went like a cloud, dissipating during sunny breaks only to reappear again, dark and foreboding, as though it had coalesced into a storm over the ocean. I could feel the industry's expectations piling up on me now that I had decided to commit myself to modeling, and while I had never worried about failure when I believed I wouldn't model for very long, I now began to fret over the idea constantly. I started to wonder if I was pretty enough for the job—I had already convinced myself I wasn't thin enough. I also felt as though I had to spruce myself up to look like the Christie Brinkley people may have seen on covers, in commercials, and on talk shows, which took time when there were so many other things I'd rather be doing. But modeling was no longer just a fun side hustle. It was my career now, and one I needed to sustain with the same degree of success.

In 1979, I bought our rental apartment on Sixty-seventh Street, and the one next door. At first, owning an apartment (not to mention two) was thrilling, especially for two formerly struggling artists who'd fallen in love in a Paris atelier that didn't have a kitchen or bathroom. The morning after we closed, Jean-François jumped out of bed naked and, brandishing a hammer, knocked a hole in the wall between the two apartments. He then called me over so we could see into our future, the two of us standing there naked, peering through the hole while imagining our new, larger life once the renovations were complete.

When I started writing checks for two monthly mortgages, however, my excitement turned into increasing financial pressure. For the first time in my career, I couldn't afford to lose jobs because I was too "full-figured" or no longer the "new" girl. Several weeks after we closed on the apartments, I became so anxious about work and money that I booked out for several days to go to a health spa upstate, where I paid good money to drink green juices and starve myself, hoping it would settle my nerves while I lost a few pounds in the process. It didn't work. Weeks later, I was still uneasy, although now it wasn't only my mortgage and modeling career I was worried about.

I couldn't put my finger on what was causing my shifting anxiety, but I thought it might have something to do with my husband, who had been nothing but wonderful and supportive—so that I could be upset with my marriage was a paradox in itself that confused me, intensifying my uneasiness. But because Jean-François was so upstanding and chivalrous, he was uncomfortable that I was paying for our apartments and other things he wouldn't have been able to afford on his own. At my insistence, we had opened a joint bank account, and while I'd said many times that my money was his money, he was noble and proud and kept meticulous track of what he contributed financially. For the same reason, he didn't want to go on trips with me anymore, saying he felt like a *maquereau* ("mackerel," in English, or slang for "pimp") for hanging about idly while I worked.

Around the same time that Jean-François became more reluctant to share in my success, I became increasingly eager to experience everything that came with that success. I was officially a top model now—the same year as my first *Sports Illustrated* cover, *Harper's Bazaar* named me one of the most beautiful women in the world in its inaugural "supermodel" issue. Also, the job was offering me more of the world in ways it never had before, and I wanted to see that world. What I didn't want to do was rush home because Jean-François, with a deadline and needing to draw, wanted me by his side while he worked. This had begun to occur more frequently, and the more successful I became, the more I understood what I was missing by speeding home to keep him company.

I also began to think about how we had first met, how I had been only nineteen and in Paris for a metaphorical minute before I fell in love. Since then, it had all unfolded like a fairy tale, from the moment Jean-François saved me from *les clochards* that one evening in 1973, to the night he proposed to me in a New York City apartment, to the day we were married in Kona Village with our feet in the waves and a song on the wind. It had all been a dream, except now I felt like I was waking up, and I started to wonder what else—and who else—might be out there. Also, in the six years I'd known Jean-François, I'd changed considerably, transforming from a girl from Malibu bound for Paris with only a backpack, paints, and bohemian ideals to a top model with two mortgages, an endless zeal for adventure, and one big career that, like the meteor I had seen in Seychelles, was taking me higher into the ether. Having grabbed onto the tail of that meteor, I now wanted to hold on for the ride.

Then I went to St. Barts with *Glamour*. I had never been to the island before, and the experience changed me. St. Barts immediately felt like home, its hills reminding me of the hills in Malibu, and its villages, ocean vistas, and spoken French taking me back to Cap d'Antibes, on the French Riviera. When I opened the windows of my hotel room, I had the same feeling I once had in Paris, as though I were standing inside a Matisse painting and looking out at the same scene the artist had painted so often, full of bright flowers, colorful homes, and happy little sailboats bobbing in the distance like seabirds. From that moment, I knew St. Barts would play a major role in my life, and it has. The island was where I first met Billy Joel, where I became enchanted by a sea captain, and where, during that initial trip, I began to wonder if being single might be better than being married.

THAT JUNE, Jean-François and I went to Malibu to visit my parents, as we usually did in the summer; I was also booked to film several TV commercials there. A few weeks into the trip, Jean-François went back to New York to sign escrow papers on our apartment and complete a few assignments. As soon as he left, the anxiety I had felt all year came rushing back, narrowing into focus in a way it hadn't before. I spent hours on the beach thinking about our life together, wondering if our paths had veered apart and realizing that we now seemed to be going in very different directions. Many mornings, as I watched the waves break against the wet sand, I thought about our dreams and how dissimilar they now seemed. I began talking about my anxiety out loud with my parents, admitting for the first time that I thought I might be feeling this way because Jean-Francois and I were on opposite life paths.

In August, I told him I needed to stay in California to think about things and that he should stay in New York. Finally, as summer faded into fall, I did something I never thought I would do: I asked Jean-François for a divorce. Neither of us contested the separation, and while I constantly worried that I was making a mistake, within weeks, our marriage dissolved as quickly and as effortlessly as our love had first sparked.

That fall, I decided to stay in Los Angeles, hoping the change would be restorative, and on a whim, I bought an apartment on the same street where I had grown up, Old Malibu Road, right on the beach next to my beloved Pier and Volcano rocks. I moved in right away, using storm lanterns to light the living room and an inflatable raft for a bed, which was perfectly fine by me. The apartment had a wonderful sundeck that jutted out over the ocean, and in the mornings, I would bait a line with cheese and hang a fishing pole there to try to catch fish for breakfast, a meal of which Eileen Ford would have been so proud. Whenever I looked out at the vast ocean from that deck, it felt like my future was the same—big, wide, and expansive— and while I had no idea what would happen next, I was ready for the adventure. For the first time in months, I felt free of anxiety and full of excitement, like anything and everything was possible.

Motivated by that feeling, I started taking scuba diving lessons again, and the day of my first dive off the Channel Islands, just west of Los Angeles, I noticed the captain of the dive boat staring at me.

"You look familiar," he said, squinting his weathered eyes at me. I was thinking he'd say he'd seen me on a certain magazine cover, commercial, or TV show when he lifted a finger in the air as if testing the breeze. "I know it!" he cried suddenly. "You're that kid who discovered the sea monster!"

I couldn't have been more pleasantly surprised. But he was right. I *was* that kid who had discovered a sea monster, and the captain had seen the photograph of me at the local aquarium. The day it happened, I was ten years old and already in my pajamas for bed when I looked out from my parents' apartment and spotted on the beach what I thought was a giant mass of seaweed. When I ran down onto the sand, I realized the seaweed was actually the body of an enormous, eel-like beast, with a huge head that looked like a horse's, framed by a shaggy red mane. The beach was empty that evening, except for my friend North, an elderly artist who lived in a shack near us and who, like me, was also staring at the creature. North enlisted the help of a few other neighbors, and somehow we all managed to lift the dead monster up on top of North's Volkswagen Bug and drive it off the beach. When the newspapers came to take pictures, I sat on North's car in my pajamas, looking like a tiny sprite next to the giant beast, which was so gigantic, its body draped over the windshield and off the hood while its other end dangled off the back fender.

Later, I learned that the creature wasn't a sea monster, but an oarfish, which is so rarely seen that, in some cultures, it's known as the doomsday fish because people believe that seeing it is a sign of a calamity to come.

But I've never believed in calamities to come. And I certainly wasn't about to believe one would befall me after seeing, touching, or even posing with the oarfish. Instead, I only believed that, *Christie, baby, you write your own script.*

LIVING IN Malibu didn't slow down my modeling career. Quite the opposite, magazines and advertisers were eager to come to Los Angeles to work with me, and that included *Glamour*, which once descended on my apartment for hair, makeup, and breakfast as Hops and I acted as short-order cooks to feed the crew.

Later that fall, I flew to Tokyo for Calvin Klein's first-ever fashion show in Japan, which ended up being a big deal, with Calvin flying all the top models there (a flight that alone produced an endless supply of gossip for the industry). At the end of the show, the Japanese gave us each a wooden box of sake, with which we had been instructed to toast the audience from the runway. I had never had sake before, and wanting to be gracious to my hosts, I drank what I was given, in addition to more sake at a sumo wrestling match afterward and multiple flutes of champagne when everyone ended up at a discotheque later that night. The next morning, I woke up with one of the worst hangovers I've ever had, and while I managed to avoid vomiting on the car ride to the airport, once I got there, I ran through every security line and straight to the ladies' room, where I promptly got sick. I felt immediately better afterward, but as I left the bathroom, my relief turned to horror when I saw the airport police standing there waiting for me, ready to arrest me on suspicion of a bomb threat. They proceeded to search me, my luggage, and the bathroom until I was able to convince them that the only thing about to explode had been me, thanks to all the sake and champagne.

Never again.

Still, I was trying new things. I was seeing the world. And I was having adventures, just like I wanted. Some of those adventures steered my life in wild new ways, both professionally and personally, including one adventure that took place much closer to home, in the beautiful, barren desert outside Palm Springs.

If someone were to narrate that adventure, the voice-over would start like this:

"These are the magic faces. Superstars of the modeling world. A pretty face can earn two thousand dollars a day, three hundred thousand dollars a year. It's a fifty-million-dollar business, all based on illusion . . ."

These are the opening lines of *Beautiful Baby, Beautiful*, an HBO documentary on the life of supermodels that I filmed in Palm Springs with Jerry Hall, Janice Dickinson, Iman, and a handful of other models, along with the famous photographer Elliot Erwitt. The movie, which aired in 1980 and was watched by millions, starts with a quick montage of magazine covers before cutting away to me, posed

182

kneeling while dressed in a snakeskin swimsuit, as the voice-over continues:

"We call our fairy tale *Beautiful Baby, Beautiful*. 'Beautiful baby, beautiful' is what the photographer says when he captures that moment of illusion . . ."

I'm the first supermodel featured in the documentary, and I'm posing in the high desert for a poster shoot with photographer Mike Reinhardt:

"Christie Brinkley has hooked the brass ring on the modeling merry-go-round. At twenty-five, Christie grosses up to two thousand dollars a day. This golden girl from California has rung up the astounding record of appearing on more than one hundred magazine covers."

While the documentary helped boost my fame, what affected me most about the experience was my newfound friendship with Janice Dickinson, which the film helped to launch. At the time, Janice was dating Mike Reinhardt, with whom I had worked many times since initially meeting him in Johnny Casablancas's Paris office during my first-ever modeling interview. We'd been friends for years, but now that I was divorced, I was more available to do the crazy, spontaneous things she and Mike did, and after the *Beautiful Baby, Beautiful* shoot, I started hanging out with them whenever I was in New York. Mike owned a house in the Hamptons, and the two started inviting me there for weekends, which is where and how I first met French photographer Pierre Houlès.

It wasn't love at first sight. I was introduced to Pierre, whom I called Houlès, in the back seat of Mike's car after he picked us both up in the city to drive the several hours out to his house at the end of Long Island. Mike and Janice had already sung Houlès's praises, in the hope of setting us up, and while I liked him, I also found him arrogant and pessimistic at first. At the same time, he had a beautiful

Parisian accent, icy blue eyes, and the kind of dark, curly hair I always found attractive. And with apartments in both Paris and New York, he seemed more sophisticated and worldly than the American men I knew—an impression he reinforced by wearing only cashmere sweaters and dark-wash jeans and keeping nothing but expensive champagne in his refrigerator. He wasn't very talkative, but when he did speak, he would often say something sexy and authoritative, like "*Voici*, this is the best restaurant" or "This is the only *parfum* a woman should wear." Houlès also belonged to a group of fashion photographers known as the French Mafia, which included Patrick Demarchelier and Gilles Bensimon, and while he didn't work as often as they did, they all considered Houlès the genius, the one who knew which lens to use, which settings worked best, what lighting produced *l'éclairage parfait*.

Oh starlight, star bright
You've got the lovin' that I like all right . . .

ONCE WE started dating, I found myself in the middle of the modeling industry in a way I'd never been before, hanging out with top photographers in their studios turned apartments over Carnegie Hall, where Houlès had a place and would talk shop with other photographers for hours while smoking cigarettes and sharing photos. I found this exhilarating, to be so deeply and directly immersed in the industry with people who were passionate about doing great work.

When I wasn't in the city, Houlès started writing and calling me in California, asking me to come back to New York or to visit him in Paris. Eventually, he, Mike, and Janice talked me into joining them on a winter ski trip in Sils Maria, Switzerland, a snowy village outside St. Moritz where Mike and Janice had rented a cabin for several weeks.

That trip was otherworldly for many reasons, beginning with the train that took me there, which looked like it had been lifted from the pages of *The Polar Express* before dropping me off in the bustling village of St. Moritz. From there, I had to cross the town by taxi to get a sleigh to take me to Sils Maria, where there were no cars, and riding on the sled over the snow as it creaked and rasped under the runners, I was stunned by how majestic the mountains looked, bathed in a magnificent blue light, as if a photographer had slanted a reflector at just the right angle to catch the moon and cast it back onto the peaks. The scene reminded me of the illustrated Christmas books I had loved so much growing up in sunny California, and I wouldn't have been surprised if, in that moment, I had seen Santa's sleigh crossing the night sky.

When I got to Mike and Janice's cabin, they were both standing outside in the snow, where they greeted me with shrieks, howls, and a gift of warm winter boots. The next morning, everything outside my window looked like a Currier and Ives print: wooden chalets topped by gabled roofs and cafés that served so much glühwein, or "mulled wine," you could smell the cloves and orange in the icy winter air.

After Houlès joined us, we spent the week skiing, taking the gondola up the mountain, then swooshing down, stopping along the way at wooden huts where we'd eat lunch on white tablecloths and drink hot glühwein while listening to the pleasant chatter of Italian, French, and German all around us. When there was too much snow for downhill skiing, we skied cross-country. In the evenings, we took turns cooking dinner, and then ate by the fire, warmed as much by the glühwein as we were by the flames.

Soon, though, Houlès had to go back to Paris. The morning he left, I joined him in his bath—which we never finished, walking dripping instead to his bedroom, where we made love. I could tell something had changed, though: I was starting to develop feelings for Houlès, which frightened me, coming so shortly after my divorce. I could hear my mom's voice inside my head—*Honey, you gotta play the field. Don't settle down so quickly!*—and afraid of getting too serious too soon, I decided I wouldn't show my feelings for him. While I didn't mind sharing my body, I wasn't ready to give anyone my heart again.

The day Houlès left, Janice and I went for a walk, and while tramping through a corridor of trees, their branches bent into a canopy above us under the weight of so much snow, we met a young Swiss man named Matthias. He was gorgeous—tall and handsome, with big blue eyes and a sweet, shy smile. The three of us chatted on the trail for some time before he invited us back to his parents' chalet, where we kept talking until four in the morning, sealing our friendship for the rest of the trip.

The more I got to know Matthias, the sweeter and more endearing I found him, and one evening, I went over to his chalet alone. Inside his bedroom, we talked again for hours, when, eventually, he admitted bashfully how he'd made love only once and that it hadn't gone well, to the point where he was afraid to try again. He then said how much he liked me and asked if I, an older woman with more experience, would show him how to enjoy it. I trusted his sincerity, and taking his big hand in mine, I leaned over to kiss him. Then slowly, shyly, and tenderly, we made love. Afterward, he cried with relief as he held me, the moon pouring in through the windows illuminating our bodies in shafts of surreal, silvery light.

As wonderful as Matthias looked and felt, the experience didn't distract me from Houlès, as I had hoped it might. Confused and missing the Frenchman even more, I decided to fly straight from Switzerland to Paris to see him, even though I wasn't sure he wanted me to visit. But when I landed, there he was in the airport, leaning against a window like some Parisian James Dean, and in an instant, we were talking and laughing as we crisscrossed the city in his miniature

Renault. We didn't go to his place, but instead to the Hôtel Rue des Beaux-Arts, where Oscar Wilde had lived at the end of his life and where I had wanted to stay ever since first visiting the city as a teenager. The hotel was the epitome of luxury, and I loved to imagine I could see Wilde's ghost everywhere in our room—sitting under the rich velvet drapes lining our windows; relishing our marble bathroom, which was bigger than my entire Paris atelier had been; and smoking his signature cigarettes out on the room's little balcony as he gazed wistfully over the city's rooftops.

AFTER SPENDING a week in Paris, I realized I had fallen in love with Houlès. When I got back to California, I didn't want to be in Malibu anymore. While I adored my apartment overlooking the ocean, it was far from the Hollywood studios and everywhere else in the Valley I had to be for work, which required me to spend at least half the day in a car, something I dreaded. I had also started traveling regularly to Paris to see Houlès, staying with him there once for nineteen consecutive days at a time, and visiting him whenever he was in New York. Suddenly, it didn't make sense to be on the West Coast anymore, where it was more challenging to work and absolutely arduous to fly to France, and five months after buying it, I put my Malibu apartment up for sale.

Once I got back to New York, though, I realized that despite owning three places, I had nowhere to live, because they were all now under renovation. *Oh well*, I thought, throwing a sleeping bag onto the sawdust-covered floor of one of the Sixty-seventh Street apartments, and camping there amid the sawhorses and sledgehammers, I felt like a pioneer on the frontier of Upper West Side living. The apartment didn't have a working toilet, and I had only the clothes I had been able to squeeze into a carry-on in California, but I kept appearing on magazine covers looking like some glamour queen, all while feeling like a squatter in something that resembled a warehouse more than a home.

At the same time, I wasn't in the city very often because I was always flying out to meet Houlès or go elsewhere in the world for work. Several days after moving back to New York, I was on a plane again, this time to Acapulco with *Glamour*. I then flew to the British West Indies with NBC Sports for a made-for-TV special about the 1980 *Sports Illustrated* Swimsuit Issue, which was about to hit newsstands.

Up go the flaps, down go the wheels . . .

It was on a plane, the scene of so many life-altering experiences for me, that I first heard the news: I had made the cover of the 1980 Swimsuit Issue. Again. It made me the first and only model ever to appear on the cover two years in a row.

I was bound for the British West Indies with the photographer John Zimmerman and other models from the issue when I heard the news, and all the other models, who had become my friends, hugged and screamed with me. On the cover, I'm wearing a white bikini and leaning against the trunk of a palm tree, with the cover line "Christie Brinkley Brightens the British Virgin Islands" inching out from my waist. Another cover and another mention of my full name.

Back in New York, *Sports Illustrated* threw another party for me. I hadn't unpacked a single bag and had nothing to wear, yet somehow—in between go-sees, CoverGirl commercials, contractor problems, and a miscommunication with the agency that the party was actually happening within minutes, not later that night, as they had originally told me—I managed to make it to the event on time, wearing an outfit I had plucked out of a suitcase while doing my own hair and makeup in the taxi to the Time–Life Building. I felt chaotic and disorganized as I took an elevator to the top floor, where I was surprised to walk into a room full of three hundred people, all clapping and smiling while standing in front of china plates superimposed with my cover shot. I could only smile and go with the flow, and after lunch and autographs, someone steered me down a hall and through a set of doors, which opened into another room, where another three hundred people started singing "Happy Birthday" because it was right around my birthday, and the editors had remembered the date. *Sports Illustrated* then presented me with another giant cake, decorated by yet another frosting-piped picture of me from the magazine cover.

I loved the party, which included a level of fanfare, graciousness, and generosity I had never expected. But as I smiled and sipped champagne from one of the twelve French crystal flutes the magazine gifted me, I kept eyeing the iced version of me on the birthday cake, blurring and weeping around the edges, and began to wonder whether my life wasn't like that image, too.

After the party, I didn't even attempt to deal with all the boxes, crates, and construction issues I had at home, but flew out instead to Paris to see Houlès, whom I had missed desperately after being away with *Glamour* and NBC Sports, turning down an opportunity to do a TV ad for Timex to make the trip. But once I got to Paris, I realized I shouldn't have given up anything because, on that trip, I learned that the entire time we had been dating, Houlès had been sleeping with another woman, a model named Valerie.

Oh starlight, star bright
You've got the lovin' that I like all right
Turn this crazy bird around
I shouldn't have got on this flight tonight.

I heard Joni Mitchell's "This Flight Tonight" again in my head, as I had once heard it in Seychelles. But now, as I flew back to New York after being in Paris with Houlès, still reeling with emotions after learning about Valerie and dizzy from all the champagne a kind stewardess kept serving me, likely out of some unspoken female solidarity, Joni's lyrics seemed prophetic:

> *I'm drinking sweet champagne*
> *Got the headphones up high*
> *Can't numb you out*
> *Can't drum you out of my mind*
> *They're playing, "Goodbye, baby, baby goodbye,*
> *Ooh, ooh, love is blind."*

I should have ended it with Houlès the moment I learned there was another woman. But I didn't. Instead, high on champagne and miles over the Atlantic on that flight back to New York, I tried to convince myself that maybe he needed time, maybe she was a great girl whom he had known for a while when he developed feelings for me, or maybe, just maybe, I was wrong for wanting more, even if "more" meant monogamy.

But as much as I tried to convince myself that I was okay with disloyalty, I couldn't. At least not for long, and months later, after continuing to see Houlès and even meeting Valerie, who was lovely, I ended my relationship with the French photographer.

Goodbye, baby, baby, goodbye.

Because while love may be blind, as Joni says, ultimately, I am not.

12

Los Angeles may have had the Brown Derby, but New York had something even more spectacular, as it still does. The Plaza Hotel.

The grand dame of Fifth Avenue, the crown jewel of Central Park South, and what may be the world's most famous hotel, the Plaza rises like a French château amid Manhattan's steel-and-glass canyons, sitting like a polished lady in her white marble coat and green-tiled roof on the lip of one of the largest urban parks and the edge of Midtown, the biggest central business district in America. Inside the hotel, the hush of the Plaza's foyer falls over you like a veil, separating you from the honking taxis, noisy tourists, and obscene rush of the city outside and leading you like a shrouded bride into a Shangri-la of marble, mosaic floors, a thousand crystal chandeliers—the hotel originally had 1,650 installed—and a million more secrets, which have caused the wallpaper to pucker and peel, not from old age but from the weight of what's happened between those walls.

F. Scott Fitzgerald once said, "Nothing unimportant ever happens at the Plaza." Geez, was he right.

For years, whenever I went shopping on Madison Avenue, I stopped for lunch at the Plaza, where no one went for the food, necessarily, but to taste the Old World elegance radiating from its constellation of high-society restaurants and bars. The Plaza was where Houlès and I had our first romantic rendezvous in the city, which I memorialized by drawing it in my journal, with me lying in a hotel bed wearing very little while holding up a wineglass as Houlès stands over me, fully clothed, with a bottle of champagne as the room's chandelier spins above us. The Plaza was also where my daughter Alexa Ray Joel would earn a musical residency, in the Oak Room, singing in a voice as sumptuous as the oak-paneled bar itself.

But years before Alexa or Billy was in my life, something else monumental happened at the Plaza: I had an encounter there that, while not entirely by chance, led me inside an all-male world of brutality, sweat, and sport that, in an odd role reversal, put me on the other side of the camera.

Because nothing unimportant happens at the Plaza.

One afternoon in late August 1980, after shopping at the models' mecca better known as Bergdorf Goodman, Hops and I went for lunch at the Plaza's Edwardian Room, which, while no longer open to the public, has one of the best views in the city, with floor-to-ceiling windows overlooking what I liked to call the "action corner," the intersection of Fifth Avenue and Central Park South, where you could often see celebrities and socialites threading around the Pulitzer Fountain or going in or out of the Sherry-Netherland hotel, Bergdorf Goodman, or, back then, FAO Schwarz, the toy store where Tom Hanks dances on an oversize piano in the movie *Big*. (One Christmastime, the manager of FAO Schwarz closed the entire store for several hours so Billy and I could shop there for Alexa, an extravagant gesture that amazed us both.)

In those days, to make a proper entrance into any of these Fifth Avenue destinations, you had to walk right past the Edwardian

Room's windows, where Hops and I were sitting that afternoon, people-watching and picking over our grapefruit salads when I suddenly jumped up from my seat.

"Oh, my god, there's Muhammad Ali," I cried, as the world's most famous boxer and easily one of the most recognizable athletes of all time crossed Fifth Avenue and headed toward the Plaza.

Leaving Hops slack-jawed at the table, I pushed my chair back and ran out of the room, through the Plaza's revolving doors, and out onto the hotel's red-carpeted exterior steps, where I eyeballed the crowd until I spotted Ali. I could see that he was walking with sports agent Mark McCormack, who created International Management Group, better known as IMG.

"Muhammad Ali!" I yelled from the steps over the crowd like a starstruck child.

"Yes?" he asked, looking up and turning his body toward me.

"I love you!" I blurted out, overwhelmed as I watched the iconic apparition walk toward me.

"I love you, too," Ali said, giving me a big grin as I realized that he also recognized me as *that* model.

"All we can talk about is your fight," I continued excitedly, referencing his upcoming bout with Larry Holmes, his first fight since announcing his retirement from the sport the year before. The Last Hurrah, as the match was being billed, had already been rescheduled several times, which had only increased the hype around Ali's return to the ring, but the bout was now set for a little more than a month away, on October 2, 1980, at Caesars Palace in Las Vegas.

"I've been looking everywhere for tickets to see you," I hurried on.

"And I've been looking everywhere to see a woman like you," Ali joked, keeping up his banter as his smile spread from ear to ear.

"We can definitely find you some tickets," Mark McCormack said, stepping in and handing me his card.

"Oh, thank you! I'd love to be on the shoulder, if I can, so I can take pictures," I added, the words spilling out of my mouth as I took his card.

"We'll see what we can do," Mark said, giving me a little grin before the two continued walking west along Central Park South.

After waiting a second, I sprinted back inside to the Edwardian Room, running faster through the Plaza than anyone likely ever has.

"Guess who just got two tickets to the Ali–Holmes fight?" I exclaimed proudly, lifting my champagne glass off the table and holding it up to Hops. "And guess who's coming with me?"

Viva, Las Vegas.

I had gotten into boxing through Houlès. He and the other French Mafia photographers were obsessed with the sport, talking about it all the time and watching as many matches as they could on TV. While I didn't like the violence, I admired the sport's intensity, its solemnity, and the sultriness that emanated from the ring like cigar smoke. I also loved the fighters' backstories: for many athletes, the sport was the only way out of challenging circumstances like poverty or crime. There was also something about these chiseled men weaving, ducking, and dancing around a ring while hundreds of flashbulbs popped off that reminded me of what I did, strutting, posing, and performing in a small space as multiple cameras clicked.

A little more than a month after our lunch in the Edwardian Room, Hops and I were sitting ringside at Caesars, along with more than 25,000 other people who had come to watch a match that would set a new boxing record that night for the highest-grossing live gate. Every seat in the arena was filled, some taken by the famous as well as the infamous, including O.J. Simpson, the legendary boxer Sugar Ray Robinson, Sylvester Stallone (who played the eponymous role in *Rocky*), and his brother Frank, who told me that night, "You could be really cute if you lost a few pounds."

Sucker punch. While I knew I was going to see guys throwing jabs all night, I never thought I'd be on the receiving end of such a cheap shot.

Because we were staying at the Flamingo Hotel, I decided to dress in all pink for the fight, wearing a rosy pink V-neck, baggy pink shorts belted at the waist, pink high heels, and glittery pink rhinestone earrings, with my black Canon camera slung around my neck. After the preliminary bouts were over, the buzz in the arena was so thick, you could reach out and touch the excitement. When the main event finally started, I was so nervous that I didn't know if my hands would function well enough to point, shoot, advance the film, and shoot again. But somehow, I managed to control the camera and even change rolls—the feats of manual photography—eventually catching the shot that defined the match: Ali with such a stunned expression on his face that seemed to say he had forgotten how much it hurt to get hit.

After that punch, Ali never recovered, as Holmes dominated the older athlete so much that commentators thought the referee should have called it long before Ali's trainer eventually did, giving Holmes the win. I was heartbroken. I had meant it when I told Ali outside the Plaza that I loved him. While I didn't know him beyond our brief encounter, I admired his athleticism, his politics, and how he always stood up for his beliefs. After the fight ended, Hops and I staggered outside the casino, where we sat down under a big stone fountain and watched the water rise and fall as we both wept for the end to the career of one of the world's greatest living legends.

While wiping away my tears, I saw Don King, the notorious boxing promoter, leading several other celebrities back into the casino through a side door. Desperate to meet him, I grabbed Hops, and after using some line on the security guards, telling them we already knew Don, we slipped right inside one of boxing's best after-parties.

Once there, I set out on a mission to find Don when I was stopped instead by the sportswriters Bert Sugar and Randy Gordon, who ran boxing's best magazine at the time, *The Ring*.

"Christie Brinkley! What brings you here?" Bert asked, chewing on an unlit cigar, his signature accessory along with a perpetually present fedora.

"Muhammed Ali, of course," I said, surprised that the sportswriter had recognized me. "I took a ton of photos! And I'm just devastated he lost."

We then launched into a detailed debate about boxing, and because I had memorized "the tale of the tape" (the nickname for the measurements taken of all boxers), I think they were astounded by how much I knew. After more than ten minutes of straight boxing talk, they asked if I would tape a segment that night for *The Ring*'s radio show and, the following week, photograph a match at Madison Square Garden.

"Of course I will!" I exclaimed, surprising them both with my enthusiasm.

Afterward, I tried again to find Don, whom I eventually discovered in a back room surrounded by a coterie of celebrities. At the first break in conversation, I stuck out my hand and introduced myself, and while we didn't speak for long, when he learned how much I loved boxing photography, he asked if I would cover the Super Fight—big bouts got big billing in those days—between Sugar Ray Leonard and Roberto Durán a month later in the Superdome, in New Orleans.

"Of course I will!" I exclaimed immediately. Although unlike Bert and Randy, Don King wasn't surprised.

A week later, I was ringside for *The Ring* at Madison Square Garden, thrusting my camera in between the ropes to capture the fighters as they hit each other, then hit the canvas in absolute agony. That evening, I also went inside the men's locker room—this at a time when being a woman inside a men's locker room was not only uncommon but also controversial. But I did it several other times, too, at MSG and at other stadiums across the country, and during my tenure as a sports photographer, I never once experienced anything other than mutual respect: the athletes were just as happy to meet me as I was to meet them.

Afterward, I started covering regional fights and hanging out at New York boxing gyms that smelled like leather and sweat and were plastered by yellowing posters from old fights, interrupted only by beat-up boxing gloves dangling from rusty nails. My boxing photographs were published in *The Ring* and even *Sports Illustrated*, and a few of the fighters even became my friends. Today, I can say I have run with Sugar Ray Leonard, shopped at a big-and-tall store with Larry Holmes, had dinner with Ali and his wife, and even photographed Roberto Durán sparring with prisoners inside a New Orleans jail.

I also like to say that I may have been the only ringside photographer who had a boxer wink at her after he was "KO'd" to the floor.

Of all my friends in boxing, my favorite was Don King. It was Don who, years later, at a party at the U.S. Open Tennis Championships during my very nasty (and very public) divorce from my fourth husband, Peter Cook, made a speech to a roomful of celebrities on how I was a woman of great character, strength, and femininity whom no man had the right to treat the way Peter was treating me.

Don, I know I already said so, but I really appreciated your speech that night. I still do.

AS FOR modeling, the industry couldn't get enough of my stint on the other side of the camera, and when I went to cover the Super Fight at the Superdome for Don in New Orleans in November 1980, French *Elle* sent a team there to shoot me for a special fashion feature. I didn't even have to pose: the photographer simply snapped pictures of me taking pictures of the boxers, even though that photographer, as it turned out, was Houlès.

By that point, Houlès and I weren't seeing each other anymore. Earlier that year, after I discovered he was sleeping with Valerie, I tried to end it with him several times. But like a hummingbird drawn to a colorful, yet poisonous, plant, I kept getting pulled back. The sex was amazing, I told myself, and I kept coming up with excuses for not ending things—like that maybe I needed to learn how to embrace our differences or be more "open-minded" about his lack of monogamy. But things remained contentious between us, and one day in Paris, I walked out of a shoot with French *Elle* where Houlès was the photographer because I was so furious with him. Days later, I wrote a long letter of apology to the magazine, feeling especially penitent because the editors had planned to shoot me—and only me—for the entire issue in a way that the reader wouldn't know I was the only model in every shot.

After the *Elle* mishap, I flew to the Hamptons to visit Mike Reinhardt, whom I had started hanging out with more since he and Janice broke up shortly after our Switzerland trip. The two of us had also decided to sue Johnny Casablancas together after the agent circulated a poster of me from a photo Mike had taken that neither of us liked and without asking our permission. (During the lawsuit, I switched agencies several times before eventually going back to Ford Models with my tail between my legs.) With Mike, I could also talk about Houlès, and that year, we spent so much time together that rumors began to spread that *we* were dating, which we both found funny—we always had been and would only ever be good friends.

In the Hamptons, I learned that Valerie was also out east for the weekend, staying at a mutual friend's home. Encouraged by Mike, I called her, and after a surprisingly pleasant conversation, we agreed to meet in person at the beach the following day, both of us bringing wine and cigarettes to calm our nerves. I immediately liked her as much in person as I had by phone, and after sharing distressingly similar stories about Houlès, we realized he'd been using the same lines on both of us. I felt played, as did she, and I knew in that moment that I could never trust anything he said again and that, finally, I was done with the relationship. Several months later, when he showed up at the Super Fight as my photographer, I surprised him by not paying him much attention other than what was necessary from a professional perspective.

WHEN ONE door closes, though, another one always opens—and after Houlès, I was pleased to discover that the door that opened led me into the arms of a dashing, young Italian hotelier named Filippo.

I met Filippo in January 1981 in Costa Careyes, Mexico, where I first went for a photo shoot. Back then, the town wasn't really a town—and it still isn't today—but rather a small oceanside enclave built into rugged, jungle-cropped cliffs on the western coast of Mexico, ninety minutes north of Manzanillo, three hours south of Puerto Vallarta, and a world away from the rest of human civilization. The resort had been developed by an Italian banker named Gian Franco Brignone, who, on a tip from a friend, flew a tiny plane over the area in the late 1960s and bought up eight miles of land, even though there were no roads or nearby towns, calling it Careyes, which means "tortoiseshell" in Spanish. The property also had no houses, other than a handful of hacienda-style bungalows that Gian Franco painted pink, yellow, and other floral colors, and above these bungalows, on the most commanding cliff, he built his own home, which he called

Mi Ojo, Spanish for "My Eye," because he had only one eye, the other made from glass.

The day we arrived for the shoot, Gian Franco invited us all to Mi Ojo for cocktails on his terrace, and while holding a glass of wine as the sun slipped below the Pacific, I felt as if I were standing on the edge of the world, where a rock face fell hundreds of feet to the ocean below me and, behind me, a swimming pool and palm trees gave way to the Mexican jungle.

Gian Franco had two sons, Giorgio and Filippo, and while both were sophisticated, gracious, and handsome, it was Filippo who charmed me, showing us the property's rustic stables and offering us the use any of his family's horses during our stay.

"And maybe you would like to go on a sunset ride with me to-morrow?" he asked me after I lagged behind the others to admire a beautiful gray mare.

"I'd love to," I said, noticing how much Filippo's eyes sparkled, even in the hushed light of the stables.

After work the next day, we met at the stables, where Filippo helped me up onto the gray mare before we rode bareback out onto a beach that curved, empty and expansive, for miles under Careyes's rocky cliffs. When Filippo realized I knew how to ride, we began galloping through the surf as the sun dropped down next to us, our horses' hooves splashing up so much golden sea that it felt like we were riding through a wheel of water and light. Hours later, long af-ter the sun had set and the stars had already fallen over us, I knew I wouldn't be sleeping in my own room that night.

For the next two weeks, I spent all my free time with Filippo. One afternoon, he drove us in a jeep through the jungle to a deserted beach where we could swim alone for hours, and another day, while riding horses, we discovered a stallion trapped in mud that we rescued us-ing ropes and pulleys. Every day was a new adventure with Filippo, who was always upbeat and optimistic—a welcome change from Houlès—and whenever he laughed, which was often, his shaggy brown hair fell into his eyes, making him look even more handsome. In these moments with him, I felt like anything was possible—and oftentimes, with Filippo, it was.

"Does Careyes have a marina? Or any sailboats?" I asked him one afternoon, thinking that if it did, the resort would combine everything I loved into one single swath of land: ocean, forest, horses, and sailing.

"No, it doesn't," he said, a smile spreading across his face. "But you know what? We need a marina! Let's ride horses and find the perfect place for one."

So, we did, cantering up and down craggy trails to various beaches before finding the ideal spot. Another afternoon, we played polo, just the two of us, on a rough field south of the resort that Filippo said, one day, he'd turn into an actual polo field. Years later, the beach we spotted together would be a marina, and that field where we played polo, only the two of us, is the largest private polo field in all of Mexico.

The day after my twenty-seventh birthday, I flew from Manzanillo back to New York, where there was a telegram waiting for me on my apartment door: "Welcome back to New York. I love you, Filippo."

And just like that, I had fallen in love again.

For the next several months, I began traveling to Careyes as often as I could, making the two-flight trip from New York to Houston, Houston to Manzanillo, before taking a ninety-minute ride through the jungle up the coast. I went so often to Careyes and stayed there long enough that magazines and advertisers began meeting me there, especially because the location was so stunning for photos. Whenever Filippo could leave Mexico, he came to New York and stayed with me, sometimes spending weeks at a time.

That summer, I booked out to stay in Careyes, living with Filippo in his little casita on the lip of a lower cliff. The house had no walls, which I loved—it meant I could be outside all the time—and an infinity swimming pool that made it difficult to tell where the pool ended and the ocean began. The place was beautiful, and I felt so much at home that I even adopted two pet birds, whom I named Al Pesto and Al Fresco and who would sit on my shoulders, unharnessed, or flap about the casita without a cage.

EVERYONE WANTED to come to Careyes that summer, including a steady stream of aristocratic Europeans whom Gian Franco knew, in addition to many of my friends, some of whom traveled to the enclave for magazine shoots while others, like Hops and actress Lois Chiles, the Bond girl of the moment, came simply because they wanted to see Filippo and me.

Of course, no adventure in Mexico would have been complete without a little black magic, and that summer, we all got a taste of it when, one afternoon, Filippo came home with a big rash across his face, which the locals told us was the result of a curse cast by a jealous businessman. The only way to reverse the curse, they said, was to see a powerful witch doctor who lived deep within the jungle, hundreds of miles away, and eager for adventure—and a cure—Filippo and I took off with our gang of friends as though we were off to see the Wizard, as the song goes, in *The Wizard of Oz*. The journey entailed driving jeeps down muddy roads, through thick rainforests, and under torrential thunderstorms, and at one point, we discovered an elephant wandering through the jungle as part of a traveling circus. When we reached the coast again, our jeeps promptly got stuck in the mud, so off we set by canoes down a river, portaging our boats when the water got too shallow. But as we kept saying with a laugh, you do what you have to do to see the witch doctor.

When we finally got to the village where the witch doctor lived, we were instructed to bring a chicken's egg to her hut, where there was already a long line of people, each with his or her own egg, waiting patiently to receive their medicine or miracle. When it was Filippo's turn, I went inside with him, where we discovered an old, withered woman who began waving her hands manically around Filippo while muttering incantations, gesturing as though trying to push all his problems into the egg we'd brought. Afterward, she told him to open the egg, which emitted a tiny plume of smoke, and by the time we got back to Careyes, Filippo's rash was gone.

Many other incredible things happened that year, most notably when I got back to New York in February 1981, right after I met Filippo for the first time, and found out, much to my astonishment, that I was on the cover of the *Sports Illustrated* Swimsuit Issue again. It was my third year in a row—1979, 1980, and 1981—and something no other model had ever done before or has done since.

The aftermath was insane. I did all the talk shows, including Johnny Carson, and what felt like a hundred other interviews and press events. The agency phoned to say they couldn't keep up with calls from clients, including brands like CoverGirl and Chanel, both which wanted to renew their contracts with me, and advertisers outside the beauty and fashion industry, like MasterCard and Natural Lite beer, both which wanted to book me for new commercial campaigns. Also, Simon & Schuster offered me a book deal, and *Sports Illustrated* began planning the first-ever Christie Brinkley calendar.

Suddenly, I was my own brand. No longer were the magazines and clients calling the agencies to ask for a blond, blue-eyed girl with an all-American look. Now they called and asked for me by name— and sometimes *only* me. If I thought about it in boxing terms, if my first two *Sports Illustrated* covers had been a one-two punch, my third cover was nothing short of a knockout. I felt as if someone had grabbed my hand and was now holding it up in the air while parading me around the ring victorious. I wasn't as beaten up as a boxer, even though I had endured the pain of constant dieting and anxiety . . .

Sports Illustrated threw another party for me, but this time, I wasn't fixated on the frosted facsimile of me on the cake. Instead, the magazine asked me to perform in a play with Norman Mailer, the iconic author whose book *Miami and the Siege of Chicago* had inspired me to become a vegetarian at age fourteen. The opportunity was remarkable for many reasons, least of all being that Norman, who was brilliant, liked to take little nips from a bottle of booze during rehearsal, and when we performed the actual play in front of an audience of Time–Life executives, he was quite tipsy. In the play, I had the role of Margaret Bourke-White, a well-known Time–Life photographer, and in the opening act, the curtain rises on me as Bourke-White, snapping pictures inside the empty office of *Life* magazine publisher Charles Whittingham, who was played by Norman, and eventually standing up on his desk in a pencil skirt and high heels to get a better shot. When Norman walked in as Whittingham, I as Bourke-White told him I was "on" his calendar—a double entendre because not only did my character have an appointment on Whittingham's calendar to see him, I was also literally standing on the calendar on his desk, which happened to be the 1982 *Sports Illustrated* Christie Brinkley calendar.

It was the first calendar I ever did, featuring a picture of me in a swimsuit for every month of the year, and when it was published that fall, *Sports Illustrated* hosted a huge party with Ford Models at Studio 54, the now-legendary nightclub frequented by celebrities like Andy Warhol, Truman Capote, Jacqueline Kennedy Onassis, and Mick Jagger. It was the most prestigious party ever thrown for me, and the only date I wanted to take, in addition to Hops, was my mom. It was a major coincidence, then, that I met two men at the party that evening who would both come to play major roles in my life, one as my future husband and the most tortured relationship I've ever had and the other as my future lover and one of the saddest losses I've ever endured.

Before the party, Hops styled my and my mom's hair while Sandy Linter, a top makeup artist and my friend to this day, did our "glam" (meaning our makeup). Right before the event, the magazine sent a limo to pick up my mom and me, and when I stepped out of the car in front of Studio 54, a thousand lightbulbs all went off at once, momentarily blinding me before I could see what the magazine and Ford had done. Lining the entryway to the club on either side were brightly lacquered red lockers like you'd find in the hallway of a high school, every door open and hung with a different month of my calendar, amounting to a full year of Christie Brinkley by the time anyone got inside the club.

As I walked over the red carpet and through the arcade of red lockers, a man with sandy-blond hair suddenly reached out and touched my arm. "On behalf of Ford Models, I'd like to say congratulations," he said as he leaned forward and kissed me on the cheek.

"Oh, thank you," I said, taken aback a bit and thinking how considerate it was that Ford had arranged a delegate to greet me.

But the man wasn't a delegate, nor had Ford arranged for him to be there, I later learned. He was Peter Cook, a Ford model who had simply wanted to meet me—and would do so again years later, when we were set up by a friend, then married, before the relationship became one of the most tormented experiences I've ever had.

But I wasn't thinking about the sandy-haired man as I walked deeper into Studio 54, where hundreds of people had packed the most notorious nightclub in New York, all to celebrate me. Everywhere

I turned, someone was handing me a glass of champagne, grabbing my elbow to steer me in another way, or whispering into my neck how thrilling it all was, and for hours, I felt as though I were on a Tilt-A-Whirl, spinning from person to cocktail coupe to camera flash.

Even as the room spun around me, I still saw him: the man with dark, curly hair who was walking toward me, eagerly but not intently (as Peter had been), rather, waiting for the sea of people to part around us so we could meet, seamlessly and naturally. He was quite handsome, and soon everyone else in the club had fallen away and it was just the two of us, standing there smiling at each other.

"I just wanted to tell you congratulations," the man said kindly, tilting his head toward me and speaking softly in a lilting accent— which, of course, wasn't just any accent.

"Oh, my god, you're French!" I cried, switching to speak with him in his own language.

Surprised, the man smiled and leaned closer, and for a moment, I felt like we were in a bustling bistro in Paris, not a crowded nightclub in New York City, as we talked excitedly in French about how much we both adored the city where he was born. I could tell he was authentically happy for me, and when other people tried to wriggle into our conversation or get my attention in other ways, the handsome man didn't act covetous or demanding, but instead told me how pleased he was to meet me and that I should go enjoy my party.

The rest of the evening was a blur of meeting new people and talking with old industry contacts, and at one point, I even ended up behind the club's turntable, dancing and helping the deejay entertain the crowd. But when I realized the sun was already starting to peek through the skyscrapers and pour down onto the avenues below, I knew it was time to go home.

I HAD slept only several hours when I heard a knock at my apartment door. When I opened it, all I could see at first were sprays and sprays of white flowers in the hallway, as a rush of perfume flooded the doorway. But through the shroud of flowers, I finally made out one of the building's doormen, holding the biggest bouquet I'd ever seen and carefully trying to pass it to me without bending or breaking any of the several dozen white tuberoses, famous for their intoxicating scent. Struggling to wrap my arms around the bouquet, I thanked him, then carried the flowers inside my apartment, where they immediately perfumed the entire room. Pushing aside a few stems, I found a stylish enclosure card, which I opened and read: "Avant que ces quelques fleurs s'évanouit, j'espère te revoir. [Before these flowers fade, I hope to see you again.] Olivier Chandon."

I didn't wait, but picked up the phone straightaway to call Hops.

"Hops!" I exclaimed as soon as he picked up, not bothering with any of the typical "how are you" pleasantries. "You know that cute guy with the curly brown hair whom I was talking with last night? He just sent me the biggest bouquet of flowers I've ever seen!"

"Oh, my god, you got flowers from Olivier Chandon?" Hops squealed.

"Yes! Why? Do you know him?" I asked. "Is he some kind of actor?"

"No, he's Olivier Chandon de Brailles of the Moët and Chandon family—you know, Christie, they make our favorite champagne!"

"Oh my gosh!" I cried in disbelief. "What an incredible coincidence! I thought about champagne when he first told me his name, but I would have never in a million years . . ."

Hops didn't wait for me to finish. "He's a count, too, Christie. *Count* Olivier Chandon de Brailles, and he's the heir to the Chandon fortune."

"*Mon dieu*, I wouldn't have expected," I said contemplatively. I had met many celebrities and even royalty in recent years, but Olivier had been different: demure, engaging, and friendly, not stuffy, arrogant, or affected.

My white tuberoses, which now looked to me to be the same creamy color as champagne, hadn't even fully bloomed, let alone faded, when Olivier called to ask me to dinner. I said yes, thinking for a moment about Filippo. A few weeks before the Studio 54 party, he and I had agreed that, while we liked each other very much, our relationship wasn't sustainable since we lived on different sides of the world, where we had to remain for our jobs. At the same time, it was only dinner with Olivier, a man I'd met for five minutes at a nightclub well known for sparking connections that were just as ephemeral as they were electrifying in the moment.

The day of our dinner, I spent most of the afternoon getting ready, fussing over my hair and trying to make it look as big and bouncy as the flowers Olivier had sent. But all that effort was for naught, it turned out, when I saw him pull up outside my apartment astride an oversize motorcycle, looking even sexier than I'd remembered. I thought briefly about my mom, who would have a nervous fit if she ever saw me riding around Manhattan on the back of a bike, but I climbed on anyway, wrapping my arms around Olivier's waist and gripping his torso, surprised to feel so much muscle under his suede jacket.

The two of us then weaved south and east through the city to Café Un Deux Trois, a French bistro in Times Square frequented by actors, producers, and other theater people after the Broadway shows emptied. As we walked in, Olivier seemed to know nearly everyone there, greeting the owners in French and talking to several other tables in Italian, German, or English—he spoke five languages fluently, I learned later that night. We sat at a table in the back, and over dinner, we talked about everything, sharing stories in a way that felt as organic and genuine as when we first met at Studio 54. I learned he had grown up spending time in Île de la Cité, an island in the middle of the Seine where the Cathédrale Notre-Dame sits and which I visited many times when I lived in Paris. He then served in the French Air Force before coming to the States to study at New York University. While he now worked for a technology company that installed elevator banks in high-rise buildings, he didn't like the job and, with a rush of passion, told me his real dream was to be a race car driver.

The dream made sense. I had known, even before Olivier told me, that he had grown up immersed in the sport: his family's champagne, Moët et Chandon, sponsored all the Formula 1 races and was synonymous with the circuit, where all winning drivers popped and sprayed a magnum of the brand's best off the champions' podium. As a teenager, Olivier had raced cars himself, but his parents stopped him, fearful of how dangerous the sport could be, encouraging him instead to pursue a corporate career. But nothing about Olivier was corporate, I could tell that right away, and just like Hops, I knew Olivier was what I call a "liver," someone who lives life to the fullest, leveraging each and every second. And now that he was in the States and outside his family's influence, he told me he wanted to pursue what he felt was his destiny.

We ended up talking a lot about dreams and destinies that night, remaining at the restaurant long after we had finished eating and nearly everyone else had left, which was when Olivier also told me, in a careful and cautious way, what else he believed to be his destiny. Ever since he was young, he said, he had had a profound fear of death and a premonition that he would die prematurely and tragically, so much so that he wanted to face the fear in the hope of conquering it, which was why, he told me, he continually put himself in harm's way.

When I first heard him say it, my heart dropped. And when I heard him say it later, again and again when we were alone, I became as haunted by his premonition as he was.

Olivier, baby, you write your own script. So, don't write it in a way you don't want it to end.

A YEAR and a half later, when his worst fear had become our worst reality, I found myself somewhere I didn't want to be—inside a dressing room in a Paris shop desperately trying to find something to wear to Olivier's funeral. I don't remember much about the day, other than that, amid what felt like crushing grief, an American song suddenly came on the radio inside the clothing store that caught my attention, the melody alone haunting and mournful, as if every note was saturated with the pain of loss. "We met as soulmates on Parris Island . . ."

That was all I needed to hear. I collapsed to the floor sobbing uncontrollably until Hops, who had accompanied me to France, burst into the dressing room, scooped me up, and held me in his arms for what felt like hours. We left the store much later, after it was already dark outside and I couldn't find my way around the city I had once known so well.

It wasn't until months later that I realized the song I'd heard was called "Goodnight Saigon," about a boot camp in South Carolina where young men were sent before being shipped off to Vietnam. And the man who sang the song was Billy Joel, the same one who would help me find joy again after Olivier died, leading me to believe that I could do what Olivier would have always wanted me to do: live each and every day to the fullest.

Olivier, if you're near me now, you knew the perfect flowers to send, the way to move my heart, and how to send an angel when I needed one most.

CHAPTER

13

All right, Christie, let go!"
"I can't let go!" I shouted.

Over the roar of the plane's engine and the whoosh of outside air, I could barely hear the instructor.

"You have to let go. You have to let go *now*! It's too dangerous to come back in. You won't make it!"

"I can't let go! I'm coming back in!"

Hovering on the struts of a single-engine prop plane ten thousand feet over the Hudson Valley, I saw my life flash in front of me, spiraling over a sea of tiny trees and toy houses, through layers of cloud and sky while trying to pull a ripcord that wouldn't budge before my body eventually hit the ground at terminal velocity.

No, not today.

But I was already out on the wing strut, one foot dangling precariously off into open air, the other planted on the thin metal bar of the plane, and a bulky parachute pack fastened to my back. Getting back inside would be perilous, but at the same time, I didn't see why anyone should jump out of perfectly operational aircraft in the first place. And what about all those people who mustered the muscle power to lift burning cars off loved ones? I could do this. I *would* do this. Using all the strength in my standing leg, I pushed myself back inside the Cessna, falling backward onto the floor of the rickety old aircraft from the weight of the parachute pack.

I could hear the instructor speaking again, although his tone was much calmer now that we were both inside the airplane.

"You know, it's going to take more guts to face the crowd on the ground than it would have if you had jumped," he said a little patronizingly.

"That's okay," I said, grinning. "I'll take my chances."

Minutes before I found myself dangling out on airplane struts, I had watched Olivier crawl into the same spot and jump into a chasm of open sky. "I'll look for you in the air!" he'd yelled over the drone of the engine right before he jumped, his smile as big and as wide as the Cheshire cat's.

I knew he'd be disappointed when he saw me walking over ground to meet him rather than falling from the sky, and he was, insisting that we go up the next day so I could try again. In that moment, I was a little disappointed in myself, too.

The next day, I put the jumpsuit and parachute pack back on and went through the same ground crew briefing I had received only twenty-four hours earlier, although now the instructor asked me to demonstrate a "jump and roll" for the benefit of the other students—perhaps his own way of chiding me for not taking the plunge the day before. I had already done a perfect jump and roll, but that afternoon, when I leapt off the training platform and hit the ground, I felt something in my knee give out. That's when I knew that I couldn't jump out of an airplane that day or anytime the entire week—no way would I be able to sustain the landing with a bum knee. I explained the predicament to the instructor, who immediately agreed, and then to Olivier as I took off my parachute and gave it to another student.

Several days later, I heard a rumor that the parachute pack I had worn before my second jump attempt had what's called a "Mae West," a malfunction that causes the suspension lines to strangle the canopy so it doesn't open properly. My intuition—and my knee—had been right. A few years later, when I had knee surgery to repair the tear, I took a small bit of comfort knowing that if the rumor was true, the injury might have helped save my life.

Helicopters, airplanes, averted accidents . . .

Flirting with danger, though, was what life was about with Olivier, who, days after we met, moved into my Sixty-seventh Street apartment. I was smitten, and so was he, as I realized I was in love with everything about him—not just how handsome he was, but also how smart, sophisticated, and fun, and perhaps more so, how he had more joie de vivre in his little finger than most people had in their entire bodies. He was happy and eager to experience everything life had to offer—and life was offering me a lot in 1982—and not only did Olivier not mind being in the spotlight, but he also knew how to handle it, having grown up in it himself.

SEVERAL WEEKS after I met Olivier, I flew to Careyes to shoot a cover for *Life*. I had never modeled for the magazine before, and it felt like a big breakthrough. *Life* wasn't a fashion or beauty journal, but a serious publication well known for its investigative journalism, groundbreaking photos, and seminal covers featuring musicians, actors, politicians, and other power brokers. Moreover, *Life* was iconic. When I was a kid, my parents always had a copy of it on the kitchen counter, and while my friends scanned the back of cereal boxes over breakfast, I read the magazine from cover to cover, devouring the stories with more interest than I did my toast or bowl of cereal. Before that, it was the magazine

I had stuffed into the seat of my pj's to protect myself from Herb Hudson's belt.

When *Life* asked if I would do the cover in Careyes of all places, and with the famous French photographer Patrick Demarchelier, I couldn't say no. That the *Life* shoot was taking place the same time as the trip for that year's *Sports Illustrated* Swimsuit Issue didn't matter, or so I assumed, given that both publications were owned by the same company, Time–Life.

I already knew the most stunning place for photos in Careyes was on Gian Franco's terrace, where I'd first experienced the thrill of the area, and in the pictures Patrick took there for *Life*, I look like I'm flying through the air as the sun sinks into the ocean behind me (one of my specialties as a model was having a long "hang time," meaning I could leap up and hold myself in midair). The pictures that made the magazine remain some of my favorites today, while the cover shot of me, looking sultry in a shiny, red one-piece swimsuit, helped sell more copies than nearly any other issue.

While in Careyes, I saw Filippo. We had already decided to be good friends, and one night, while having drinks on his father's terrace, we made a pact to remain *amigos, siempre y para siempre*— "friends, always and forever." I kept that pact, too, even bringing Billy to meet him in Careyes years later and arranging to have lunch or drinks with him whenever he was in the city.

Everything about that trip to Careyes was wonderful—except for when I learned that Jule Campbell, *Sports Illustrated*'s swimsuit editor, was upset that I would be appearing on the cover of *Life* the same time her Swimsuit Issue hit newsstands, in February 1982. Over the years, Jule and I had become close, and when I heard through industry friends that she was hurt I had "chosen" *Life*, I got upset, too. I would never do anything to hurt or disappoint Jule—I adored, respected, and appreciated her so much.

But either way, I didn't do another *SI* swimsuit shoot for several years.

At the same time the *Life* issue went viral, I began seeing myself all over newsstands for another reason, surprising me every time I saw the photo or accompanying article. As soon as the tabloids caught wind that Olivier and I were together, they pounced on the information like a cat on a feather, coming up with all sorts of monikers for our relationship—like "the model and the millionaire," "the model and the count," or, as *People* put it on the cover of a March 1982 issue, "supermodel and her millionaire." The paparazzi started following us everywhere as we zipped about Manhattan on Olivier's motorcycle to various restaurants and nightclubs, creating a literal procession, with the media behind us in hot pursuit, desperate to get a shot of the dark, dashing count squiring his blond model around on the back of his BMW bike. We caused quite a stir, and soon enough, when nightclubs learned we were coming, they started opening the doors of their private parking garages so we could scoot right into the party like royalty. Talk about making an entrance. It didn't matter that I was usually underdressed, wearing just a tee or a blazer over jeans: they still treated us like celebrities. And for the first time in my life, I didn't mind, in part because I was dating a man who didn't mind the attention but also didn't seek it out, either—a rare amalgam, I've learned over the years.

In many ways, Olivier was everything I could ever have wanted: playful, joyful, and carefree, yet also sophisticated, intellectual, cultural, and constantly curious. In my apartment, he kept a stack of books on poetry, philosophy, psychology, and other abstract ideas by our bedside, reading every night before waking up early in the morning to practice tae kwon do, so often that I eventually installed a boxing bag so we could practice together whenever I was home. We also went often to art museums and the ballet, which Olivier loved nearly as much as he did driving cars. He knew all the prima ballerinas by name and would watch their rehearsals, often helping them with their leaps and jumps if the male dancers wanted to save their arm strength for the evening's performance.

Olivier was also extremely supportive of my work in ways I hadn't experienced before. In the spring of 1982, for example, he came with me to Annapolis, Maryland, to film comedian Bob Hope's annual birthday TV special, which featured James Coburn, Brooke Shields, Charlton Heston, and a handful of other celebrities. I had done the TV special before—and would do so again the following year, shortly after Olivier died, when Bob turned eighty and Brooke Shields, Cheryl Tiegs, and I ended up singing for President Reagan and the First Lady in Washington, DC. But I cherish the time more when Olivier was right by my side, helping me practice my lines and holding my hand encouragingly everywhere we went.

Because Olivier was so supportive of my work, I felt indebted to be the same for him when he joined the Formula Atlantic circuit and began racing, spending hours at the track so he could practice while courting sponsors. Although I had started to have the same feelings that his parents did about his driving—I was terrified for his safety and suggested he get involved in the sport in any other way—I also knew how happy it made him, and over time, his excitement became my excitement.

That year, after Olivier got his first race car, we started traveling to speedways all over the country, and while I was anxious every time he climbed into the low-slung helm of a car that was far more dangerous than any commercial vehicle on the road, it was also inspiring to see him completely in his element. He knew all the drivers personally, including the British Formula 1 legend Jackie Stewart, who once gave me driving tips—"Christie, the most important thing you can do is keep your hands on nine and three"—and they all knew him, fondly calling out "Olivier!" whenever he stepped onto the track. We started socializing with his driver friends, many of whom also became my friends, including Rupert Keegan, an amusing, rakish Brit who was my life support after Olivier died; and Elio de Angelis, an Italian Formula 1 driver, and his actress-model girlfriend, Ute Kittelberger. Three years after Olivier passed away, I cried for days when I learned that Elio had met a similar fate, cartwheeling off a speedway outside Marseille and dying hours later from smoke inhalation.

The first time Olivier ever competed was in Detroit, in June 1982. I still remember how wide-eyed he was that morning, waking up in our hotel room overlooking the track and turning to me with an eager, hungry look. "Listen, Christie," he whispered, staring out the window while gripping my bare shoulder with one hand. "Can you hear it?"

I could. It was the drone of the cars outside as they did practice laps. And there was Olivier, just as entranced by the roar of the engines as I was whenever I heard the din of crashing waves when I was near the ocean. His speedway was my waterway, and while I was nervous the entire time he zipped around the track at inhuman speeds, I knew I could never stand in the way of something that brought him so much joy.

A WEEK after the Detroit race, we went to Montreal to watch a Formula 1 Grand Prix. Olivier wanted to meet with potential sponsors there, so I brought along my camera, thinking I'd take photos while he networked. Once we got to the track, we split up—he to hobnob and me to snap—and I started taking photos of the pre-race briefing, which was when I noticed one young Italian driver who kept looking all around him, including at me, without paying much attention to the briefing. His stare was eerie, and with his one look, I felt a thousand premonitions, which was disturbing to witness only moments before he climbed into a car designed to exceed one hundred miles per hour around a tightly turning track.

Seconds after the race started, I watched in horror as the young Italian slammed into another car in the pole position, hitting a low guardrail only feet in front of me, causing his engine to explode into smoke and flames. In an instant, all I could see was thick, black soot, so thick and black it looked like night had suddenly descended. But I continued shooting the scene, feeling compelled to capture it, as safety crews ran out and doused the Italian's car in fire extinguisher foam, then manically worked to free him. By the time the doctors pulled him out, the Italian was dead, passing away just two days before his twenty-fourth birthday. For months afterward, the image of his stare haunted me like a ghost, appearing like an omen whenever I thought too long or too much about Olivier in his own car.

As much as Olivier loved danger, he also loved adventure, and that summer, we had plenty of both when we traveled to Europe, eventually ending up at his parents' country home on the Amalfi Coast—or the Costiera Amalfitana, as they say in Italy. The house was gorgeous, carved into the top of stone cliffs that fell into the Tyrrhenian Sea, and if I had wanted to, I could have jumped right out of Olivier's bedroom window and into the ocean below.

Olivier kept a small Boston Whaler there, so small it didn't even have a center console, and one beautiful, sunny day, we decided to boat along the coastline, hugging the shore while we merrily stopped along the way to see several of Olivier's friends, including Italian movie director Bernardo Bertolucci, who had a charming house on his own island, with rocks perfect for pulling up a Whaler and hopping out to say hello. Farther along the shore, we docked at an adorable restaurant where they served you your very own ball of fresh mozzarella: warm, gooey, and topped by juicy tomatoes, leafy basil, and local olive oil, it was my favorite meal in the world at the time. While we were eating, I kept staring through the salty haze to the island of Capri, several miles across the ocean and where I'd never been before, despite listening many times to Frank Sinatra's "Isle of Capri," which captivated me with its lyrics of sitting "beneath the shade of an old walnut tree."

"Do you want to go?" Olivier asked, following my gaze and smiling at me.

"Oh, yes!" I cried, and off we went in his Whaler, skipping across the water like a child's stone.

But halfway there, the sea suddenly shifted, as it often does, the wind picking up as huge swells started to roll in, tossing our little boat around like a toy and threatening to capsize us in the middle of the crossing, too far from any port to swim to shore. Gripping the gunwales so I wouldn't bounce out, I kept my eyes on Olivier as he tried to carve the boat through the trough of waves, steering us in the same direction for as long as he could, as though we were riding in a wagon forced to travel in the grooves of a well-worn trail. As frightening as it was, I trusted him, as I repeated in my mind what I had learned in my California sailing classes about what to do when a vessel capsizes in open ocean.

When we finally made it into the harbor of Capri, it was dusk and we were rattled, but we had no choice: we had to spend the night, as there was no way of boating back across the dark, inky sea. The only problem was, we had no money, no shoes, and nothing other than the clothes on our backs. For Olivier, that meant a pair of swim trunks, while I had on only a bikini top and a peasant skirt.

Just then, Olivier's eyes popped open. "I have an idea!" he said, a small smile forming on his lips as he began to throttle the Whaler toward an enormous yacht.

"Nabila! Nabila!" he started yelling as soon as we pulled up alongside the ship, our Whaler looking like a little tern floating on the waterline next to the towering white hull of what I later learned was the biggest private yacht in the world.

Eventually, a small face peered over the top railing.

"Please tell Nabila that Olivier Chandon de Brailles is here to see her!" Olivier shouted, cupping his hands around his mouth so that his words would carry up the side of the immense ship.

A few minutes later, the face reappeared, still small but now smiling. "Come around and dock near the tenders!"

And that's how we ended up on the *Nabila*, the yacht owned by Adnan Khashoggi, a Saudi billionaire and, as I later learned, an arms dealer who had named the boat after his daughter Nabila, whom Olivier had known since childhood. When Olivier explained to Nabila what had happened—that we had been caught by the storm and now had no money, clothes, or a place to go—she offered to have her helicopter take us to Rome, so we could go shopping there. After we insisted that we hardly needed a helicopter, she folded a wad of liras into Olivier's hand and asked one of the deckhands to take us off the boat and into town, where we could buy something to wear so we could join her and the yacht's other guests for dinner on the island before spending the night on her father's ship. We thanked her profusely, then darted off to town, buying the first outfits we found before heading back to the ship. Once we were back on board, a boatswain gave us the grand tour, where we learned the yacht's staterooms were all named after different jewels—the Ruby Room, the Sapphire Room, the Emerald Room—and decorated to look as costly and precious as the gemstones themselves.

Several hours later, we were sitting in cocktail attire at an elegant dinner in Capri with Adnan, Nabila, and dozens of their guests, listening to the pleasant tinkle of different foreign languages while looking out on the sparkling lights of the homes up in the hills of the island. I couldn't quite believe our good fortune, how hours before, we'd been cold and wet, only now to be at one of the most exclusive dinners on the Amalfi Coast.

The next morning, though, after we woke up on the yacht as it began to steam and chug out of the harbor, we quickly realized that Adnan was preparing to throw one of his notorious parties, complete with high-class escorts and models he often flew on board to allegedly "entertain" his male guests. In a heartbeat, I returned to the time when I was just twenty and the agency had asked if I wanted to fly to the French Mediterranean to do a "modeling job" on a yacht, where my only task would be to wear something pretty and "be nice" to all the men on board. Now, aboard Adnan's yacht, I didn't want to be confused with anyone who would accept that kind of job, so I told Olivier we had to get off immediately, even if it meant swimming to shore. I was incredibly grateful to Nabila, her family, and their staff for all the kindness they had showed us, but when things started to seem a little fishy, I decided I'd rather have to swim through the sharks than spend a night surrounded by men who acted like them.

LATER THAT summer, after we went back to New York and Olivier started racing again, my life took a synchronous turn.

I didn't even really read for the part of "the Girl in the Red Ferrari," the role I would play in the movie *National Lampoon's Vacation* that helped to launch my film career and spike my fame, especially among Middle Americans. (If they didn't know me as "that model," they soon recognized me as the flirty blonde in the fast convertible.) It happened very quickly after my acting agent called to tell me that a group of casting directors had a part for which they thought I'd be perfect, and after a brief meeting in the city, I had the role.

Soon enough, I was on a plane to the southwestern United States, where we were scheduled to film for the next several weeks. I was ecstatic, eager to explore everything I'd dreamed about the Wild West ever since I was a little girl watching Westerns starring Roy Rogers, Dale Evans, and Trigger the Horse. But as excited as I was, I was also nervous: I had a speaking role in the film, a billing with the credit "introducing Christie Brinkley," and a photographer from the popular French magazine *Paris Match* trailing me for the first week, taking photos for an article on my cinematic debut. I also wasn't quite sure how it would all work, and after we arrived at a little roadside motel in the middle of the mountains of Colorado, I unpacked my things into a knotty pinewood dresser, sat down on the orange flowered bedspread, and wondered what on earth I was supposed to do next. There was no filming schedule and, in that motel, there were no amenities like room service to make it easier.

Just then, the phone rang. "Christie, this is Beverly D'Angelo," a female voice drawled on the other end.

I already knew who she was. Not only was Beverly playing the part of Chevy Chase's wife in the movie, but I had also seen her in several other movies, including *Coal Miner's Daughter.*

"Welcome to Colorado!" Beverly said enthusiastically. "A couple of us are going out for dinner and wanted to know if you'd like to join us. And I wanted to give you my number in case you had any questions. You can call me anytime!"

Immediately, I was touched by Beverly's warmth and kindness, and with that one call, I felt more at ease.

Then I met Chevy Chase, whom I had idolized from *Saturday Night Live*, one of my favorite television shows to this day. He was just as welcoming as Beverly, asking me for my "beauty secrets" in his own hilarious way: "Christie, you gotta give me tips to make my hair look thicker!" As funny as he was, he was also shy, a combination I found endearing, and we quickly developed a playful chemistry that translated on-screen.

In the film, I play a flirtatious blonde in a red Ferrari convertible who keeps running into Chevy's character while he's driving cross-country with his wife and kids to visit an amusement park. I did all my own driving for the movie, which is unusual in Hollywood today, and even took driving lessons from Chevy's *SNL* co-star Al Franken. I also spent six weeks on location for the movie, which I never expected to do, but the film's production team mandated that we shoot my indoor scenes only when it was rainy—and it was a very sunny summer in the Southwest that year, much to my delight, despite the dismay of my modeling agency.

The most memorable part of filming was the scene where I bump into Chevy's character at a motel pool and talk him into going skinny-dipping, which we shot at two in the morning. That's when the production team asked me to go topless for the shot, but I wasn't comfortable with it: I knew very well by then that part of my appeal as a model was that men had to imagine what was underneath my swimsuit, and I wasn't about to give that away for what I thought would be a small, goofy movie. (None of us at the time ever suspected *National Lampoon's Vacation* would take off the way it did.)

When the production team asked again about the possibility of nudity—and I couldn't blame them for trying—Beverly walked out onto set in the nick of time. "I'll do it," she said. "I'll be the one to go topless! You'll get your titties."

I couldn't have loved her more in that moment. And in my opinion, the scene between Chevy and me is funnier and cleverer because I throw my bra and panties at him from off camera, and all that the viewers can see are his oversize facial expressions.

AT ONE point, Olivier joined me while we were filming, and we stayed together in a little log cabin in a field of wildflowers by the side of a stream, all of it looking like a postcard that would have read, "Welcome to Colorful Colorado." Olivier had never spent any time in the Southwest, and he loved it as much as I did, which only made me love him more, and one morning, after we saw wild horses grazing outside our window, he announced that he was off to ride one. When I asked what he would do for reins, he told me horses always know what to do when an expert rider mounts, but nevertheless, he ended up with a huge shiner after the first horse he jumped onto reared its head right back into his face. Still, the idea of adventure never failed to thrill Olivier, who also insisted we go whitewater rafting and mono-skiing (where you waterski on only one ski), as he wore his black eye around Colorado like a badge of honor.

By the time the film came out the following summer, the black eye was long gone—and so was Olivier. Five months after he died, *National Lampoon's Vacation* was released, and I had published my first book, *Christie Brinkley's Outdoor Beauty and Fitness Book*, which I had written, illustrated, and dedicated to Olivier and which made the *New York Times* Best Seller list. I had also been asked to partner in opening a chain of fitness centers, which I turned down, but accepted an offer to create and launch my own clothing line, which I did in 1984. And by that time, I had started dating, slowly and cautiously, one of the most famous rock stars of the century, Billy Joel, who changed my life irrevocably.

Either way, what I learned that year is that life turns on a dime, and the best way to navigate the twists and turns, as Olivier's friend race car driver Jackie Stewart once told me, is to keep your hands on nine and three, steer as best as you can, and smile.

CHAPTER

14

Tall and tan and young and lovely
The girl from Ipanema goes walking . . .

sang the song in Portuguese, then danced the samba. And I wasn't even in Rio de Janeiro.

Instead, I was more than three thousand miles north, in St. Barts, a tropical oasis where I've found magic nearly as often as I've seen sailboats glide in and out of the island's enchanting blue bays. The night I first met Billy Joel there, singing for him long before he sang for me, in a rundown motel bar where thousands of mosquitoes danced around the lightbulbs while an undiscovered Whitney Houston and the model Elle Macpherson sauntered by the bar's ancient upright piano, was nothing more than magical. That the night had hardly started out that way made our meeting feel all the more serendipitous.

Life turns on a dime. Grab the wheel, steer as best as you can, and smile.

The night before I met Billy in January 1983, I had called Olivier from my hotel room in St. Barts to say again what I had already said before—that it really was over between us—as my heart sank into my stomach, my eyes swam with tears, and I placed the phone receiver slowly and deliberately back into its cradle. I was still in love with Olivier and didn't want to break up with him, but weeks before I left for St. Barts, my intuition had overwhelmed me, and like a sudden rainstorm that floods a river, I knew in a second something was wrong.

When I first told him I knew there was somebody else, pretending I had overheard him talking to a friend about an encounter with another woman, Olivier didn't deny it. Instead, he told me that I deserved the truth and that it was just a fling, not lasting more than one night, and while he had always loved me, he said, he was still young and had a lot to learn about relationships. He said all the right things, but the only thing I heard was confirmation of his infidelity, no matter how brief it might have been. After my roller-coaster ride with Houlès, I wanted someone who wanted me, definitively and unequivocally. Olivier's betrayal stung all the more because he had swept me off my feet so entirely, introducing me to a love that felt as breathless and giddy for a year as it had the evening of our first date, when I climbed onto the back of his motorcycle, wrapped my arms around his waist, and trusted him fully as we careened through the crowded streets of Manhattan.

If I overlooked his fling, though, I would be going back in time— and I wanted to go forward. So, I asked Olivier to move out of my apartment, and after pleading with me, he eventually did, renting his own place several blocks away while making me promise that, one day, if we couldn't be boyfriend and girlfriend again, he could at least ask me out on a date again.

D'accord, Olivier.

SHORTLY AFTERWARD, I flew to St. Barts with *Self* magazine. It was my second trip to the island in less than a month and what felt like my umpteenth trip since I first went there with *Glamour* four years before. In the 1980s, St. Barts was to models and magazines what Aspen has always been to skiers and the wintertime jet set, and at any given moment, there were at least several magazines shooting on island, which created a fun, collegial atmosphere.

During that trip with *Self*, though, I wasn't feeling particularly fun or collegial. Instead, I was devastated by what was happening with Olivier, which made me feel sadder and lonelier than I had in a long time. But it was a great job where I got to work all day on a gorgeous sailboat at sea, which felt restorative.

After work one day, Hops and I decided to venture into Gustavia, the island's capital, which has always had great restaurants, but that night, we opted to have dinner at a small hole-in-the-wall café, where we assumed we would be alone to talk about loneliness—how it can sometimes engulf you like the ocean tide, then recede just as quickly, leaving in its wake a smattering of life lessons that, like seashells, are found only in the ebbing. But not even small hole-in-the-wall cafés were immune to the industry camaraderie on the island, and we hadn't even finished our appetizers before a stylist from another magazine came rushing into the restaurant, his face flushed and his hands waving excitedly, causing the jewelry on his wrists and fingers to tinkle together like wind chimes.

"Billy Joel is at the bar at the PLM!" he cried to everyone in the café as though he were a court page delivering an important message from the king to the masses.

"Oh, my god, we have to go!" Hops said, giving me a sudden wide-eyed look as he pulled me up from the table and fished around for money to pay our bill.

I stood up and straightened my sweater. "*Who's* at the PLM? Billy who?" I asked, unfamiliar with the name.

"Billy *Joel*," Hops exclaimed, giving me an incredulous expression. "You must know him! The Piano Man? He's very famous. A rock star! Let's go!"

I still didn't understand who or what Hops was talking about, but his excitement was infectious, and in the moment, I figured I could benefit from a little Hops-onian adventure.

The PLM was a threadbare motel with a bar and a gorgeous view of the Baie de St. Jean, one of the bigger bays on island, with snow-white sand and seawater the color of blue butterfly wings. Otherwise, the place was a real dive, but because it was so cheap, and there weren't many other options on island, the magazines often put us up there. This meant I'd be awake half the night listening to the pitter-patter of bugs, mice, and other creepy-crawlies, which populated the motel more than people did.

After dashing across town with me in tow, Hops slowed to a stroll as soon as we walked into the PLM, trying to look cool and casual as he subtly motioned to a man in a Hawaiian shirt sitting at the bar with two other people. The man was sunburned to a crisp, his face the same color as cranberries and unctuous with oil, which he'd undoubtedly slathered on to soothe the burn, topped by what I like to call the "Long Island Bubble": a carapace of curly, shellacked hair popular in the 1980s in parts of suburban New York.

Hmmm, I thought to myself, *he doesn't look very much like a rock star.*

Hops didn't wait for an opening or invitation, but walked right over to the bar, sidled up next to Billy, and struck up a conversation as I took a seat next to Billy on the other side. The other two at the bar were Billy's best childhood friend, Billy Zampino, and Zampino's wife, Teresa. As I later learned, it was Billy's first trip to St. Barts—or anywhere in the world—since divorcing his first wife, Elizabeth Weber.

Immediately, I found Billy charming and hilarious as he cracked jokes about his "tan" and made other self-deprecating remarks that were both amusing and endearing. When he first introduced himself, offering his hand to make my acquaintance, I gave him a funny sideways glance—I wasn't sure if his name was Billy Joe or Billy Joel, and not wanting to insult him, I decided to play it safe.

"You look like a 'Joe' to me," I said, squinting at him as though sizing him up. "I'm going to call you Joe!"

"My mom calls me Joe," Billy said, leaning back in his chair in genuine surprise.

"You're kidding!" I said, my grin growing into an authentic smile. "Well, you're now 'Joe' to me, too."

And I did call him Joe, not only that first night at the PLM but for the eleven years we dated and were married.

At the end of the bar was an upright wooden piano, undoubtedly out of tune and obsolete, but hoping to "work some magic" on me, as he later admitted, Billy got up from his drink and sat down at it, which caused a salvo of cheers to go up around the room.

"Sing us a song, you're the piano man!" someone yelled.

"'Only the Good Die Young'!" another chimed in, as the energy in the bar became as frenetic as the mosquitoes above us, darting in and around the exposed bulbs hanging from the room's rafters.

But Billy didn't touch the keys. Instead, he looked directly at me and patted the bench next to him, suggesting I join him there, which I did, scooching beside him on the narrow seat.

"What do you want to hear?" he asked, flashing me a sly smile.

"'The Girl from Ipanema'!" I cried, naming my favorite song, which I had just learned to sing in Portuguese—and which surely wasn't what he expected, indisputably disappointing the crowd, too.

But at the time, I figured that if Billy was the "Piano Man," as everyone called him, he must want to play the piano while others sang.

And Billy did play, more beautifully than I had ever heard anyone play the piano before, as I crooned the Brazilian classic, singing breathlessly into the microphone as I had once done when I was six years old at Deb's home the night I burned my lips on her parents' cigarette lighter. But the only flames I now felt were from Billy and his superstardom, as the mosquitoes still swarmed above our heads and the room swayed with alcohol and anticipation. In one dramatic moment, I even threw my head back and onto Billy's shoulder, hamming it up for the audience as he looked over and leaned into me.

Flash, click . . .

In that instant, someone snapped our photo, which I still have, and so began a wonderful relationship with one of the most incredible men I've ever known.

After I finished singing, a tall, pretty girl with rich café-au-lait skin approached the piano and, looking at Billy, announced that she could sing, too. *Go away, kid—I'm trying to work my magic here*, Billy thought, he told me later, but always the consummate gentleman, he simply nodded and started playing what she asked him to, which was "Respect," by Aretha Franklin. After she began belting out the soulful tune, within seconds, the bar had fallen completely silent, as everyone sat stunned, paralyzed by the power of her voice.

That young woman, as it turned out, was Whitney Houston, a nineteen-year-old model from New Jersey who, in January 1983, was in St. Barts for a shoot and, one month later, would sign a worldwide record deal that put her on the path to becoming "the Voice" and one of the greatest singers in music history.

At that point, word had spread that Billy Joel was at the PLM, and while Whitney was singing, another nineteen-year-old model walked into the bar, one who would also go on to get her own one-noun nickname: "the Body." At first, Elle Macpherson draped her beautiful body over the back of a chair, then eventually, right across the piano, making eyes at Billy, who was popular in her native Australia.

By now, the bar was packed, and because Hops and I had to wake up early the next day for a shoot on a sailboat, we decided to head back to our hotel, saying goodbye to Billy and promising to be his official tour guides while he was in St. Barts, so he wouldn't end up in a dump like the PLM again.

Oh, but the thrills that dump provided that night! Once I got back to my room, I wrote about the day in my journal, ending the entry with the enthusiasm we had all felt inside the PLM:

We go into the bar in the PLM for one last drink and meet Billy Joel. We end up dancing and singing at the piano, Hops and I doing backup. I even attempt a samba while Billy Joel plays. Billy Joel and I become fast friends. Just when I thought I'd die of loneliness, life is great again!

At the time, I wasn't thinking romantic thoughts about Billy—I just knew I wanted to be friends with him forever.

Forever is a funny word, of course. Some people say it has no meaning, but what I know is that, more than forty years later, I am still friends with Billy, and for that, I'm forever grateful.

After we were married, Billy and I joked that when we first met in St. Barts, we both went home with the wrong people: he had a few dates with Elle, while I became enthralled with a young sailing captain named Clay.

I first spotted Clay on the deck of the *Zakanya*, pulling in the lines of the sailboat with his tan, muscular arms, which he then used to lift me up onto the sloop like a knight helping a handmaiden onto his white horse before riding her out onto the open seas. *Self* had chartered the *Zakanya* for two days for a shoot, and instantly, I found Clay

231

handsome, with his bronzed skin and curly mop of dark blond hair, bleached white at the tips from all the sun and salt water. I knew right away that he had seen many adventures on the high seas by how well he could handle the boat, sailing her "off the hook"—without the help of an engine—and making sure we were all safe and comfortable even after the winds picked up and frothy sea-green waves began to break across her bow.

Our first day on the sloop, our photographer, Alex Chatelain, pulled me aside to tell me that he was planning a dinner that evening with several people on the island, including Elle, whom he had a crush on, and Billy, who had promised to come only if "Christie doesn't stand me up." Laughing, I agreed, and asked Alex if he would invite Clay, too, which he did, prompting Hops and me to spend the rest of the afternoon devising a seating plan for that night's meal. When we got to the restaurant, though, our strategic design evaporated as the evening turned into a comedic game of musical chairs, everyone maneuvering to sit somewhere else, with Elle trying to sit next to Billy, Alex following Elle, and me trying to keep Clay on one side and Billy on the other.

At some point, I think Billy realized I was interested in Clay, and after dancing dinner off at a nearby nightclub, everyone parted ways, Billy presumably with Elle and me with Clay, accompanied by Hops and a few other friends, all of whom went to the beach to talk and laugh. Shortly before dawn, I ended up falling asleep on the *Zakanya*, where a nearly full moon illuminated the ocean and, floating there on its waves, Clay and me alone on the deck of the sailboat—a far better bed, in my opinion, than any berth below, where you can't see the stars or taste the salty air.

The night after our dinner with Billy, Clay, Elle, Alex, and me, Hops and I planned a happy sendoff for Billy the next day, going to the St. Barts airport the same time he was catching his flight back to New York. The airport was and still is a single-runway affair, with one of the most exhilarating (or terrifying, as some might argue) takeoffs and landings in the world, given that half the runway slopes down a mountain while the other ends abruptly on the beach. In those days, there was no airport terminal—only a folding table under a tree—and anyone could stand on the hill right near the runway, which they often did to watch the planes make their thrilling arrivals and departures. That's where Hops and I stood that afternoon, madly waving palm fronds and blowing kisses toward Billy's plane, and when his aircraft finally roared down the runway and zoomed overhead, I could see Billy's face framed in the tiny porthole, laughing and waving back.

After the *Self* shoot wrapped, I didn't leave St. Barts as planned. I had become enchanted by Clay, and when he invited me to stay on the *Zakanya* as long as I liked, I said yes, eager to continue what we'd done the past several days, which was sail, make love, and eat all our meals on the boat's deck while watching the sun rise above or sink below the Caribbean. When I thought about all the hurt I felt around Olivier and my empty apartment back in New York, now devoid of the man I loved so much, it made me want to ease the pain with someone else, which made Clay as emotionally attractive as he was physically handsome.

On February 2, 1983, the day I turned twenty-nine, I woke up on the deck of the *Zakanya* for the eighth consecutive morning with Clay. He kissed me softly and surprised me with a beautiful and tender poem he had written for me for my birthday, in addition to a pretty brass shackle from his boat, which I stored in my purse as a keepsake of our romantic week together.

The next day, I had to fly back to New York, and soon after, Clay began writing me long letters full of poetry and passionate invites to join him sailing around South America. We talked several times ship-to-shore by phone whenever he was in port, and I really thought I might meet him as he navigated around the Argentine Basin or over the Patagonian Shelf. But a month to the day after I turned twenty-nine, Olivier died, and Clay's letters eventually stopped, I'm sure, when he heard the terrible news of Olivier's accident, since all the published reports, which were numerous, included my name.

WHAT HAPPENED after I flew back from St. Barts before Olivier's death was, in some ways, similar to what many couples face: a rough patch, a tough spell, a painful time when love and hurt blur together so much that it's difficult to discern the difference between the two. When I was in St. Barts, I thought I was resolute in my decision to end things with Olivier, but once I got back to New York, I discovered that he had written me a raft of letters in my absence, all of which he never sent. Sitting in my bedroom in my apartment, as the city's lights filtered in through the casement windows near my bed, I began reading his letters one by one, and I started to cry, laugh, then question everything about my obstinacy to end things. What he had written in those letters was all the things I wanted to hear: "I'm trying to be the best I can be to make you proud and make you come back to me" and "If I cannot win you back, the one thing I ask is that you believe that my love has always been true and sincere." And in a letter dated January 23, 1983, the day before I met Billy, he'd written, "You must be sleeping safely in a little bungalow—alone, I hope, with the sound of little wavelets licking the beach. Now don't forget, watch the giant clams, scorpions, bugs, and mosquitoes that could attack your little body. Sleep tight, my darling. I love you."

The entire time I was in St. Barts, Olivier barely left his apartment, he told me, reading and writing at home and venturing out only to see art exhibits and hear classical music at Lincoln Center, which was only a few blocks away. While other men may have drowned their sorrow in alcohol, Olivier immersed himself in Vivaldi's *The Four Seasons* and Gershwin's *Rhapsody in Blue*, regardless of whether he was upset or happy. During our time together, I heard *Rhapsody in Blue* so often that I nearly fell out of my chair when Billy played it again years later, after we were married, using it to open his international concerts.

Olivier's letters melted my heart, to the point that I suddenly felt more confused and didn't know what I wanted anymore—I knew only that I loved Olivier and always had. At the same time, I wasn't ready to forgive him, so while we began seeing each other again, and he moved back into my apartment, I also wanted to hold him at arm's length.

Life may turn on a dime, but human emotions don't always work the same way.

AT THE end of February, I flew to Los Angeles to meet with casting directors and screen-test for several different movie roles, including for the part of the mermaid in *Splash*, a film that, after it was released one year later, became a worldwide hit. *National Lampoon's Vacation* hadn't even aired in theaters yet, but nevertheless, I was getting a ton of attention for acting, for which I was excited and grateful.

While in L.A., I stayed with my parents, borrowing their car to drive to the studios in the Valley. One afternoon, after auditioning for the role of Sheena in *Sheena: Queen of the Jungle*, I decided to stop in at the clothing store Maxfield, in West Hollywood, where I had shopped for years, ever since I first went there as a teenager with my mom.

When I walked into the store, the assistants were surprised and thrilled to see me—"Oh my god, Christie, it's been so long!"—asking if I wanted a glass of champagne or a cup of tea while setting me up in a dressing room, where they insisted on bringing me an array of outfits to try on. Shopping at Maxfield was as much a major to-do as it was fun, and I loved seeing the new styles popular on the West Coast.

Inside a fitting room, as I cheerfully pulled on different dresses and blouses, I remember feeling so exhilarated, excited by the prospect of landing a new movie role, in addition to all the other positive things that seemed to be moving through my life. But in the next moment, one of the store's assistants tapped lightly on my dressing room door, then opened it slowly and tiptoed in as quietly as a ghost, looking as pale as one, too. "Christie, your mom just called looking for you," she said cautiously, biting the side of her mouth. "Don't worry, your parents are okay, but your mom needs you to come home right away."

Oh no, oh no, oh no . . .

I quickly pulled on my own clothes and rushed out of the dressing room, my mind spinning through dozens of images of what could have happened to my parents. If my mom had thought to call one of my favorite spots in Los Angeles to find me, something terrible must have happened, I assumed, and after gushing a heartfelt thank-you to the assistants, I ran out of the store, climbed into my parents' car, and steered out onto Melrose Avenue.

As I sped down the avenue, the idea that something could have happened to Olivier floated briefly into my mind like a strange apparition. We had just spoken by phone an hour before, so nothing could be wrong, right? He had called from a speedway in Palm Beach, Florida, where he was testing race cars. The last time I'd seen him was in New York, on the street outside my apartment, where I had climbed into a taxicab as he tried to kiss me. But I had turned my cheek, causing his lips to land on the side of my face—I was still upset with him, and I wanted him to know it. If something had happened to him on the track . . .

No, why would my parents call me, I anxiously thought again as I veered onto their street and the sun began to set behind the palm trees and stucco-style homes.

When I walked into my parents' house, both my mom and dad were standing motionless inside the door like sentries, waiting for me to arrive. There were no lights on inside the house, and the window slats, which were partially closed, cast an odd louvered light onto their faces, striping them in orange from the glow of the setting sun, then gray—much grayer than I had ever seen my lovely, bronzed mom—where the slats screened out the outside glare. Before either could say a word, I knew the news was worse than I expected.

"Honey, it's Olivier," my mom said slowly and softly, so soft that I could barely hear her.

"Oh, my god, is he okay? Please say he's okay!" It wasn't a question so much as a gasp, as I held my breath, pleading with the universe for any answer other than the one I feared most.

"No, honey, he's dead."

Suddenly, everything around me stopped, and just like that, the movie of my life, the one that had been playing in my mind since I was a little girl, reverted back to black and white. The world looked wobbly, grainy, and distorted, jumping around and blurring at the edges like a silent film, one where the only sounds I could hear were the words "he's dead" pounding in my head over and over like a migraine.

"Take it back! Don't say those words to me!" I started shouting, covering my ears and desperately trying to push back what my parents had just said—if I didn't hear it, I thought, it couldn't have happened. "That can't be true!" I started to scream, as my parents tried desperately to comfort me. "I know that it can't be true!"

I felt crushed by something I didn't want to be real, as the room started spinning in a monochromatic blur—from lamp to table to louvered faces, lamp to table to louvered faces—and I fell to the floor, sobbing, unable to stand it anymore. I let out a guttural scream I'd never heard from my own mouth before, as my mom and dad wrapped their arms around me and held me there, on the floor, for a long time. I later realized that my mom had called every possible shop and restaurant to try to find me—she hadn't wanted me to hear about Olivier's death on the radio while I was driving and suffer the kind of breakdown I was having now.

Oh no, oh no, oh no . . .

I kept looking around the room and wondering why things continued to exist when Olivier didn't. Why was the lamp still there and he wasn't? Why was that potted plant by the door thriving when Olivier was gone? Nothing made sense anymore, and for a while, I thought that if nothing made sense, then it couldn't be true.

BUT IT was true.

For days, I didn't know how Olivier had died because I didn't want to know: knowing the details would finalize his death, making it real in a way I wasn't ready to accept. But then, when I did learn what had happened, guilt overwhelmed me because if I had been there, maybe I would have been able to save him.

Olivier had traveled to Palm Beach alone, though, and on his second day at the speedway, he crashed into a retaining wall, causing his car to catapult into a canal. The impact didn't kill him, and he survived to hit the water, where his car began to sink through the murky gloom. I can only imagine what he must have thought as his car sank farther into the hypoxic water, when he realized that his foot was trapped so badly in the buckled metal that he couldn't escape. When rescue crews finally reached him underwater, he was alive, gripping the shoulders of the first diver who tried to pull him out. But they were unable to extract him, and by the time crews lifted the car out, it was too late.

Official cause of death: asphyxiation by drowning.

I've always been able to swim faster and hold my breath underwater longer than most people—a benefit of my Malibu upbringing. And if I had been at the speedway that day, I thought, I would have jumped into the canal, swum down to Olivier, and found the strength to free his foot. It took me years to realize that I wouldn't have been able to do anything differently than what the trained rescue crews did and that his foot was trapped so tightly that, when they finally did pull him out, it was mangled beyond recognition.

After Olivier's death, I was supposed to go back to New York for work, but I didn't; I couldn't because I wasn't able to stop crying, screaming, and aching. Instead, I stayed in California for days, unable to get out of bed. I couldn't bear the idea of being inside my apartment with all of Olivier's things—the philosophy books he'd never finish, the journals with the thoughts and musings he'd never have again, the clothes that still smelled like him. Every morning, I woke up in my parents' guest room screaming, still in shock that his death had actually happened, that Olivier was really gone. I couldn't stop sobbing, not enough to leave my room, and eventually, my parents' doctor gave me something to sedate me just so I could function. I remained this way until the Chandons called, asking me to come to France for Olivier's funeral.

Even though I hadn't left my room in days, I immediately told them yes—I knew I had to for Olivier. My mom offered to come with me, but I didn't want to put her through any more anguish: she had suffered enough watching me endure the throes of grief. I asked Hops instead, who didn't hesitate, helping me pack my things after I flew back to New York and holding my hand the entire flight over the Atlantic.

Olivier's funeral was a blur. What I remember is that we spent one night in Paris before driving with two of Olivier's friends several hours southwest to Laferté-sur-Aube, in the Vallée de la Marne, which is famous for its champagne and where Olivier's family had a home. I had met his parents before, and they had always been lovely with me, but I couldn't believe how dignified and gracious they were now, after losing their only son. We spent the night in their home, where I felt compelled to tell Olivier's parents how much I had loved him, even though he and I had been going through a rough spell before he died, causing me to wonder if he knew how much I loved him.

"Christie, *ma cherie*, he knew you loved him," his mother said tenderly, clutching my hand in hers and looking at me with affection. "Those things happen, but he knew you loved him."

The next morning, we walked from the family's home to an old stone church in the village, into which men carried Olivier's casket on their shoulders, everyone solemn and grim. After the ceremony, they buried Olivier in a cemetery behind the church where all the Chandons had been buried for centuries, Olivier's body sinking into the ground slowly, interminably, and forevermore, from where he'd never again see the sun, moon, or stars.

Forever is such a terrible word.

The night before he was buried, I wrote Olivier a letter from my little room at the Chandons' family estate. I still have it today, after keeping it stowed away in a folder inside a box that, for decades, was too painful to open.

That letter begins:

My darling, amore mio, my love, Oliver, Ollie, Olivier Chandon.
Tomorrow, you'll be buried. That fact is too painful to accept.

I have never felt or imagined such absolute grief, pain, sorrow, or loss. . . .

You're my lover. My friend. My joy. We were teammates.

You'll never read these words. I'm broken. But I promise I'll always keep you alive.

I made that promise so long ago, Olivier. Have I kept it?

All I know is that I still see you sometimes, the sun shining in your beautiful brown eyes as you beam at me from the wing strut of an airplane, tempting me to gather my strength, face the challenge, and take the leap, if not from the airplane, then into life—hands out, heart first, and letting everything else follow as it may.

15

Hi, Christie, It's Joe!"

"Well, hello, Joe! Whoa, where are you? It sounds soooo loud!"

"I know. Isn't it great? I'm at the Grammys! Hold on, I want you to hear something . . ."

The Grammys? Billy Joel was calling me from the Grammys?

But there was no time to think, because in the next second, all I could hear was the roar inside Los Angeles's Shrine Auditorium, where the crowd was going wild, and, a moment later, piano music as clear as a bell, as though Billy were holding up the receiver from a pay phone backstage—and maybe he was—when a voice I recognized as Ray Charles's started to sing.

"Oh, wow, that's incredible!" I jumped to my feet, suddenly becoming part of the thrill in that auditorium in L.A., even though I was 2,700 miles across the country, in my apartment in New York. "That's Ray Charles, right?"

"Yes, it is!" Billy said gleefully, shouting so I could hear him. "But wait, because Little Richard, Jerry Lee Lewis, and Count Basie are also playing piano with him, and they're about to sing, too!"

I could tell the phone receiver was back up in the air and out toward the stage again, as I heard four of the greatest rhythm and blues players sing Charles's legendary song "What'd I Say." Swaying to the music coming through the receiver in the quiet hush of my apartment, I suddenly felt so flattered that Billy, in the middle of all that energy, action, and talent, had thought to call me and share the moment.

"Are you playing tonight?" I asked.

"No, I'm up for an award," he said, the receiver now back to his mouth. "Album of the Year, for *The Nylon Curtain*."

The Nylon Curtain? I thought. *Do I know that one?* No, no, I didn't—not yet, at least.

Since meeting him a month before in St. Barts, I had bought only one Billy Joel cassette—his iconic album *The Stranger*—which I had played nonstop on my Walkman whenever I ambled around the city, usually rewinding it again and again to my favorite song, "Vienna."

It wasn't our first time speaking by phone. At the PLM in St. Barts, Billy had given me a phone number where I could reach him in New York, which was at the Hotel St. Moritz, on Central Park South, just a few doors west of the Plaza, where he owned a duplex apartment. He'd also given me a pseudonym that I needed to use when I called the hotel—"That's my road name," he told me somewhat sheepishly, self-conscious that his fame had reached *that* level. Yet, somewhere between sailing around the Caribbean with Clay and falling in love again with Olivier, I'd lost the teensy slip of paper on which he'd written both his number and the fake name. Eager to retain our fast friendship, I called the St. Moritz anyway, explaining to the concierge that I was a friend of Billy's and knew he lived at the hotel under a different name, which I couldn't remember.

"I'm so sorry, madame," the concierge said politely, if not a little disdainfully. "I have no idea what you're talking about."

I spent the rest of the afternoon wondering if I'd ever speak to Billy again, but only hours after I tried to reach him at the St. Moritz, my phone rang.

"Hi, is Christie there?" a distinctive voice drawled on the other end, his New York accent instantly giving him away.

"Joe! I can't believe it! I tried to call you today, but I couldn't get through. I'm so happy you called!"

Not only was I happy, I also couldn't quite believe how serendipitous his call was, that he had thought to ring me the same day I had tried him, especially given that I hadn't shared my name with the concierge and that no one at the St. Moritz had told Billy a female caller had tried to reach him. It was kismet, I thought, or *quelle coincidence*, I told myself at the time, smiling on the other end of the line.

I WAS even happier when Billy continued to call again . . . and again and again, as we quickly developed a cheery phone friendship, speaking regularly and sharing what was happening in each of our lives. We continued to talk frequently. Then, one day in early March 1983, after Olivier had died, Billy's call took on a slightly different tone than the others.

"Hi, Christie, it's Joe," he said slowly before pausing, maybe to make sure I wasn't too upset to speak. "I've been wanting to call you, but I didn't want to bother you. But I just feel so awful about what you're going through, and I want to let you know that if you ever need someone to talk with or if I can distract you in any way . . ."

I could tell his sympathy was sincere, and the more we talked, the more I opened up about what had happened and all the agony and grief I had experienced since Olivier's death and how I had barely left my apartment after returning from his funeral in France. I was touched by Billy's sympathy and sincerity, and in that one call, the lyrics of "Vienna" began to wash over me like a lullaby:

Slow down, you're doing fine,
You can't be everything you want to be before your time.

After that, Billy started calling me every day, making it his mission to cheer me up in any way he could, whether it was with a joke, a song, or a funny poem he'd written. While he told me he was perfectly okay with my being as miserable as I wanted to be, he was also perfectly okay with making me laugh and smile as much as he could, which worked. By the time he coaxed me into venturing out again, it had been only several weeks since Olivier's death, but to me, it felt like an entire year. And it was Billy who had helped ease the agony. I felt so grateful to him for his friendship, which he offered unconditionally, no strings attached.

Billy wasn't the only one calling. Two of Olivier's oldest friends, Simon Gaul, a proper Brit who owned a bookstore in Notting Hill (yes, that bookstore from the eponymous movie), and Rupert Keegan, a rakish British race car driver who liked women as much as he did fast automobiles—and together, they made quite the odd couple—phoned me every morning, at first to cry with and console me, then to encourage me to get up and get out. "You've got to seize the day," Simon always said in his genteel way before Rupert chimed in, in his gruff Essex accent, "Come on, Christie, Olivier wouldn't want you lying around the house. Get out! Meet someone!"

When my friendship with Billy started to turn into something more, Simon and Rupert were the first ones to encourage me to pursue it, acting like giddy girlfriends at the notion. I knew they were right, and I welcomed the courtship carefully, like a child visiting the ocean for the first time, wading in slowly and getting a little deeper each time we met. I knew it was what Olivier would have wanted: for me to go out and enjoy myself rather than staying home, paralyzed by his death. In my mind, I could hear him whispering, *Get up, get out, live your life. There are no guarantees, so live each day like it's your last . . . because it could be.* And if it was going to be my last day on earth, I figured it was all right to have a first date with Billy, who asked me out in early April.

As soon as I said yes, I called my mom.

"Is it too soon after Olivier to be dating?" I asked, explaining how Billy and I had first met in St. Barts, when I thought we'd be friends forever.

"No, sweetie, it's what Olivier would have wanted," my mom said, echoing Simon and Rupert.

"But I've never dated anyone like Billy before," I said, rushing through my words as my brain spun into overdrive. "He's so old-school New York, and I hate to be superficial, but I'm not really crazy about his shoes . . . But I'm also having the best time with him, and whenever he calls, he's so sweet and knows exactly how to lift me up when I'm down."

"What's the problem, then?" When it came to matters of the heart, my mom was great at getting to the heart of the matter. "Listen, honey, you can change a man's shoes or you can change a man's hair, but he has to have a good heart and a good sense of humor. And if he has both, he's a keeper."

A few months later, after we'd dated for a while, I found the opportunity to change Billy's shoes. He was shooting the cover to his album *An Innocent Man*, so I asked my friend Patrick Demarchelier to be the photographer and a stylist friend to pull together different clothes and (more stylish) shoes for him. Afterward, Billy looked incredible. (Now, when I see pictures of myself from the same era, with my super-high 1980s hair and electric '80s makeup, I wish someone had thought to give *me* a few style tips, too.) And then, when I first heard him sing onstage, I found myself undeniably attracted to this physically hot and intellectually charismatic man.

Billy didn't sing for me on our first date. Instead, he asked me to dinner and to see the musical *Little Shop of Horrors*, which a friend had recommended he take me to: "You can put your arm around her when the plant comes out!" the friend told Billy. "She'll cozy right up to you!"

The trick worked.

Our second date was even more spectacular, when Billy took me to see the Beach Boys perform at a stadium in New Jersey. When we got there, he led me through a dark, drab maze of hallways and up and down concrete stairs until we were suddenly backstage with the band—I quickly learned that Billy knew almost every famous musician—and when the group opened up with "California Girls" onstage, they pointed to me in the front row as they crooned, "I wish they all could be California Girls." I couldn't believe it: Beach Boys songs had blared out of every transistor radio on the beaches where I grew up, overheating car radios up and down the Pacific Coast Highway, and now Billy was bringing all those memories to life for me in a way I could never have imagined.

Being serenaded by the Beach Boys wasn't the best part of the evening, though—not even close. At one point, the band called Billy up onstage, and when he finally relented, the audience went wild, screaming for him at first, then roaring with approval as he sat down at the piano. I'd never seen Billy perform—I'd heard him play only briefly at the PLM, in front of a ragtag crew—and when I saw his hands float across the keys in front of tens of thousands of shouting fans, then heard him cover "Help Me, Rhonda" and the classic Beatles song "Rock and Roll Music" with the Beach Boys, I felt entranced, not just by his talent, the scope of which I already knew from listening to *The Stranger*, but also by his stage presence, which was both confident and extraordinary, with a kind of charisma and charm I had never seen.

BILLY'S MUSIC had a lot to do with my early attraction to him. It was exciting to listen to his songs while knowing intimately the person who was singing them, and it was exhilarating to discover his different music styles, each of which revealed another part of his personality and voice. Some of his songs were so tender and sweet, while others were electrifying, classic rock and roll.

I didn't yet know all his music, though, when I went back to his penthouse apartment in the St. Moritz for the first time. It was late at night, and when he pushed open his front door, all I could see initially were the lights of other high-rise buildings glittering in the distance through his apartment's giant oversize windows, which looked out over Central Park, lying dark and leafy between the Upper West and Upper East Sides, separating the two neighborhoods like an inky, green sea.

Directly in front of the windows was a grand piano, where Billy sat after we had walked in and, flashing me a smile, began to play a song I had heard before.

"Oh, my gosh, I love this song!" I said as soon as I heard the soulful piano intro. "It's Ray Charles, right?"

"Nope, I wrote this song," Billy said, looking up at me as his hands continued to dance across the keys. "It's my song, but I had Ray Charles in mind when I wrote it."

"Oh, wow, I can't believe that I've loved this song for so long without ever knowing who sang it," I said, more than a little dumbstruck by the man playing so beautifully for me.

I sat down next to Billy on the bench as he kept playing "New York State of Mind," mesmerized by the sight and sound of this great musician singing his own song about the city he loved so much against one of the most magnificent backdrops of that city itself. In that moment, I felt I was inside the song's lyrics, the music painting the air all around us as the city twinkled in the distance, both of us very much in a New York state of mind, a phrase that had been coined by Billy. I couldn't believe how lucky I was to be able to experience this moment with him, which I've remembered my entire life.

As soon as Billy and I started to date, flowers began to arrive daily at my apartment, and if he ever missed a day, I'd get two arrangements the following day. He sent flowers for every occasion and non-occasion—even though it was always an occasion whenever I saw him—and attached to every bouquet was a little card with a preprinted message that Billy would turn into something clever and sweet with his own added text, like "Happy Birthday *for the third time this week*!" or "Wishing you a speedy recovery *from your bad dream. I adore you, Joe*," or "Congratulations *on your new arrival back to New York . . . and me. Love, Joe*." Or my favorite one, "Because you said *oinks*," since I once said I loved "oinks" while pointing to an onyx table, mispronouncing the beautiful stone.

Not only flowers and cards, Billy also gave me cakes and funny little songs, not all of which he sang. For example, at every dinner at every restaurant, I never failed to be surprised when a quintet of waiters danced out with a cake while serenading me with "Happy Birthday to You"—Billy liked to pretend it was my birthday every day, thinking it would lift me up and make me smile, which it did. He engaged in lots of other cute antics, too, like the Easter Sunday he showed up outside my door wearing bunny ears and a bunny tail pinned to the back of his suit while carrying a huge basket of chocolates and flowers. I was awestruck, wondering just how many famous musicians would deign to walk through the streets of Manhattan with a pair of big pink bunny ears flapping over their head.

Another day, Billy handed me a soft velvet box, and when I opened it, I was dumbfounded to discover a delicate and beautiful diamond bracelet inside. I loved it, but what was far more precious to me was something else he gave me at the same time, written in black ink on regular lined notepad paper:

Once I thought my innocence was gone
Now I know that happiness goes on
That's where you found me
When you put your arms around me
I haven't been there for the longest time
For the longest time
I'm that voice you're hearing in the hall
And the greatest miracle of all
Is how I need you
And how you needed me too
That hasn't happened for the longest time.

I cried when I first read the verses, which described our relationship perfectly: we both needed each other, me because I was devasted after Olivier's death and Billy because he was still reeling from his recent divorce. And when he first wrote down these lyrics, he and I were still tentative with each other, feeling each other out—and admittedly, liking what we felt.

As our relationship grew and deepened, Billy kept giving me lyrics, which wove music into our lives and our lives into his music in an incredibly beautiful and synergistic way. One month later, he handed me another sheet of simple notebook paper with a few more verses, all of which finally became the song "The Longest Time," which he released in August 1983 as part of his new album, *An Innocent Man.*

When I went to Los Angeles for a job that spring, Billy and I spoke by phone every night. All I could think about was him. We were falling in love, and everyone but us knew it. On my last day in L.A., I gathered up the nerve to tell him over the telephone that I couldn't wait to see him. He offered to pick me up at the airport, and during the entire flight back to New York, I combed my hair over and over, wanting to look perfect for Billy, who was waiting in the airport just past security with a handful of balloons. He then led me to a limo filled with more balloons, a bottle of champagne, and a cake with lettering wishing me a happy Sweet Sixteen, an occasion Billy knew I had never celebrated as a California kid.

Even though I was falling in love with Billy, I still felt sad about Olivier. Whenever I did, Billy was understanding, offering to tuck me into bed and bring me my meals there, "bothering" me only if I wanted company. He had also had a recent past after his divorce and, more recently, dating model Elle Macpherson. Once he and I started seeing each other, he insisted on calling Elle, while I was on the line, to tell her that he was going to be exclusive with me. I kept telling him it was completely unnecessary to call her while I was there and that I certainly didn't need or want to be on the line. He kept insisting, and while I refused to pick up an extension, he held the phone away from his ear, and when I heard her voice, she sounded indifferent. Still, that didn't stop rumors from circulating that she was waiting for Billy in his apartment the first time I ever went there, which wasn't true (the media seemed always to want to pit models against each other, even though there were more friendships in the industry than anything else).

The more I got to know Billy, the deeper I fell for him. It didn't take me long to discover that he was incredibly smart, with an encyclopedic knowledge of world history, all self-taught, since he had never finished high school, reading voraciously instead while opting to pursue music—"I'm not going to Columbia University, I'm going to Columbia Records," he always said. And he did.

If I had been worried at first about our differences, once we started to date, those differences started to fascinate me, especially how much he lived and breathed the old-school New York lifestyle, with his own rough-and-tumble street smarts and a lexicon of urban slang. His expressions, like "that's copacetic" instead of "that's cool," were so different from anything I had known growing up in coastal California. And even though I had lived in the city for nearly a decade when I first met him, Billy showed me a side of New York I'd never seen, taking me to new restaurants, neighborhoods, concerts, and jazz clubs, where I met everyone from Bruce Springsteen to Stan Getz. He also brought me to opening day for the Yankees, where we met the players—an experience made even more thrilling by the fact I'd never been to a Yankees game before.

Another afternoon, Billy picked me up in his jeep, and because it was a beautiful day, he had taken off both doors and the roof, so I threw on a T-shirt, a pair of shorts, and a baseball cap, which matched his outfit and made us look like two teenagers in love—exactly how we felt. He then told me he was taking me to Coney Island to ride the Cyclone. I had never been to Coney Island or even heard of the Cyclone, a rickety old roller coaster that dips and twists like a ribbon right over the Atlantic. After one ride, I was so delighted by the experience that he told the attendants to spin us again and again, and that day, I think we must have ridden the Cyclone no fewer than eight times before we teetered off, finding our sea legs again by walking the boardwalk nearby, where we stumbled past hot dog stands, clam bars, and surf shops that looked like they had been plucked from another era. That afternoon, it felt like Billy had taken me not just to Coney Island but to another time and place, which he kept doing over and over again, in his own way.

WEEKS AFTER we started dating, Billy began recording the album *An Innocent Man*, and every chance I could take, I went to the studio with him. To me, music is like fine art, and when I watched him record, I felt like I did whenever I stood in front of a Matisse—as though I had suddenly been transported to another world where I could hear, feel, and taste everything more richly and deeply. I loved seeing the camaraderie between Billy and his band. They were always laughing and never took anything too seriously, oftentimes singing his songs with fabricated lyrics, like when they changed the words to "Just the Way You Are" to "She took the house, the kids, the car . . ." And they did all this while recording what would become one of the most successful albums of the decade.

Perhaps even more magical was watching Billy write songs in real time, some of which began as simple poems to me, like "The Longest Time," while others came out of everyday conversations between us. One night, for example, he said something so sweet to me, then made a joke in the next breath, reversing the romance in an instant, which he had done several times before, perpetually concerned he had said too much.

"Billy, do you realize that every time you say something sweet, you follow it with a joke?" I asked that evening. "It kind of kills the mood."

"Yeah, I guess I should leave a tender moment alone," he said somewhat bashfully.

From that conversation, the song "Leave a Tender Moment Alone" was born, beginning as a single verse Billy gave to me before he added more and more lines, eventually recording it as a song for *An Innocent Man*.

Another day, Billy called me while I was working in Los Angeles to tell me he was thinking about using my name in a song, but he was worried "Christie" didn't sound "rock and roll" enough.

Giddy with the idea of being immortalized in a Billy Joel song, I suggested he add my middle name, "Lee."

"That's your middle name? 'Lee'? 'Christie Lee'? That's like 'Stagger Lee'!" Billy said, referring to the 1950s song by R&B singer Lloyd Price. "Now, *that's* a rock-and-roll name!"

Days later, Billy was back in the studio, recording the song "Christie Lee," which, because he knew how much I loved Stan Getz and the saxophone, he wrote about a sax player who could hit a high note only when he played for Christie Lee.

There was truth in his lyrics, too. Metaphorically, Billy had started to hit the high note after we began dating the spring and summer of 1983, prolifically writing songs for *An Innocent Man* while telling me he felt a joy he hadn't in a long time. We were in love, after all, so much so that we began calling each other "Badabing" and "Badaboom," because we both had butterfingers and kept dropping things, distracted by the passion we felt for each other. We were so clumsy, in fact, that we even concocted a hilarious agreement that I could fumble and drop things from 9 a.m. to 5 p.m. while Billy would take the evening shift, and each day we'd alternate.

While dating Billy, I continued to work at an exhilarating pace, appearing on cover after cover, doing TV commercials, promoting *Christie Brinkley's Outdoor Beauty and Fitness Book*, and celebrating the success of *National Lampoon's Vacation*, which, after its release in July, became a box-office hit.

Six months into our relationship and one month after *An Innocent Man* started dominating the airwaves, we did something that would change my life and characterize us as a couple for the rest of our relationship: we made the music video for Billy's new song "Uptown Girl." Unlike what many people think, Billy didn't write the hit about me—at least, not initially—nor about Elle Macpherson, but about someone who was as much fantasy as "the Girl in the Red Ferrari."

I'm not sure how "Whitney" found Billy's phone number, or if "Whitney" was even her real name, but she started calling him, along with a handful of other well-known musicians and music industry executives—which Billy learned much later, when he realized she had fed them all the same story. Whitney's story was that she lived in a sumptuous penthouse on the Upper East Side with a wealthy father who wouldn't let her leave because she was too beautiful to be seen wandering the streets among common men. When she told Billy this, she did so in a sexy, breathless voice, taking advantage of his empathy by describing her situation as though she were some poor, imprisoned rich girl—the Rapunzel of the Upper East Side, the Cinderella of the ultra-wealthy—while telling him things that made him feel as though he were the sexiest man alive. But whenever he asked to meet her in person, she had a million excuses, which only increased her mystery and intrigue. Eventually, though, Billy got sick of the shtick, especially after learning she had a reputation among musicians as the mystery girl who "gave good phone," but not before he had already written a few lines about an uptown girl who lived in her uptown world.

After he stopped taking Whitney's calls, Billy shelved the lyrics . . . until one day, when we were out in his home on Long Island, which overlooked Oyster Bay Harbor, and he suddenly turned to me with a smile on his face that grew wider as he spoke.

"I just realized something about this song that I started writing a while ago about someone I was imagining," he said hurriedly, his thoughts far ahead of his words, as he gave me a look of surprise and delight. "And now I'm looking at you here, and I don't have to imagine her anymore—you're right here in front of me, *you're* my real uptown girl."

He then told me the entire backstory as the sun sank into Long Island Sound, getting up only when he realized he could finally write more verses. Several days later, he had finished "Uptown Girl," a song about a working-class "backstreet guy" who falls in love with an uptown girl who's looking for her "downtown man."

In many ways, the song fit. Billy had grown up in what was known as a "Levitt house," in Hicksville, a working-class suburb of Long Island made up mostly of blue-collar Italian Americans. There, hustling was as much a part of the social fabric as the suburban ranch homes in which Billy's family and most others in the town lived. By comparison, I had grown up on the beach in Malibu, which was about as good as it gets for Los Angeles, and had attended private school, which, where Billy was from, was a luxury only for the super-affluent. I didn't swear, snap gum, or talk loudly like many of the girls Billy had grown up with—instead, I spoke fluent French; had impeccable manners (thanks to my mom); loved fine art, jazz, and classical music; and was interested in other cultures. When we met, I had also traveled much of the world, and altogether, it made me seem elegant and aristocratic in Billy's eyes. To him, I was the epitome of a sophisticated California beach girl, while he was the motorcycle-riding, smart-talking punk from a hard-knocks part of New York.

When it came time to make the music video for "Uptown Girl," there wasn't much discussion over who should play the titular role. When Billy suggested me, everyone in the band and his music production team nodded in agreement, and after he asked me, I didn't think twice about it. To me, it seemed like we were just a group of friends getting together to make a little film for Billy's soon-to-be hit song, all of which felt organic, collegial, and creative—which was why I didn't think to tell my agency or acting manager, even though, after the video came out, I almost lost my Screen Actors Guild membership because the video that changed my life was, technically, an "unpaid" appearance.

WE HAD to shoot "Uptown Girl" in Manhattan, of course—there was nowhere else imaginable—but when you want to film live on the streets of New York, you have to do so at odd hours, which is how we ended up shooting the whole video over two consecutive nights, until seven in the morning one night and the next night until two. Our location was a working gas station at the corner of Bond Street and the Bowery, right across from the iconic music club CBGB (where punk was the order of the day and where people had more pins in their faces than I had down the back of my dress). In the dark downtown streets in the middle of one of the busiest cities in the world, it was magical and mystical to film overnight, when New York felt like another place, under the shimmering glow of the windows of those still awake, those just getting up, or those doing whatever else people do in the city that never sleeps. For the shoot, our little block was lit up like a Christmas tree, under a hundred floodlights, and at times, it felt like we were the most animated block in downtown Manhattan, especially when we left the set the same time as the bleary-eyed stragglers from the nearby nightclubs.

For the shoot, the video's directors had erected a fictitious billboard over the gas station—an image of me modeling for the made-up brand "Uptown Cosmetics"—which became the opening shot for the video before the camera panned down to a trio of mechanics harmonizing the song's intro. The camera then stops on Billy, dressed in a mechanic's suit, as he slicks back his hair in front of his locker in the staff breakroom, the locker open to reveal a taped page from my most recent swimsuit calendar. After one refrain, a chauffeur pulls up in an old Rolls-Royce, with me in the back seat wearing a black boater, a strapless black-and-white dress, a pair of black pumps, and drop earrings that continually catch and sparkle under the station's bright lights. After the chauffeur parks, mechanics polish and clean the car while I roll down my window, smile, then get out of the car, strutting around the station and acting uppity— "More hoity-toity, Christie," I remember the director repeatedly telling me—before we all start dancing together. Toward the end of the song, I take Billy's arm and climb onto the back of his motorcycle before we ride off together into the New York City streets. As I shake my hair out from under my hat, the video ends on the same shot it opened with, panning up to the billboard of me.

While we were filming, a thousand thoughts ran through my mind, including the memory of the gas station scene from *Les Parapluies de Cherbourg*, the movie I watched as a little girl that launched my love affair with France, and the recollection of climbing onto the back of Olivier's bike so many times, just as I do Billy's motorcycle in the video. While it was already early September when we filmed "Uptown Girl," these were some of the hottest days that summer, so hot that the heels of my shoes kept sinking into the melted asphalt. Many times, when I kicked my leg up to dance, I was surprised to see my bare foot, the heel of my shoe stuck behind in the smoldering tar.

I loved everything about "Uptown Girl," and after the video become an MTV hit alongside the song, Billy and I became known as the downtown guy and the uptown girl, the street-smart New Yorker and the sophisticated supermodel, each of us complementing the other like Bonnie and Clyde. Wherever I went, they played "Uptown Girl"; it became my theme song on every talk show and at every party and public event, including when I took my seat on camera at the U.S. Open. Similarly, the press punned the name in nearly every headline—so, when my photo was taken swinging our daughter, Alexa Ray, upside down, I was suddenly the "up-clown girl"; when I bought an apartment below Fourteenth Street more than thirty years after the video aired, the headline read "Uptown Girl Moves Downtown."

The video surprisingly overlapped with other areas of my life, too. Three decades later, Gary Chryst, who choreographed the "Uptown Girl" video and played one of two motorcyclists in the background, became the dance director when I starred in the Broadway musical *Chicago*, which also featured another dancer from Billy's music video.

More than four decades later, while I don't necessarily think of myself this way, I'm still an uptown girl in many ways. I'm still the woman whom Billy first met at a dive bar in St. Barts, the one who likes sophistication, culture, and art, but who also likes to take risks, try new things, and shake her hair out on the back of a bike every once in a while. And I'm also someone who says yes to love whenever and wherever it happens, no matter whether that's uptown, downtown, or somewhere in between.

CHAPTER

16

Standing inside the tiny terminal of the Farmingdale airport, I watched as the Gulfstream III touched down in front of me, the sleek plane looking like a white heron gliding across black water as it breasted the runway, then edged its beak toward the gate. I grabbed my bag, pushed open the terminal door, and walked across the tarmac, smoothing down my pencil skirt as my high heels clicked across the cold pavement and the crew unfolded a small stairway from the jet's fuselage. There was no line to board: I was the only one getting on the private plane to fly from Farmingdale, Long Island, to South Bend, Indiana, where Billy was performing a sold-out show for his newly launched *An Innocent Man* tour.

The date: February 2, 1984. The occasion: my thirtieth birthday.

When I first started modeling at age twenty, I never imagined I'd still be doing it at thirty. Not only did I think modeling would last me only as long as the next fabulous trip, but all the agents and other models had told me I'd be chewed up and spat out by the time I was thirty, just like most of the women before me. But there I was, getting on a private plane sent to me by my rock star boyfriend while modeling more than ever, doing covers and commercials, and designing my own clothing line with the apparel brand Russ Togs, in addition to a swimsuit line with Monika Tilley, whose sexy swimsuits I had worn in the pages of *Sports Illustrated*. I was also putting together my fourth consecutive swimsuit calendar, this time with my friend, the photographer Patrick Demarchelier, and getting regularly asked onto talk shows and to make other press appearances.

The day before my birthday, I had to work until late at night on my swimsuit designs, and even though every day was my birthday with Billy, he was adamant that we celebrate the actual calendar day together—and because it was a big birthday, he sent a private plane so I could make it to South Bend to see him before the show.

As soon as I landed, he picked me up in a limo and whisked me away to an early dinner, where the waiters came dancing out with an even larger, more elaborate cake than when he just pretended it was my birthday. We then rushed off to the arena where Billy was performing, and while I swayed to the music from the front row, he and the ten thousand fans there sang "Happy Birthday" to me, making it the biggest birthday song Billy had orchestrated yet. Later, when he pulled me up onstage for "Uptown Girl," the crowd went wild. Afterward, I thought how so few people were ever able to have their love publicly celebrated like that, which amplified how we both felt about each other that night, making us almost dizzy with love. After the show, the band gave me a cake, the crew handed me a big bouquet of roses, and Billy slipped me another soft velvet box, this time with a bracelet inside dotted with diamonds, emeralds, and rubies, all just as bright and brilliant as Billy had been onstage that night.

That spring and early summer, I toured with Billy as much as I could, eventually joining him in Japan, where they adored him as much as they did in New York, to the point where some people had even handcrafted little Billy Joel dolls. It was fascinating to see the effect Billy's music had on people in other cultures, and I felt fortunate to be inside his work with him like that and to be able to experience the world with him in such an intimate, unforgettable way.

Touring with Billy wasn't all private planes, though, which were the exception, not the rule. Most of the time, we shuttled around on big tour buses, which not only felt very real—like I was living the movie *Almost Famous* more than a decade before it was released—but also a ton of fun. The guys in Billy's band were always joking, laughing, singing, and teasing one another, using their own secret language and special road names so no one would overhear something juicy that might make it into the tabloids. The band also went out of their way to make me feel welcome, saying they'd never seen Billy so happy before. By the time I joined them in Japan later that spring, I had become so close with the band and crew that we would start each day with what we came to call the "dream club," meeting every morning in our kimonos in my room to have breakfast together and share the crazy dreams we were all having, which we believed were caused by the delicious but unusual foods we were eating.

After Japan, Billy and I flew to Paris, just the two of us, and wanting to show me a new, extraordinary side of the city that I had called home for so long, he booked the premier suite at the Hôtel de Crillon, a five-star palace of a place located in an actual eighteenth-century palace at one end of the Place de la Concorde. We spent the entire weekend there, acting like two kids in a candy store by hamming up our good fortune in front of our recently purchased video recorder by lounging around on the suite's ornate Italian sofas. I can still picture Billy picking at a fruit plate in our room that looked as though it had been painted by the nineteenth-century Prussian American still-life artist Severin Roesen, occasionally asking me to peel him a grape or fan him with a French silk pillow. We felt so fortunate to be able to experience that kind of luxury, a gratitude we retained every time we traveled together or did decadent things, neither of us ever taking for granted what we had—not then, not later, and not now.

In Paris, Olivier's family came to see us, not only to meet Billy, whom they adored, but also to show me that they supported our relationship, which touched me to the core, in the most tender part of my heart. I was also so thankful to Billy, and whenever he insisted upon splurging on fancy hotels, private planes, or expensive jewelry for me, I told him he'd already given me the greatest gift of all, bringing me back to life after Olivier's death. While I constantly reminded him that I loved him for him and that I didn't need or want anything else, Billy was bighearted, always doing generous things like buying motorcycles for the guys in his band. This kind of largesse was not just part of his personality but also his reaction, I think, to the reality that he had become rich and famous, which, for the entire time we were together, he never quite believed and still continually amazed him.

From Paris, we flew to London, where Billy had a string of sold-out shows at Wembley Arena and where I was looking forward to seeing Olivier's and my dear friends Simon and Rupert, who had now become Billy's dear friends, too. One day, after Billy left for a sound check at Wembley, I was trying to organize all our messy stuff in our hotel room when I got a call from the two lads.

"Hey, Fat Face!" one called out, using their favorite nickname for me. "Care to pop over to Buckingham Palace for tea?"

"We'll pick you up in ten," the other shouted, as they handed the receiver back and forth between the two of them. "Dress smart. And practice your curtsey!"

Ten minutes to get ready for tea at the palace? I had just enough time to do my hair before grabbing my purse and running out the door . . . only to discover Simon and Rupert had pulled up outside in a convertible. So much for my hair.

As soon as we arrived in front of the palace, its famous gold-and-iron gates parted, admitting our pint-size convertible inside one of the most regal courtyards in the entire world. We then solemnly drove past rows of standing guards, who looked more like toy soldiers, toward the grandest arch I'd ever seen.

"All right, Lady Brinkley. Show us your curtsey," Rupert called after I'd popped out of the convertible.

As I bowed with a flourish, I heard laughter, then saw Prince Andrew standing under the arch, watching us with a smile and great amusement. He then ushered us into the palace and upstairs to his sitting room, eager to serve us tea and share his photos of the Falklands, "accidentally" slipping in a few of his ex-girlfriend, the American actress Koo Stark—"Ooh, you don't want to see that," he giggled—before showing us pics of his helicopter. Afterward, I took the liberty to share with him some pictures of my favorite subject: Billy.

"You know, I've never been to a rock-and-roll concert," the prince said wistfully.

What? I couldn't believe it. I called Billy's tour manager on the spot and told him I was bringing the prince to the show that night.

When we got backstage at Wembley, the crew and band walked right past Prince Andrew and, looking to me, asked where "Prince" was, saying how excited they were to meet him.

"*The* prince, not Prince," I whispered under my breath, much to their dismay.

Afterward, we all went out—the prince, my parents, Billy, and the band—to the club Tramp, which was renowned for protecting celebrities from the paparazzi. That night, they served me a plate of food carved into letters that spelled "Uptown Girl," the number one hit on the UK pop charts at the time.

WHILE I loved being on tour with Billy, it was always a juggling act with my work, and every day I was on the road with him, I felt like I had three balls up in the air, with me in the middle, trying to smile and look supermodel-ready after the usual cavalcade of cars, concerts, buses, airports, and airplanes. I remember one stretch when, after busing around the Midwest with Billy and his band, I flew to New York for an interview with Barbara Walters (who made me cry on national TV when she asked me about Olivier, even though I had told her beforehand that the subject was off-limits), then flew again that night to Los Angeles, where I presented the award for best sound at the fifty-sixth annual Academy Awards alongside Michael Keaton. The next day, I shot a TV commercial for Diet Coke in which I held up a copy of my bestselling *Christie Brinkley's Outdoor Beauty and Fitness Book* (can you imagine a better plug?), and as soon as that wrapped, I was off to the airport to get back to New York so I could attend a party for Russ Togs at the Metropolitan Museum of Art. The next morning, I shot the cover of my 1985 swimsuit calendar with Patrick Demarchelier, then rushed to Dallas, where Billy had suddenly landed in the hospital with a kidney stone, despite continuing to play sold-out shows. But that was typical Billy, who always insisted that the show go on.

And so did I.

After a night or two in Dallas, I flew back to New York to tape five segments for *Good Morning America*, then got back on a plane to Los Angeles, this time flying Regentair, the luxury airliner that was all the rage in the 1980s, with no more than thirty passengers per plane, a full bar, and banquette tables topped by white linen and buckets of champagne. On that flight, I sat at the jet's bar, and within minutes after takeoff, I met the musician Rod Stewart, who invited me back to the private compartment he was sharing with a friend. The three of us proceeded to have the most fabulous lunch, complemented by lots of champagne, although when the plane hit a patch of turbulence, Rod switched to vodka, telling the stewardess to leave the entire bottle on the table (which she did), and on every bump, we took a slug. At one point, Rod even did an upside-down yoga pose in his seat, which his friend and I tried to emulate, but couldn't since we were laughing too much. But not even upside-down yoga could mess up Rod's great head of hair, which was envy-inducing, and during that flight, I was sure to get all his top styling tips and product recommendations.

After we landed, a convoy of limos was already lined up on the tarmac immediately outside the plane, three of which were for each of us, so everyone climbed into their respective cars, and we created a procession of limos from the airport to a tropical-themed restaurant in Marina del Rey that had a giant, manmade waterfall at the front door, which Rod decided to scale, climbing its faux rocks to the tippy top. All the while, I kept thinking that if this was what thirty was like, I was in for the ride, literally and figuratively, not to mention that my 1980s high hair never looked better after that evening.

THAT SUMMER, after Billy capped his long tour with seven sold-out shows at New York's Madison Square Garden, he and I spent an extended stretch of time together at Gate Lodge, his home on the North Shore of Long Island, where I had already planted a flower garden, we had adopted a cat named Little Richard, and from where, at his request, I took seaplanes into the city whenever I had to work. That July and August, we went swimming almost every day in a saltwater pool Billy had built into the seawall, warming up afterward in his steam room and boating up and down the coast or into Manhattan in Billy's tiny skiff, a little Popeye motor launch that barely had a center console but that we thought of as a super-yacht.

That July, we took a navigation course together, and after earning our captain's licenses, we used parallel rulers and those divider compasses that walk across maps to plot a course to Martha's Vineyard, off Cape Cod, roping Billy's best friend, Billy Zampino, and his wife, Teresa, both of whom had been at the PLM when I first met Billy, into taking the trip with us, even though Billy's skiff could barely fit four pieces of luggage, let alone four people.

On our first day boating, the Long Island Sound was beautiful and placid, and we made it all the way from Gate Lodge, in Lloyd Harbor, to Montauk, at the very tip of Long Island, where we spent the night in an old motel Billy had booked by the Coast Guard station. The next day, we cruised to Block Island, a charming Victorian gem of an island untouched by time, off Rhode Island. Finally, we set course for Martha's Vineyard, singing and laughing all day until we spotted the marina where we wanted to moor, which was when Billy radioed the island's harbormaster to announce our arrival.

A tinny voice picked up on the other end. "How many feet is your yacht, Captain?" the harbormaster asked, his voice scratching out from the boat's center console for all of us to hear.

"Twenty feet, sir!" Billy shouted into the handset.

"That's your *tender*, Captain," the harbormaster said, using the term for a smaller boat that ferries people, luggage, or other items back and forth from larger ships. "We want to know the size of your *yacht*!"

"This *is* our yacht!" Billy said, flashing us all a smile.

Not even the harbormaster could believe we had boated all the way in Billy's tiny skiff from the North Shore of Long Island to Martha's Vineyard, and when we hit a huge squall on our way home, getting doused by waves that sloshed over the small prow of our Popeye, we all felt lucky to be alive. But Billy was proud of his skiff—and I was proud of him—and I still have pictures of him standing on the bow of the boat as though he were manning the wheel of HMS *Victory*. I loved him for loving boats as much as I did, and we used to joke—because we were always joking—that I was the rag bagger (or sailor) in our relationship while he was the stinkpotter (motorboater), and between the two of us, just like the old nursey rhyme about Jack Sprat and his wife, we licked the waters of the world clean.

On August 7, 1984, I was sketching designs for my clothing line in Billy's office on the top floor of Gate Lodge when I heard him padding softly up the stairs. That afternoon, the sun was dancing off the harbor, spraying up sunlight into his office like a child throwing handfuls of golden coins into a fountain, and as soon as he walked in, the summer light caught his smile as he beamed down at me with soulful green eyes.

"I was going to wait until tonight, but this thing is burning a hole in my pocket," he said as he handed me a single sheet of notepad paper.

On the paper was the last and final verse of "Leave a Tender Moment Alone," the song he had written about our relationship when we first started dating, which had already been released on *An Innocent Man*. But this verse wasn't part of the original song—nor would it ever be—and at first, I read it slowly, then with awe and surprise, before I couldn't read it out loud anymore because I was sobbing:

> *Guess I must be in love much more than I thought I could be*
> *Yes, I'm sure I'm in love, so please say that you'll marry me*
> *I know the moment isn't right for such a traditional thing*
> *I couldn't wait another night, I just had to give you this ring*
> *So that's how I feel and it's the best feeling I've ever known*
> *It's undeniably real, Christie, never leave me alone.*

I looked up through my tears. Billy had dropped to one knee and was holding out a radiant-cut diamond ring, which was the most beautiful ring I'd ever seen as it caught and spun the light around the room just like the summer sun had done with Billy's smile.

"Yes, Joe," I whispered through tears. "Yes."

FOR THE next several months, after our engagement made the magazines and newspapers, I felt like all of New York City was celebrating with us. Wherever I went, whether with friends or with Billy, restaurants surprised us with bottles of champagne and women gushed over my ring. Even Bono, the lead singer of the band U2, brought me backstage when I saw him in concert with a friend so he could toast our engagement.

That Christmas, we spent the holidays at Gate Lodge, and when I woke up on December 25, Billy was grinning like a kid sitting before a pile of presents. He motioned for me to look out the window, where, at first, I assumed I would see a huge snowfall that had blown in overnight. But instead, standing on the lawn on long legs, was a magnificent white horse, the same color as freshly fallen snow, with a big, bright red ribbon tied around her neck. For some time, all I could say was "What? What?," my eyes so full of tears of joy that I could hardly see what I couldn't believe I was seeing—that Billy had given me a horse for Christmas. But he kept smiling and saying, "That's for you, my love." When I finally understood what he had done, that I had my own horse and that the animal and I were to be best friends, I wrapped myself around Billy and began to cry. Ever since I was a little girl and Trigger carried me away from anguish into a more magical world, I had always dreamed of having my own horse. Now Billy was bringing that magic into my everyday life. Her name was Belle Star, and I loved her.

After the New Year, in the middle of planning for our March wedding, Billy and I went to Los Angeles, where he had been asked to record the song "We Are the World" with forty other of the world's top musicians to raise money for African famine relief. The taping took place overnight at a record studio in Hollywood, and when we arrived at 9 p.m., the security was tighter than it would be at a modern-day United Nations meeting. Shortly afterward, Billy was whisked back to the studio with the other artists, and I was shown into an enormous room that had video monitors so family and friends could watch. But after only a few minutes, a guard fetched me and led me back to the artists-only studio, and for the rest of the evening, I was one of only a handful who were able to witness in person music history being made as Michael Jackson, Bob Dylan, Stevie Wonder, Bruce Springsteen, Diana Ross, and more than three dozen other legendary musicians harmonized and collaborated on what would become the fastest-selling U.S. pop single in history. To me, the night reminded me of what it felt to be a child at a party after the piñata bursts open, as I constantly swung my head around to try to catch every delicious moment.

One of those sweet moments happened when Billy and I were standing with Bob Dylan and Stevie Wonder, and Bob, whose music I had adored since I was a teen, admitted that he didn't know how he should sing the song.

"What do you mean?" Stevie immediately chimed in. "You should sing the song like *you*! You should sing it like Bob Dylan would sing it!"

Stevie then began demo'ing the song with a pitch-perfect Bob Dylan impersonation, singing in Bob's same folky, twangy, nasally voice, "We are the world, we are the children," with all the emphasis and pauses that Bob gives his own lyrics. It was an incredible moment to witness—the best living artist of soul impersonating the best living artist of folk—and for years to come, Billy and I would relive it over and over, one of us pretending to be Bob while the other played Stevie. That night, I learned that even the world's most talented rock stars can doubt their own abilities at times.

ONCE WE were back in New York, I set about drawing our wedding invitation, illustrating a colorful card that I sent to 250 of our closest friends and family, including half of Sony Records, whom Billy had invited. The invitation featured an illustration of us as bride and groom standing on a boat between a hand-penciled Statue of Liberty and New York City, with the words "We've been waiting to do this for the longest time" floating in blue-shaded waters around cartoon skyscrapers of Lower Manhattan. Right after we were engaged, we had decided quickly and easily to get married on a boat, given that we both loved boats, and to hold the ceremony in New York because the city is synonymous with Billy and because I loved Billy and everything about him—not to mention, I had also fallen in love with New York, where my life and career had taken incredible turns.

The night before our wedding, we stayed in the presidential suite at the Carlyle, the hotel where John F. Kennedy allegedly used to sneak Marilyn Monroe into his room using a labyrinth of underground tunnels, and while we were there, I quickly realized why the hotel is known as the "palace of secrets": the staff there was so clandestine, treating us like their own children by warning us whenever paparazzi were outside—and paparazzi were always outside—and sending us out with a convoy of bellboys with oversize umbrellas that shielded us from intrusive eyes and lenses.

The day of our wedding, March 23, 1985, we got dressed in separate rooms of the suite, which had a grand piano that Billy played from time to time until I told him he couldn't see me anymore. While I didn't put on my wedding dress at the hotel—I wore white silk pajamas with Keds and a fancy necklace Billy had given me on my way to a 147-foot boat we had chartered in the Hudson River for the ceremony—I wanted it to feel special when he did see me for the first time that day. My dress was an elegant two-piece with a white satin bustier, gold tulle skirt, and Victorian white lace jacket, designed specifically for me by Norma Kamali, who created the teeny, stringy purple bikini I wore on my first-ever *Cosmopolitan* cover that had created such a stir.

Even though we were married long before social media (which has made privacy that much more challenging, since anyone with a smartphone can broadcast your activity and whereabouts to the entire world), everyone still knew that Billy and I were getting married that day; the buildup had been that intense. As my solo limo approached Chelsea Piers, where the 147-foot boat was docked, I saw hundreds of people lining the park along the river, and I could tell that paparazzi were everywhere, pointing telephoto lenses off piers, down from rooftops, and out the doors of the helicopters swirling overhead. In that moment, I could physically feel the buzz of anticipation in the air, as the roar of the choppers sent reverberations through my body. To steady myself, I clutched the necklace Billy had given me, made up of multiple stands of baby pearls anchored by a square emerald crusted by diamonds, but that didn't stop me from throwing up in the car—I was that nervous. While I knew I wanted to marry Billy, I had never hosted a party this big before.

Thankfully, I recovered in time for the ceremony, as we boated out to float just under the Statue of Liberty, which is where Billy and I had decided to exchange our vows, not only because the views of the city were spectacular but also because of what Lady Liberty represented to us—a place where people were embraced for who they were and where they went to start a new life with the help of others. To us, she stood there in the Atlantic Ocean, arms wide open, as the symbol of America itself (albeit one made in France, which delighted me) and of all things possible. Similarly, Billy and I were ready to embrace each other and the possibility of a new life together, just as many others had done who'd arrived beneath her torch for years before.

Under a simple flower arch and before a female judge, we exchanged vows in the yacht's main salon, the windows of which we lined with a thousand white tulips. As soon as we said our "I dos," a recording of James Brown's voice boomed throughout the boat from loudspeakers—"Wow, I feel good, I knew that I would"—as everyone leapt to their feet and started the party, which began early and lasted all night long. Almost immediately, someone spilled champagne down the front of my dress, causing the tulle to shrivel, but I only shouted, "Hey, that's good luck!" as I sang along with James Brown and danced. We then cruised around the tip of Manhattan to the Water's Edge restaurant in Long Island City for a sit-down dinner, where the whole cityscape framed our tables from big windows on the water. No one went home before the sun rose over the East River the following morning, and the next week, *People* magazine ran a cover story on our wedding. When we got home from our honeymoon, there was a telegram waiting for us at the front desk from James Brown, who had heard about his secondhand role in our nuptials and wrote, "Papa's got a brand new bag. Congratulations."

SEVERAL WEEKS later, on a gorgeous spring day in the middle of April, we decided to take Billy's little skiff to Greenport, on the North Fork of Long Island, where we loved going to the restaurant Claudio's, a Victorian-era eatery on the village pier perfect for lobster rolls and rosé on a sunny day. Once there, we sat at our usual table, from which we could see all the sailboats and the little ferry that goes back and forth to Shelter Island, and ordered oysters and a bottle of wine. At the same time, a little voice in the back of my mind told me maybe I shouldn't have any oysters and wine: earlier that week, I had been to the doctor, and I wanted to make sure everything was okay before I ate shellfish or drank rosé. I told Billy I wanted to call the doctor before we ate, excusing myself to use one of the old-fashioned phone booths that lined the entryway of the restaurant before mobile phones became as ubiquitous as silverware at every table.

When I returned to the table, I pushed my wineglass away and started to cry softly and silently, with the kind of tears that make no noise. "Billy, we're going to have a baby," I said, as the teardrops rolled down my face. "I'm pregnant. We're going to have a baby."

For the first time since I'd known him, Billy was speechless. We both knew we wanted to have a baby—it was one reason why we had gotten married—and I think we were amazed and delighted it had happened so quickly, our soon-to-be daughter conceived either on our wedding night at the Carlyle (a fitting prelude to her musical residency there years later) or in Mustique, a private island in the Grenadines where we had gone for the first half of our honeymoon, before spending the second half in St. Barts. Wherever it had occurred, Billy couldn't have been happier, jumping up out of his seat. Later, he took me home in the boat as carefully as he could, steering back and forth over the sea so he wouldn't hit any little wavelet that might upset the baby.

That spring and summer was a happy time for me. I loved being pregnant, as my body seemed to know instinctively what I should avoid, like swordfish and tuna, which I knew were laden with mercury, in addition to Billy's steam room (I didn't want the baby to get overheated) and any restaurant where there was even a whiff of cigarette smoke (this was long before legislation banned all indoor smoking).

I had already given up smoking months before, when I knew I wanted to get pregnant. Billy and I both went for help to a famous hypnotist who told us to lie in the same room on separate couches and imagine drifting aimlessly on the open ocean. I pictured myself in a beautiful sailboat, floating peacefully on top of the waves, and afterward, whenever I saw a cigarette, all I craved was a glass of water.

But the first thing Billy thought when he heard "drifting aimlessly" was that his motorboat must have a broken engine. Eventually, he stopped smoking only after going to an "aura changer," who somehow karate-chopped the addiction out of his body.

Even though I started to show at five months and my face ultimately became as round as Mr. Magoo's, I continued to model for CoverGirl and other clients almost until the week I gave birth. While I worked, my priorities were elsewhere, though—I was going to be a mom—and I felt a surge of creativity that inspired me to draw and paint regularly, the artistry of creating a baby inside spilling into my everyday life.

Billy and I started taking Lamaze classes together, which caused several hilarious scenes, since Billy always tried to make me laugh at the most inopportune moments, like in the middle of practicing our "hee, hee, hoos" and "pant, pant, blows." Around my third trimester, he also began wearing a stopwatch around his neck at all times, even while sleeping, so he could time my contractions and tell me whether they were Braxton-Hicks (false labor pains) or real contractions.

When my water finally broke, in the early hours of the morning at Gate Lodge, neither of us was expecting it. I had assumed our baby would be born late because my mom told me that my brother and I had both been late and that I would be just like her. But the only thing our daughter has ever been early for in her life has been her own birth: she arrived two weeks premature, on December 29, 1985. When I woke up early that morning and felt the wetness all around me, Billy sat straight up in bed next to me, hitting the Start button on his stopwatch like an anxious coach watching his top track prospect compete in the Olympics, as we both realized I needed to get to the hospital as soon as possible.

Billy drove me there a nervous wreck, continuing to time my contractions while weaving on and off service roads to avoid the city's constant commuter traffic, even at four in the morning. I filmed the whole thing—like Billy and his stopwatch, I constantly had a recorder affixed to my shoulder, so much so that he started to joke, "You gotta get that thing lanced"—and I kept filming even as I walked into the Manhattan hospital, pointing the camera down at my shoes and saying, "When I walk out the door again, these will be the feet of the mother," as nurses tried to rush me into a room. Once I was lying safely in a hospital bed, I opened the go bag I'd hastily packed at home and realized I'd brought only giant earrings and colorful berets, which made me if not the most prepared mom in the hospital, then at least the best accessorized one.

After nineteen hours of labor without any drugs, I finally gave birth to our beautiful baby girl, and when the doctor held her up for me to see, I loved her instantly, with her puffy little face and hair sticking up straight like the crown of the Statue of Liberty, making her look like a miniature Don King, only much prettier. We decided to name her Alexa Ray, a unique-sounding name at the time, with "Ray" for Ray Charles, whom Billy and I both adored.

When the nurses brought Alexa Ray back into our room in a bassinette, which Billy called "the casserole dish," someone suggested we take a family photo. Billy looked at the bassinette as he tried to figure out how to get Alexa Ray out of it, then decided to run his fingers between the glass and the bassinette's mattress before lifting Alexa Ray out of it still tightly swaddled to her bedding. He then lovingly and proudly presented her to me, mattress and all, and I held her up while he stood on the other side of the bassinette and the two of us smiled for the camera as though we were posing with a product for a commercial. That became our first-ever family picture, and I still laugh today whenever I see it—fitting, since all Billy and I did was laugh during the first few years of our marriage. Alexa Ray only amplified our joy in a way I hadn't ever imagined possible.

THAT DAY, I learned something about the human heart. Just when you think you don't have the room to fill it with one more drop of love, someone like Alexa Ray comes along to show you that the heart is vast and limitless, with the ability to expand at any time, making you feel as boundless and blissful as a seabird on a placid and endless ocean.

First a horse, now a baby girl: I've always believed in Christmas miracles.

"I carried my journal with me all over the world"

Off to See the World JOURNAL

Alongside stories, I drew little sketches to remind me of the people and places I loved.

I don't remember where I was going in this 1959 shot, but it had to be somewhere special because I have on my fancy shoes and a flouncy slip underneath my skirt.

Once every year, my mom dressed up my brother and me and took us to a professional studio to get our pictures taken, including this time, when I was three or four, wearing my favorite fancy party dress.

My parents always kissed before having wine, doing so in this shot from the mid-1960s in the living room of our Malibu home, which was lined by the paintings and other art they collected.

I still love gingham this much!

School picture day at Le Lycée Français de Los Angeles in 1968, taken in my school uniform that included a beret, which I adored.

Calling all my friends in California to say goodbye before I headed off to Paris in 1973.

Polaroid selfie of artist Joey Mills doing my makeup, most likely for *Glamour* magazine in the mid-1970s.

A mirror selfie taken with my glam team and glam cam, which I always decorated and constantly wore around my neck.

Hamming it up on the set, as usual!

During a photo shoot for one of my beauty books, I rubbed sand all over my body to illustrate just how much I loved to exfoliate. But after others said the shot was sexy, it ended up in my *Sports Illustrated* Swimsuit calendar.

© Patrick Demarchelier/Trunk Archive

This bathroom selfie shows me getting ready to go to a birthday party for makeup artist extraordinaire Sandy Linter in 1985.

A toast to my husband Jean-François on our wedding day in November 1975, adorned with fragrant pikake and maile leaves for jewelry, with our feet in the Pacific and our hearts bursting with love.

My mom and dad taking Polaroids of Jean-François and me on our wedding day in Kona Village Resort in Hawaii (and my sweet dad is holding my mom's crossbody bag).

Jean-François and me attending the 1978 International Model of the Year awards ceremony honoring Johnny Casablancas, where I was also the celebrity guest of honor.

PLEINE D'AMOUR ET DE BONN

Working the phones in my Everlast robe (and sitting next to a hotel lamp I decorated with boxing belts) to make sure all my credentials were in order before I went to the Super Fight at the Superdome in New Orleans in 1980.

Wearing all pink at the Flamingo Hotel Las Vegas—and tinkled pink to have tickets to the Last Hurrah fight between boxers Muhammad Ali and Larry Holmes in 1980.

My mom and Elvis.

Hops and I started crying after Muhammad Ali lost to Larry Holmes in the Last Hurrah—until we spotted promoter Don King walking into an after-party, so off we went.

Neither Maury Hopson (Hops), my best friend at the time, nor I had ever been to a boxing match before the Last Hurrah, and getting to our seats ringside, with the people-watching there, was an adventure in itself.

My two wild red-headed parrots, Al Pesto and Al Fresco, chose to live with me and Filippo Brignone when I stayed in Careyes, Mexico, the summer of 1981. © Patrick Demarchelier/Trunk Archive

Filippo Brignone and I taking shots of tequila while playing "The Blue Danube" for our two parrots, who loved to waltz, in Careyes, Mexico, in 1981.

Olivier Chandon de Brailles and I often took boat rides from his family's home on the Amalfi Coast in Italy, where he knew every nook and cranny of the spectacular shoreline, including where this pic was shot in 1982, at one of our favorite restaurants.

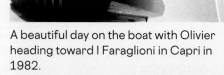

A beautiful day on the boat with Olivier heading toward I Faraglioni in Capri in 1982.

Backstage with Olivier entertaining the troops with Bob Hope in Annapolis, Maryland.

A calm moment on what was usually an electrifying ride on the back of Olivier's motorcycle in New York City in 1982.

This was just a quick snap taken in my own clothes on the Ferrari with the now-iconic license plate from the 1982 set of *National Lampoon's Vacation*. Somehow, though, it became one of the photos I was asked to autograph the most often.

Licensed by: Warner Bros. Discovery. All Rights Reserved.

DIRECTOR HAROLD RAMIS

BEVERLY D'ANGELIS CHEVY CHASE

PART OF OUR MARVELOUS CREW DANA AND MICHAEL

THE "VACATION" WAGON

I snapped this while we were filming *National Lampoon's Vacation* in 1982, then labeled the photo with everyone's name to make sure I'd never forget, not realizing at the time that both the movie and the people who made it would become lasting aspects of my life.

This Polaroid is from a photo shoot we did to help the artist draw the official promo poster for *National Lampoon's Vacation*. In the illustrated poster, actor Beverly D'Angelo clutches Chevy Chase's other leg.

chevy Chase as James Bond

January 1983, St. Barthelemy. Our first encounter. Alex Chatelaine introduced us. Hello Joe. I sang "the girl from Ipanema"... in portugese. But he liked me anyway. He wouldn't sing his own songs, but I liked him anyway. We sang. We danced. We talked. We really laughed. We had a couple of drinks and we both went home with the wrong person. But we would come to our senses.

I can't believe I still have a photo from that fateful first meet-cute with Billy Joel in 1983—and the funny thing was, he's the great singer, but look who's hogging the mic.

We had to go back to the same place where we first met during our honeymoon in 1985, where I decided to sing a little bossa nova (again) to the love of my life.

We didn't want anyone to feel left out at our wedding, so we organized to sit just the two of us before table-hopping the rest of the evening.
© Patrick Demarchelier/Trunk Archive

Whenever Billy and I dressed up, we liked to re-create the "taffeta, darling" scene from Mel Brooks's movie *Young Frankenstein*, even doing so the night we were married in Manhattan in March 1985.
© Patrick Demarchelier/Trunk Archive

Screw the taffeta, just kiss me.
© Patrick Demarchelier/Trunk Archive

Alexa Ray sitting on Billy's shoulders with Chevy Chase in the Hamptons in the summer of 1986.

At the recording for "We Are the World" for U.S.A. for Africa in January 1985 in Los Angeles with Billy and Michael Jackson, who cowrote the famous song for charity with Lionel Richie.

Billy and I were such Beatles fan that neither of us could believe we got the chance to spend time with Paul and Linda McCartney, seen here with Alexa Ray in 1987, when they came out to the Hamptons.

A few weeks after having Alexa Ray, I caught up with one of my top idols, Bob Dylan, alongside Billy at the 1986 induction ceremony for the Rock & Roll Hall of Fame in New York City.

© Zuma Press

Keith Richards and Patti Hansen, seen here in the mid-1990s, are my neighbors in the Caribbean and one of the sweetest families I know. I love when Keith plucks the guitar, and music drifts through the bougainvillea and hibiscus.

Every time I've met Bruce Springsteen, like when we hung out at U.S.A. for Africa, I've been struck by how kind and down-to-earth he is.

Patrick Demarchelier was the sweetest photographer and took these black-and-white pictures as a baby gift.
© Patrick Demarchelier/Trunk Archive

Like father, like daughter . . .
© Patrick Demarchelier/Trunk Archive

Holding my newborn baby girl and telling her how much I love her.
© Patrick Demarchelier/Trunk Archive

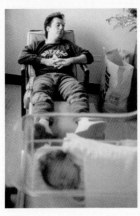

Billy was always happy to do naptime with Alexa Ray—he was smitten.

Newborn Alexa Ray and Billy grabbing a nap in the Manhattan hospital where she was born (Alexa Ray is the one in the casserole dish).

Alexa Ray and Billy loved watching the animated movie *The Little Mermaid* over and over again.

Billy and I always danced when we cooked—food tasted better like that. Here we are dancing in the kitchen of Gate Lodge on Long Island in the mid-1980s.

Painting Billy's 1993 *River of Dreams* album cover.

Sports Illustrated's Jule Campbell told me to bring Alexa Ray to Kenya in 1988 for the swimsuit shoot. So I did, and occasionally, she ran right into the shot.

John G. Zimmerman/Sports Illustrated

Giving the paparazzi a couple of shots in Paris in 1987 so they would give us the rest of the day to be tourists.

Daddy giving Alexa Ray piano lessons in 1987.

Billy and me with Alexa Ray's godfather, legendary music promoter Ron Delsener, and godmother, Ellin Delsener, who planned the best galas, at the East Hampton airport in 1990.

Alexa Ray and me riding a horse we borrowed from Robert Redford's stable to head to the Oregon Trail in 1993.

In Texas with "Lex" in 1991 for the National Cutting Horse Association Futurity championship, shopping for chinks, chaps, and fringe jackets to boot.

What goes up . . . Wedding day, Ricky Taubman, Top of the World, Telluride, 1994.
© Timothy White

Jack ran into the photo of this shoot for a magazine cover in 1996 and made the shot.
Credit: Andrew Eccles

My mom and me on my wedding day to Peter Cook in Bridgehampton in 1996.

My adorable parents doing the baby gaze with Sailor in Beverly Hills in 1998.

The best thing I ever grew in the garden of my Hamptons home were my children. In this 2001 shot, Sailor teaches me about ladybugs.

© Michael Grimm for InStyle

Sailor and Jack smiling for the camera in the Caribbean in 2003.

For Sailor's first Halloween, in 1998, I dressed her up as a bouquet of flowers so I could carry her in my arms as I took the other kids trick or treating door-to-door.

My kids and puppies were always running into photos, and the magazines, which often held shoots at my Hamptons home, loved it, including this pic of me with Sailor and Jack in the early 2000s.

Courtesy of Carlo Dala Chiesa

Jack in the arms of his godmother and my BFF, Mindy Moak, on Mustique Island, with Alexa Ray in 1996.

I got a thrill every time I saw the marquee outside New York City's Ambassador Theatre on Broadway, including this shot from 2011.

I was totally razzle dazzle every time I was lucky enough to appear as Roxie Hart.
Credit: Andrew Eccles

Playing Roxie Hart, the killer diller, from Broadway to London to Las Vegas and the rest of the US. I was truly honored by my amazing castmates and all the kind audience members I met at the stage door.
Credit: Andrew Eccles

Photo by Mindy Moak

My downtown guy whisking me away for the final scene of the music video "Uptown Girl," which we shot in Lower Manhattan in 1983.

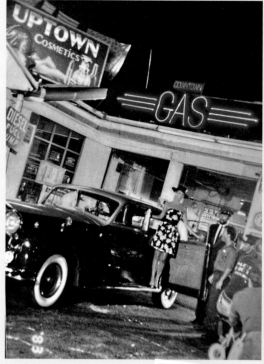

The real-life gas station where we shot "Uptown Girl" was transformed for the music video— from the billboard above to the Rolls-Royce below—and we happened to do the shoot on the hottest night of the year.

I still have the sparkling drop earrings I wore in "Uptown Girl," which also gave me a theme song for life.

Boy George meets Uptown Girl—doing my best Boy George look backstage at one of Billy's shows in 1983.

17

O h, my god, Billy, this is it."

My entire body trembled as we stood on the back lawn and looked out over the dunes, which dipped and crested all the way to the ocean, interrupted only by a sunken thicket of gnarled trees and a tiny sliver of a sandy path that led to the beach. The home itself—a rustic, French-style charmer with a gray stucco exterior and dark blue shutters—was delightful, albeit dilapidated, but nothing mattered to us as much as what we were now seeing: the biggest and best-preserved double sand dune system on the Eastern Seaboard, with fields for horses that lay between the house and the main road, all of which ensured utmost privacy.

And now more than ever, what Billy and I wanted most was privacy.

The boats had started coming up to Gate Lodge long before we were married, some full of curious fishermen while others had been hired by paparazzi, who leveled and pointed their telephoto lenses off the prow, hoping to capture whatever candid photo they could. One morning, while I was walking naked from our bed to get dressed as I always did, I saw three men in a boat aiming their cameras at me, which prompted me to drop to the floor and crawl on my stomach like a paratrooper, hoping to avoid their sight lines. While Billy cracked up laughing at my naked combat crawl, we both knew that our days at Gate Lodge were numbered and that we needed to find a new country home as soon as possible.

So began our months-long search for the perfect seaside home, which was one of the most rewarding adventures Billy and I ever took together, as all we did was be silly and enjoy each other's company. We both loved a good road trip, when we would crank up the radio and sing as loud as we could while laughing at names we found on maps, like "Lake Chaubunagungamaug" and the town of "Athol." For weeks, we puttered up and down the East Coast, hugging the shoreline from Maine's Mount Desert Island all the way down to Cumberland Island in Georgia, which was so secluded that, when John F. Kennedy Jr. and Carolyn Bessette were married there more than a decade later, the paparazzi had no clue until after the fact.

Along the way, we saw seaside towns we'd never been to before, slept in little inns, ate delicious seafood, and imagined our life together in every new home we saw. The drive was never tedious or boring because Billy and I were always laughing, doing our "schtick" by pretending to be different characters, like the old couple who've been together so long they practically share one mind, spending hours reminiscing about the time one did this or the other did that. We believed we'd be that old couple one day, and we felt perfectly sympatico the few times we came close to making an offer on a home, only to stumble upon a mountain of dead flies in the attic or to be attacked by biting bugs while touring the grounds.

Eventually, we decided that the coastline south of New York State wasn't for us—too many horseshoe crabs, not enough clear water— and while we were enamored of Maine, the cold was so cold there, and we didn't love the idea that the state also had a "black fly season."

So, we narrowed our search to the eastern end of Long Island, which was when we discovered fifty acres of waterfront in East Marion, a small farming village on the North Fork. I knew it was some sort of sign when the nearest restaurant had "The Longest Time" and "Christie Lee" as the top two songs on its jukebox, so we bought the land, which was nestled between a big pond and the Long Island Sound, with water views that reminded me of the beaches I'd been to in Greece. We spent days discussing what kind of home we wanted to build there for our soon-to-be brood of children, but after an obstinate neighbor refused to sell us the right of passage to the property, we put it back on the market and resumed our search, now focusing solely on the South Fork of Long Island, what is collectively known as the Hamptons.

ONE SUMMER afternoon while Billy and I were still at Gate Lodge and I was four months pregnant, we got a call from our dear friends Ron Delsener, the top impresario of East Coast concerts at the time, and his wife, Ellin, both of whom would become Alexa Ray's godparents. In a tumble of words, they hurriedly explained that someone named Old Man Potter had just died, leaving no apparent heirs and, as a result, his estate in East Hampton in limbo. Old Man Potter's place was located right on the ocean, on Further Lane, an exclusive two-mile stretch of leafy road lined by large country estates on the Atlantic and bookended by a private country club and the tiny village of Amagansett.

Intrigued, Billy and I drove out to the Delseners' place, which was also in East Hampton, where we all piled into Ron's big, fancy vintage car to putter over to Old Man Potter's. As we turned up the estate's long driveway, bounded on both sides by fields and a little guesthouse out front, I drew in my breath when I saw the main home, elevated over the ocean on a bluff that crested down to the water in a row of double dunes, with a dry creek that ran under a forest of twisted trees and, we later discovered, gushed with water whenever it rained. As the Delseners had promised, the property was right on the Atlantic, with acres of direct beachfront so far removed from the public eye that anyone who lived there was guaranteed absolute privacy. Standing on the estate's back lawn, Billy and I felt as though we had the entire ocean to ourselves, seeing the water stretch blue and endless from the property's edge to the horizon, before the earth tipped, curved, and fell away into the deep Atlantic water.

That same evening, we made an offer on the estate, choosing not to use our real names after learning that some sellers inflated a property's asking price as soon as they discovered the buyer was a celebrity. As it turned out, our decision to remain anonymous was smart: Old Man Potter had included a provision in his will that his estate could not be sold to a Jew or anyone in show business, both of which Billy was. But there was no way we were going to let prejudice keep us from our dream home, so we stayed anonymous while doubling down on our intent to get the property—which, despite a flurry of offers from other bidders, we managed to do, even acquiring the little guesthouse in front, which was owned separately.

THE IRONY of owning our dream home, however, was that the dream took more than five years to materialize, given that we didn't move into the main house until Alexa Ray was four and a half. Instead, we lived in the little guest house for years as renovations to the main home dragged on and on, complicated by some lofty plans of our architect and not-so-lofty plans of our first contractor, who gave away or sold some of the home's beautiful fixtures to a nearby antique store. These complications turned our East Hampton home into "the Beast in the East," as Billy called it, and months later, when he and I decided to move within New York City at the same time, trading in his penthouse on Central Park South for a more family-friendly duplex on Central Park West—or, as Billy put it, trading in our sports car because we needed a station wagon—my real estate–related stress hit the roof. I started to feel anxious, and despite being a busy new mom with a full-time job, I tried all the time to make things as perfect as possible in our two new homes while Billy was away on tour. Eventually, my anxiety became so acute that I made an appointment to see a psychiatrist, which was when Billy told me I didn't need a shrink; I needed a vacation. He booked a trip to St. Barts, just the three of us, and he was right: after a week on my favorite island, my anxiety disappeared.

DISAPPEARED, AT least, for the time being.

The summer after we bought Old Man Potter's place, too much work was being done on the main home for us even to stay in the estate's guesthouse, so we rented a cottage in Montauk, where I brought my beloved Belle Star. Once there, we spent long, idyllic afternoons exploring all the nooks, crannies, harbors, islands, and "gunkholes," as Billy called them, along the Eastern Seaboard in our new boat, the *Sea Major*, which we had personally designed to be part sailboat, part motorboat, appealing to both our aesthetics.

I loved being a new mom, so much so that I was overly attuned to every little sound Alexa Ray made, running to her the second she giggled, gurgled, or emitted even the slightest peep. But we also had a full-time nanny, which took some getting used to, since Billy and I were such private people. Thankfully, our first nanny, a proper English au pair from a UK agency, was wonderful, but after she went back to London, we interviewed so many nannies and made so many temporary hires that I used to joke that if anyone ever made a movie of my life, a different nanny would appear in every scene, floating through the background, a constantly changing cast of characters.

There was no nanny with us, though, one rainy evening in the summer of 1986, while we were staying in the cottage in Montauk, when Billy did something I've never forgotten.

That night, I fell asleep cozy, safe, and secure next to Billy, as I always did, but when I woke up several hours later, he wasn't in bed. At first, in a sleepy haze, I thought he had to be in the bathroom, but when he didn't come back for some time, I figured he must have gone down to the kitchen or was looking in on Alexa Ray, asleep in her crib in an adjacent room. But after too much time had passed, I got out of bed and went into the bathroom—*no, not there*, I realized, before tiptoeing into Alexa Ray's room. But he wasn't there, either. Growing frightened, I crept down the stairs toward the kitchen, wondering for a moment if there had been an intruder. But at the bottom of the stairs, I didn't see or hear anything unusual, just the sound of the rain hitting the windows, as my heart began to beat faster and faster. I looked out every kitchen window to see if I could spot Billy in the yard, then checked the time on the wall clock. It was two in the morning.

Where is he? Should I call the police?

I decided I needed to find out if our car was still in the shed up the hill, where we had parked it, or if Billy had left the property, so after running upstairs to check on Alexa Ray again, I sprinted through the heavy rain up the hill. The car was gone. I was stunned and bewildered, but at the same time, I knew I couldn't call the police, which would only result in an article in the gossip columns the next day. Instead, I did the only reasonable thing I could think to do at that hour: I called every local bar. Most were closed by that time, but when someone picked up at the fourth place I found in the phonebook, my heart, which had been pounding as loudly as the ocean outside, began to settle when the bartender told me that, yes, Billy Joel was there.

He wasn't dead. He wasn't hurt. And he hadn't even left Montauk for god knew where.

He was just drunk. And I felt abandoned, which is a horrible feeling.

When Billy finally stumbled out of a taxi at four-thirty in the morning, he could barely walk, and when I told him how worried I'd been, he only got angry at me and started yelling. I thought he may have been mortified for me to see him that drunk—it was the first time it had happened in my presence—and wanting to spare him even more embarrassment, I went back to bed and pretended to fall asleep, staying there until he woke up hours later, hungover, bleary-eyed, and contrite. He said he didn't remember anything from the night before and seemed horrified by his behavior, as he told me how much he loved me, how stressed he'd been writing hits for his new album, *The Bridge*, and that it would never happen again.

I believed him, I trusted him, and it didn't happen again—at least not for a while, as we fell back into an easy harmony, and things between us were wonderful again. I also took it as an encouraging sign that the biggest hit from *The Bridge*, released the same summer we rented the cottage in Montauk, was a little song called "A Matter of Trust."

I loved both the song, which Billy wrote for me, and the music video for it, which features Billy and his band jamming inside the basement of a building in New York's East Village while everyone out in the street and up on the fire escapes dances away. Alexa Ray and I are also in the video—I carry her around the basement while the band plays nearby—and to me, the video made Manhattan seem like a small town. And in some ways, it was, because everyone in that moment seemed so happy for Billy, his music, and us.

That fall, Billy launched a fourteen-month-long tour for *The Bridge* in a way only he would do, piloting the *Sea Major* several hours up the Hudson River from New York City to Glens Falls, where he was scheduled to play his first show. That morning, Alexa Ray and I woke up early to say goodbye, and just like that, our little family of three entered a new phase of life, one in which Billy was constantly touring while I juggled my own work with motherhood and our mutual desire to be together whenever we could.

AFTER ALEXA Ray was born, my work didn't slow—if anything, it picked up, especially after I lost the baby weight in a frenzy of Jane Fonda videos. (I did so many, in fact, that Alexa Ray learned to count by repeating Jane's signature couplet, "One, two, three, four, make it burn / Five, six, seven, eight, keep going.") Almost immediately, I was doing TV commercials again, for CoverGirl, Prell, Master-Card, and other advertisers, all while filming the *CoverGirl Guide to Basic Makeup with Christie Brinkley*, which film critics Siskel and Ebert named a top holiday gift in 1987. I started doing cover shoots again, too, like for *Glamour* and *Harper's Bazaar*, the latter on which I appeared holding a tiny, precious Alexa Ray. *Good Morning America* even offered me a job as a fashion correspondent, which I turned down because of the time commitment, while my clothing line continued to sell out, requiring more designs, press events, and late-night evenings juggling the demands of motherhood alongside those of fashion.

Despite my nonstop schedule, Alexa Ray and I still joined Billy on tour whenever we could—or, if I couldn't leave the city because of work, Billy flew home between shows for the weekend. I loved being on tour with him and Alexa Ray, which was an enriching experience for many reasons, first of all because Billy was the consummate performer. He was so dynamic onstage, capable of lighting up an entire arena while managing to touch every individual there with his music, magic, and charisma. Even though I covered her ears with headphones, Alexa Ray was also spellbound by the shows. From the moment she was born, she had been a musical baby, singing on her back in the bathtub and shimmying to the sound whenever I placed her little body on the lid of Billy's piano while he played. I don't think it's a coincidence, either, that years later she became a phenomenal singer and piano player in her own right.

On February 2, 1987, my thirty-third birthday, while Billy was away on tour, I received a dozen roses from my husband, along with a dozen more from "the Piano Man," a dozen more from "an Innocent Man," a dozen more from "Joe," a dozen more from "Billy Joel," and, finally, a dozen from "Alexa Ray." In total, I got six dozen roses in one day from Billy, which set a new personal record in the number of floral arrangements I've ever received in twenty-four hours from one person. Our love had never felt so infinite, and later that afternoon, Alexa Ray and I drove up to Connecticut to see Billy perform, taking a limo back the same night into the city, where Billy eventually joined us for a day or two before flying out again to rejoin the tour. But that was what our life was like, a constant kaleidoscope of commotion—and I loved it.

That spring, Alexa Ray and I met Billy in Australia for the first leg of his international tour, the three of us doing the *Today Show* together from Sydney—it made me giddy to see our little family on Australian TV. They loved Billy Down Under, and the record company went out of its way to plan a dozen different activities for us while I also took Alexa Ray to see the kangaroos, pet the koalas, and swim over the Great Barrier Reef. Knowing how much I loved horses, the record company even arranged for me to ride with the same trainers who had handled the horses for the movie *The Man from Snowy River,* flying me by helicopter to the mountain where it was filmed so that I could gallop on those trails.

It was a once-in-a-lifetime experience, but halfway back to Melbourne, the helicopter suddenly started to sputter, rattle, and shake. Without looking at me or even saying a word, the pilot began to flick the dials on the dashboard with his fingers, as I watched the needle on the fuel gauge jump from right to left before its little arrow remained fixed over the bar of red that indicates empty. The pilot then muttered, "We better land this baby now," and began to take us straight down toward the ground, as the helicopter hiccupped and gasped along the way, landing it in the middle of a playground for an elementary school. As soon as the rotors stopped circling above us, the pilot wordlessly pushed open his door and ambled out with a gas can, apparently in no rush, as a group of at least a dozen schoolchildren gathered around me, asking a million questions about the helicopter and the pilot, for which I had no answers. I still didn't have any answers by the time the pilot dropped me off in time for Billy's show, but I was overjoyed to be alive and safe.

From Australia, we flew together to Tokyo, and while I was alone in our hotel room with Alexa Ray, an earthquake shook the city. In a heartbeat, my wonder turned to terror. As a kid growing up in California, I'd experienced enough earthquakes to know the degree of death and damage they could cause—the only difference now was that I had an eighteen-month-old in my arms. But what was worse were the aftershocks, which didn't happen as a result of the earthquake, but when Billy, whom I was desperate to see, came back drunk to the hotel in the early morning—and I'd never seen him that way on tour before. Sure, he always sipped whiskey onstage, but getting drunk was different, and when he tumbled into our room, he couldn't even speak about the earthquake that had happened earlier. The next morning, it was the same as it had been in Montauk, Billy apologizing profusely while making more promises and excuses: it was the sake, he wasn't used to it, he had drank on an empty stomach, it would never happen again . . .

BUT LIFE can turn on a dime, as I learned after Olivier's death, and a little more than a month after Tokyo, something monumental happened. And while I can't say we singlehandedly brought down the Iron Curtain, I do believe that Billy—and to a lesser extent, Alexa Ray and I—played a role in helping chip away at the age-old divide between the East and the West that had existed for decades, since the start of the Cold War.

Our trip to the Soviet Union was months in the making after the country's head of state, Mikhail Gorbachev, with his progressive ideas about *glasnost* (openness) and *perestroika* (restructuring), invited Billy to perform there. At the time, only a handful of American musicians had ever played inside Soviet lines, and Billy, who insisted on bringing his own equipment and broadcasting his performances live, became the first American ever to put on a fully staged rock-and-roll show inside the USSR for the rest of the world to see. When we went to the Soviet Union in July 1987, I think we both believed Billy would be able to use his music to break down barriers and unite the world, which was a beautiful thought. What made it even more magical for me was that, along with his own keyboards, guitars, and drum kits, Billy wanted to bring his wife and young daughter, which was something not many foreigners did, and the Soviets were enchanted by Alexa Ray.

Our trip began in Tbilisi, Georgia, an ancient city of cobblestone streets and medieval churches more than a thousand miles south of Moscow, that Billy was eager to visit for its Georgian chanting, which is so strong and intense that it creates vibrations that can purportedly heal the sick. In a monastery high on a hill overlooking all of Tbilisi with an old organ grinder and a monkey who sat outside its crumbling entrance, Billy and I joined a chant circle, as the local musicians invited us to lock arms in a circle so that we could all hear and feel firsthand the power and beauty of their voices. Moved by the experience, Billy and his band returned the favor, singing the Beach Boys' "Good Vibrations," then "Georgia on My Mind" in a stunning, international exchange of music that made us all feel as though we were the same, regardless of which side of the East–West divide we lived.

Afterward, one of the local musicians hosted a big banquet dinner for us inside his private home, where the Georgian singers, eager to welcome us, wrapped us in bearskins and gave us cow horns filled with wine to drink. Knowing I was a vegetarian, Billy whispered to me to take just a sip, which I did—anything for world peace. We were then escorted to the city's old opera house, where Billy was scheduled to do only a sound check, but after he saw the hundreds of people who had turned out only to get a glimpse of him in person, in addition to the spread of food the theater had laid out for us when there was barely enough meat and potatoes to sell in the local markets, Billy felt indebted to perform. The only problem was that the opera house had no sound system or infrastructure that would have allowed Billy's crew to set one up, so he had to sing at the top of his lungs to reach the audience in the loges and balconies. By the end of the night, his throat, already strained from eleven months of near-constant performances, was shredded.

After Tbilisi, we flew to Moscow, where Billy saw a doctor who injected him with steroids, poured something down his throat, and then, with a grand, self-important flourish, produced some "very powerful American medicine," shaking out two mints from a box of Tic Tacs and telling Billy to take one in the morning and one at night. This made us very wary of everything else the doctor had just done, but at the same time, I knew Billy was desperate to heal his voice: there was a ton of pressure on him, not only from politicians, peacemakers, and music lovers worldwide but also in his own mind, evinced by the fact that he'd spent two million dollars of his own money to make sure the Soviet people got the American rock-and-roll show they deserved. Many in the West also saw Billy as an ambassador of American culture and democracy and hoped that he might be able to help bring down the Iron Curtain with the power of his voice—that is, if his voice still worked.

Pumped up on pressure and steroids, Billy played his first show in Moscow as I watched from the front row, where it became apparent to me he'd have to work extra hard to animate the "oil painting" in front of him—a term he used to describe a subdued and motionless audience. Next to me in the front row were only stoic security guards and stuffy bureaucrats, which made it more difficult for Billy to engage the crowd. I think everyone felt watched—I certainly did, corroborated by the people we had met on the street while there, including two clowns from the circus who told us they couldn't speak with us for too long out of fear of repercussions. (Those clowns, incidentally, became our friends and followed us to all the shows, where they were some of the best audience members I'd ever seen and whom Billy later wrote about in the song "Leningrad," on the *Storm Front* album.)

At his shows, Billy wanted his Soviet audience to feel safe, or at least safe enough to sing and dance, so he poured everything he had into his performances, practically doing backflips off the piano to energize the crowd. I've never seen anyone give so much of himself for his art, and his efforts paid off. By the end of the first show, everyone was on their feet and screaming, and Billy, dripping with sweat, dove into the crowd, allowing himself to be carried overhead on the hands of the Soviet people, showing them how much he trusted their enthusiasm and support.

The next night, though, it was the same thing all over again as the crowd filed into Moscow's Olympic Stadium, looking as solemn as the lonely figures in Edward Hopper's famous oil painting *Nighthawks*. I knew Billy was already past the point of exhaustion, worn down by the pressure, the press, the sightseeing, and the consecutive shows—and no number of Tic Tacs or vodka shots was helping soothe his throat, which was worse than it had been in Tbilisi. And then, when an American film crew, there to shoot a documentary on his Soviet tour, began illuminating the audience members with bright lights, causing them to freeze like deer caught in headlights, Billy snapped.

"Stop lighting the audience!" he yelled. "Stop it! Let me do my show for Chrissake!"

But the film crew didn't stop, and from the front row, I watched in horror as Billy suddenly lifted his piano and flipped it over on its side, overwhelmed by his own outrage and frustration. While continuing to sing—astoundingly, in perfect timing with the music—he then jumped to the front of the stage, ignoring his band as they kept playing, and grabbed a microphone stand and smashed it against the floor. Leaping around like a madman, Billy then snatched another mic stand and, after belting out a line of lyrics and taking a karate-like kick, beat the stand against a different piano, sending chunks of metal flying up into the air and hurtling right past my head in the front row.

I was shocked. Never before had I seen such fury from Billy, who later claimed the outburst was all part of his performance. In the moment, I was scared, though, and, afterward, disappointed, given that up until that moment, all the press on his Soviet tour had been glowing.

But like Billy, I could talk my way out of it: passion, after all, is part and parcel of great art.

By the time we left the Soviet Union, after Billy had played six shows total in Moscow and Leningrad, his tour was already being heralded as a turning point in East–West relations. That he had brought along Alexa Ray and me also showed the rest of the world that the Soviet Union was safe, welcoming, and ready to embrace all aspects of Western culture.

OTHER THINGS happened on our Soviet trip, too, and while it didn't make headlines—at least not at the time—the tour helped to confirm my suspicions about Frank Weber, Billy's manager and ex-brother-in-law. Eventually, my suspicions became the only reason Billy and I didn't end up in financial ruin, though the ordeal would place an incredible strain on our marriage.

The Frank story is a sad story, but it's one worth telling, even if only briefly.

Shortly after Billy divorced his first wife and manager, Elizabeth Weber, he appointed her brother, Frank, to take over as his manager, and while Frank was friendly enough, things with him never added up, at least not in my eyes. When I told Billy he should look into how Frank was handling his finances, he got angry—not with Frank, but with me.

"Don't even talk to me about Frank," he snapped. "Because I've known him a hell of a lot longer than I've known you."

His words burned. Wasn't I supposed to be his confidante, his best friend, his partner for life? At the same time, Billy was extremely loyal to all his friends, and while the press later reported that Frank was like a brother to him, I believe he was more like a father, filling the shoes Billy's dad had left when he deserted Billy and his mother when Billy was only eight.

For months, I didn't bring up it again, but eventually, a forensic attorney told us that Frank had allegedly siphoned more than thirty million dollars from Billy's profits over the years. In 1989, Billy sued Frank for ninety million dollars, and after months of a tiring court case, Frank's side finally settled, but with no admission of guilt. The case wore on Billy, though, and while our marriage had already been through several storms by then, Frank's betrayal changed Billy in indelible ways. He became dark, withdrawn, and stressed as he tried to pump out more hits to recoup his financial losses while drinking more—a lot more. Like a boat on a dark sea without a map or a motor, Billy became lost, and as much and as hard as I tried, I couldn't light his way back to safe harbor. For the rest of our marriage, I don't think Billy ever found land again.

One thing I've learned is that when life gets tough, people often assume other identities. The very reason Billy became "the Piano Man" in the first place, for example, was because he created a new anonymous persona in Los Angeles to escape a bad record deal in New York, when he was just launching his career. As for me, when things began to darken between Billy and me, whether I did it intentionally or not, I channeled my childhood love of Westerns and went from "cover girl to cowgirl," as one magazine put it, herding cattle on horseback in the Hamptons and dressing more like a rancher's daughter than someone attending a polo match, which is more typical of the eastern end of Long Island.

During that time, I also read the bestselling novel *Even Cowgirls Get the Blues*, by Tom Robbins. I loved the book, but unlike its title, I was determined to be that one cowgirl who never got the blues again.

CHAPTER

18

Baraaaaaaaag!

The noise was deafening, and it was all I could hear at first, booming from above as I crouched lower on the roof of the old Land Cruiser. The sound surprised me, since only minutes ago, we'd been hurtling through the game preserve, the only noises that of the coughing diesel engine and the voice of the driver as he called to me from inside the jeep to duck left or right, out of the way of oncoming bushes and branches. Just moments before, I'd been standing on the Land Cruiser's roof as we whooshed through the bush, turning back at times so that sports photographer John Zimmerman, who trailed us in another jeep, could grab shots of me posing in front of any zebras or giraffes we passed. But the shot of me that swimsuit editor Jule Campbell really wanted was with a great African elephant, which had been elusive all afternoon—until that very moment, when a great African elephant found us as much as we found her.

Baraaaaaaaag!

The elephant, standing only feet away from us, trumpeted again, and while everyone inside the Land Cruiser was elated to have finally found one of the massive mammals, those on the outside, by which I mean me—dressed only in a skimpy bikini top and tightly rolled thigh-high shorts—were alarmed. From the top of the mud-spattered truck, I could see something the others could not: a baby elephant, cowering behind the mammoth mother we'd just encountered. And if we'd learned anything from our safari tracker (the same one who had once guided Ernest Hemingway into that very preserve), it was that hell hath no fury like a mother elephant protecting her young.

"Start purring!" the tracker yelled, as the mother trumpeted again.

I immediately did what I was told, imitating the sound of a cat by rolling my tongue the way the tracker had taught us that morning, when he told us the sound can help soothe an enraged elephant, as both he and the driver began to open and close the truck's doors, mimicking the motion of the mother's flapping ears—another technique that can disarm the animal. But at the forefront of my mind was something else: I had my own young to protect.

"Please take care of my baby!" I screamed at the crew while anxiously peering down through the truck's sunroof so I could see Alexa Ray, who was sitting in the back seat, looking frightened. "Make sure she's strapped in!"

That day, I learned a lot about the matriarchal society of the African elephant and how wise, loving, and fierce the females can be, which I found inspiring. And as soon as I locked eyes with the mama, she turned around to retreat back into the bush, because I'm pretty sure she could tell she was dealing with another fierce mama, just like her.

We moms have to stick together!

For years since that day, I've participated in programs protecting elephants, working alongside the First Lady of Kenya Margaret Kenyatta and another of Africa's most notable wildlife conservationists, Dr. Paula Kahumbu.

I'd brought Alexa Ray to Kenya for that year's *Sports Illustrated* swimsuit shoot, and until that moment, my biggest worry had been her refusal to wear anything khaki. The strong cotton material can help protect you on safari from everything from stinging insects to charging animals, but she had insisted on wearing her favorite brightly colored floral Kenzo dress. It was only right, then, that such a dedicated fashionista would get herself featured as the youngest girl ever in the Swimsuit Issue, which she did when she ran into a shot, struck a perfect pose, then ran back out again, all in the blink of an eye—so fast that the moment could be captured only by a sports photographer's speed drive.

BY THE time the issue came out in early 1989, with my derriere on the back cover and the caption "Christie's back!," Billy was back in the studio, recording his next album, *Storm Front*. While I listened in the control booth as he sang "I Go to Extremes," I began to wonder what those lyrics might be saying about our relationship. Ever since he had learned about Frank Weber's betrayal, we had begun to experience some of those extremes, mostly from the pressure Billy felt to keep writing Top 40 hits and a resulting uptick in his drinking. At times, I even began to feel like liquor was the other woman in our marriage and that I had become the "bad" cop, the one who asked him to stop after one or two drinks. When he sang the lyric about "leaving the scene of the crime" in "I Go to Extremes," I began to wonder what crime he was talking about.

At the time, though, the whole world seemed to be functioning at extremes—which was the inspiration for Billy's number one hit song "We Didn't Start the Fire," also on *Storm Front*. News was circulating around the globe at rapid-fire speed, and I felt that people were more overwhelmed than ever before by what was happening in the world—the AIDS epidemic, the collapse of communism, the Space Shuttle *Challenger* disaster, Reaganomics. Even so, I chose to focus on all the positive aspects of Billy's album and what he wrote into his songs, including how he felt like he was in the "prime" of his life in "I Go to Extremes."

AROUND THE same time, I was also focused on our dream home in East Hampton, which we watched from the tiny guesthouse next door as it continued to be renovated and rebuilt. That fall, even though our house was far from being finished, we decided to throw a big party for Alexa Ray's fifth birthday a few months early, as we usually did, when it was still warm and because her actual birthday is so close to Christmas. Our house had a beautiful front yard with a huge field and a massive oak tree, under which I set up a long table topped by flowers, cupcakes, strewn candy, and big gift bags for the children, each bag bursting with fun toys and trinkets. That year, my parents had given Alexa Ray a trampoline for her birthday, which I set up in the front yard, and we also had a carousel and a pony-drawn hay wagon, so the kids could take rides across the field, along with a bar for the adults, all of which made it feel like a real carnival. It was the first big birthday party we had thrown Alexa Ray, and while everyone had a blast, she didn't want to leave her room. She was shy, and it was all way too much for her, and after that day, I learned to scale it down when it came to celebrations for my daughter.

Many of our friends were also at the party, like Chevy Chase and his wife, Jayni; the actor Kathleen Turner and her husband, Jay Weiss; *Rolling Stone* publisher Jann Wenner and his wife, Jane; and the singer Mick Jones and his wife, Ann. My parents flew in from California, too, and Billy's mom, Rosalind Nyman, whom we all called Nanny Roz, also came.

Everyone loved Nanny Roz, who was a real character, always wearing a funny little hat. But despite that Billy gave her anything she could ever want or need, she still tried to stuff as much food or other swag into her purse at every event she attended—I think she thought she was being helpful by preventing anything from going to waste. And when she arrived at Alexa Ray's party that year, she went straight for the kids' table, where she started trying to cram gift bags into her purse. To me, it was just Nanny Roz being Nanny Roz, but when I sidled over to ask her what she was doing, Billy saw the interaction and not only became embarrassed, but also mad at me for inviting her in the first place.

Afterward, when all our guests started to filter away, I turned to look for Billy, to say, "Well, honey, we did it—that was a hit," but I realized he had filtered away, too. At first, I thought he was just blowing off steam, but when he didn't come back for dinner that night, I started to call our friends—without suggesting that anything was amiss, but to ask, casually, if he had stopped by their place or was out with someone somewhere for a drink. When he didn't come home at all that night or the next morning, I began to have visions of his car wrapped around a tree and developed a panic I couldn't shake. I thought about calling the police, but because Billy was famous, I knew what such a call would bring—instant media coverage—which was why, throughout our relationship, I usually suffered through these incidents alone.

Sure enough, though, Billy finally reappeared two days later, profusely apologetic, with some story of how he had had a pain in his back and had had to take a pill for it, which had caused him to pull over so he wouldn't get into a crash. In my eyes, I was just thankful he was alive and all in one piece, and I believed his promises that the drinking would stop.

But it didn't.

AROUND THE same time Billy began to drink more, I began to ride more, spending hours at the ranch where I kept Belle Star, which was the oldest working ranch in the United States, surrounded by acres of preserved coastal park on the eastern end of Montauk—the end of "the End," which is what people still call the town today. The ranch's owners, Rusty and his wife, Diane, came from a long line of cowboys, and the three of us, along with another friend and her husband, spent many happy afternoons that summer riding our horses down to the ocean, then into the sunset. On special evenings, Billy would drive our old red truck down to meet us on a deserted stretch of bay beach, bringing Alexa Ray with him, along with ice-cold beer, fresh veggies, local fish, and firewood for a cookout. Those were perfect summer evenings, riding our horses back to the ranch under the starlight, the moon as full as our bellies. Enthralled by it all, I even bought a second horse that year, named Blue Jean, so we would have another seat on the trail for friends to ride.

The following winter, Billy went on tour for *Storm Front*, the longest tour of his career, lasting nearly a year and a half as he performed nonstop to try to earn back the money Frank had allegedly stolen from him. But now that Alexa Ray was in school, I couldn't join him as often as I would have liked. Not only was I working a ton, but Billy and I also wanted her to have as normal a childhood as possible, attending a school where she could make friends and have regular piano lessons and playdates. So, while Billy was away on tour, I stayed home, taking only a handful of trips outside work to see him.

One night while Alexa Ray and I were alone in the guesthouse in East Hampton, I was flipping through TV channels when I suddenly saw a horse doing something I'd never seen a horse do before, on a sports station I'd normally never have watched. The horse looked as if it were dancing across the screen, its two front legs simultaneously swooshing to the right, then to the left while the rider remained perfectly still, not appearing to prompt the horse in any way. For more than an hour, I watched, transfixed, as other cowboys rode their horses the same way, and I started to understand that the competition required the rider to "cut" a cow away from a herd while the horse held it there by swinging its body in between the cow and the herd, as the rider tried to appear as if he or she was exerting no effort the entire time. The sport was called cutting, and at the end of the competition, when an advertisement came on for a how-to-cut video, I scrambled to find a pen and a piece of paper to take down the phone number. The product being advertised in the next commercial, a mechanical cow to help practice cutting, sounded even more intriguing.

Minutes later, I was the proud owner of the video and my very own fake cow.

By that time, I was already fully in my cowgirl phase, hooked on Western-style riding and dressing in jeans or a long southwestern-style skirt, oversize belts, and cowboy hats and boots, a departure from the delicate florals and preppy prints typical of the Hamptons. That spring, when I brought the how-to-cut video to the ranch, it seemed to bring out the cowpoke in everyone there, and my friends and I started training our quarter horses to cut. But soon, we realized we needed specially trained cutting horses, so we all chipped in and bought a trailer on which we shipped several horses from Texas to the ranch—which is how I ended up with my favorite horse of all, Goodbar Miss, a muscular brown beauty with a white blaze and a honey-blond mane and tail. All of us at the ranch began to practice cutting every day, and soon enough, after we had outgrown our mechanical cows, we started to rent real cattle—something everyone else in the Hamptons found fascinating—and driving all over the mid-Atlantic to compete in local cutting competitions.

By the following summer, my ranch friends and I were having so much fun with the sport that we decided to hold our very own cutting competition, in Montauk. For the event, we hired professional judges from Texas and Montana and placed ads in equestrian magazines across the country, which attracted dozens of real riders. When the press learned about the competition, TV stations flooded the ranch, and the whole Hamptons turned out for the event, making it an instant hit. Billy, who got a real kick out of my cowgirl phase, brought Alexa Ray in her little cowgirl boots and ten-gallon hat, and the two of them cheered me from the sidelines.

Afterward, one of the judges sidled up to me and asked, in his long Texas drawl, if I would be interested in competing in the National Cutting Horse Association Futurity championship in Fort Worth, Texas, that December.

"Whoa, Nelly, what did you say? You want me to come to Texas?" I said, stunned and delighted at the same time. "But what will I do about a horse to ride?"

"Don't worry," the judge said. "I'll set you up with our best trainer, Punk Carter, and he'll put you on his best horse, and you'll have the best time."

Sure as shootin', he was right: I did have the best time. And while I was there, I figured this tenderfooted city slicker ought to win the futurity by hook or by crook.

On the day of the actual competition, I was more nervous than I'd ever been for any modeling shoot or TV commercial. That year, I ended up finished third in my category, which was astonishing, while I won the event outright the following year—and along with it, a championship belt I still wear everywhere with everything, from sundresses to evening gowns. I also won a saddle and a trip to Hawaii, which I gave to Punk and his wife as a token of my gratitude.

In my eyes, I've always been part cowgirl, part sailor girl, and shortly before the futurity, Billy bought me a sweet wooden sloop, rigged to sail singlehandedly, which I kept in Three Mile Harbor, in East Hampton, near where we docked our fishing boat. We both loved being out on the water and had always done so together, but after the Frank Weber incident, Billy started to take more fishing trips with the guys, while I started sailing with friends. We still shared many beautiful moments together, but there were some jarring events that became more difficult to ignore or excuse, including one that occurred in a New York City restaurant one night.

That evening, Billy, Alexa Ray, and I had gone out for a cozy dinner together and had just sat down and ordered food. Sometime in between the salad and the main dish, Billy excused himself to go to the bathroom. When our dinner began to turn cold and he still hadn't returned, I asked the waiter to check the men's room to make sure he was okay, but he told me that Billy wasn't there. I was so confused as to where he could have gone, and after I looked around the restaurant to see if maybe he had bumped into a friend, the maître d' came over and whispered that someone had seen Billy going into the bar next door, where he was having a drink. As soon as he told me, I thought I was going to faint, and when Alexa Ray looked at me inquisitively, asking where Daddy had gone and whether he was okay, I felt like everyone in the restaurant was suddenly wondering the same thing. Without touching the food, I paid the bill and left with Alexa Ray to go home, leaving Billy next door to drink.

OUR LIFE went on, though, and enough time passed between these incidents with Billy that it felt more like a wonderful marriage than anything else. But when the rumors of his possible affairs started, it made sustaining the wonder even more difficult.

I was in our New York City apartment when Billy called from San Francisco to tell me I would see something the next day in the newspaper that I wouldn't like—and he was right. The day after he called, the *National Enquirer* ran a story with the headline "CAUGHT—Billy Joel Two-Timing Gorgeous Wife Christie Brinkley," with incriminating photos of him holding a bottle of champagne while getting into a limo alone with a woman. According to Billy, the woman was just a good friend's girlfriend, and the press hadn't included the friend in the photographs expressly because they had wanted to create a sensational story.

That sounded possible, but I wasn't 100 percent convinced. And I didn't like that feeling.

"You're so big on calling the other girl while I'm on the phone," I said crossly, referring to the time he asked me to be on the line when he called Elle Macpherson to tell her that he wanted to be exclusive with me. "Why don't you call this woman now and ask her about her boyfriend while I'm on the line?"

But Billy refused. And because I desperately wanted to make things work, I refused to think about it anymore, choosing instead to believe him.

The summer of our cattle-cutting competition in Montauk, Billy and I finally moved into the main house in East Hampton, more than five years after we bought it. People say real estate stress can kill even the best marriages, so the fact that we lasted nine years through so much real estate stress, both in renovating the Hamptons house and moving multiple times in the city, was testament, I think, to the strength of our relationship.

Either way, when I finally saw our dream home completed, rising fully formed from the ocean's edge like Venus from her seashell, I felt both overjoyed and overwhelmed. The house still needed a ton of work to make it our own, which, for Billy, meant raising his own yardarm. He had always loved a good yardarm, having pointed out every single one we ever passed during our road trips, so it was a big moment the day our flag went up on the pole outside our East

Hampton home, indicating to him that he—and we—had finally found our place.

For me, our home was all about the garden, and enchanted by many of our neighbors' lawns, I had started to learn how to grow flowers like foxglove and thistle, along with vegetables that we could pick off the vine and eat, which launched what has become a lifelong love of gardening. Hoping to reduce the huge tick population around our property, I also bought a dozen guinea hens—during my trip to Kenya with *Sports Illustrated*, I had learned they like to eat ticks—in addition to an incubator, so I could hatch my own chicks. (In part due to my zeal for guinea hens, Stony Brook University conducted a study that showed I was right about the birds: they do help control ticks on the Eastern Seaboard. This prompted Rep. George Hochbrueckner, a U.S. congressman from New York, to introduce legislation allowing the hens to be used for that purpose throughout Long Island. Shortly afterward, *Time* ran a story about me and my guinea hens, which felt like a big win.)

THAT FALL, I decided to stay in the Hamptons rather than move back to the city, enrolling Alexa Ray in a school at the end of Further Lane. By that time, Billy was constantly away on the *Storm Front* tour, and as the days turned shorter and colder and all our friends trickled back into the city for good, I found myself very much alone with my little girl, the two of us in a big house far from people in the middle of winter. While I loved being by the ocean and surrounded by nature, I had always thought I'd share the experience with my husband. Now, though, the only ones I was sharing it with were my growing flock of nearly one hundred guinea hens—that incubator!—along with the little foxes that ran through our fields, and as Billy's tour stretched on and on, so did my feelings of loneliness and isolation.

305

After the winter holidays were over, eager to escape the seclusion, I took Alexa Ray to Fiji for a short stopover before we were to meet Billy in Australia following his show schedule in the Philippines. But on our last day in Fiji, after I came dripping wet into the hotel lobby from a scuba diving expedition, the concierge told me that all flights into and out of the Philippines had been grounded indefinitely because war had broken out. In the hotel's little thatched-hut lobby, I learned that the United States had just declared war on Iraq and that America needed to be able to deploy all servicepeople, ships, and aircraft out of the Philippines to the Gulf War. That meant Billy was now stuck in the Philippines, and anxious for international news, nearly every evening, I'd join others gathered around a shortwave radio inside a grass hut on hotel grounds to listen as the scratchy voices of the world faded in and out, the radio operator turning the dials until he found a station that would give us the updates we all wanted to hear.

Eventually, Billy was able to fly out of the Philippines, and the three of us joyfully reunited in Australia, where he was scheduled to start a seven-week tour. Because he and I had been to the country so often on tour, we had a home away from home of sorts there—that is, the same suite at the same hotel on Sydney Harbour. After we landed, we stayed there for a few weeks while Billy did shows in the city, then headed to Perth, where he was booked for more shows. When we returned to Sydney, though, we discovered that the hotel had given our favorite suite to Frank Sinatra, who was also there on tour, accompanied by his wife, Barbara.

After Barbara somehow learned we'd been displaced, she insisted on having Billy and me up to their suite for dinner, where the hotel staff had set up tables topped by dozens of platters of gourmet dishes and finger food. While we were having cocktails with Barbara, Steve Lawrence and Eydie Gormé, who made up the musical duo Steve and Eydie, and who had just opened for Frank, came bouncing into the suite, amped up on the kind of energy typical of musicians after a performance. As they mixed themselves drinks, they told us hurriedly how Frank had been a little displeased that night because his prompter had broken mid-performance, but never mind, they said, as they sat down at a piano inside the suite to play and sing for us.

But right when Eydie hit a high note, the door of the suite suddenly swung open, and Frank Sinatra himself walked in.

He paused before turning his head slowly to scan the room, eventually stopping his gaze on Billy and me. "Who the fuck are these people in my room?" he said with a sneer.

"Why, honey," Barbara said with an effervescent smile, "this is Billy Joel and Christie Brinkley."

"I don't care who the fuck they are," Frank grumbled angrily. "I want everyone to get out of my room now!"

Billy and I didn't hesitate to slip out, giving Barbara a look of understanding and mouthing a silent "thank you" as we closed the door behind us. Once we were in the elevator, though, we doubled over in surprise and even a little bit of delight that the great Frank Sinatra had told us to get the fuck out.

The next day, while Billy was performing, I went out for dinner with my friend Sue, who was married to Billy's Australian music producer. Afterward, while we were waiting for our husbands to join us in the hotel bar, none other than Frank Sinatra walked in. I braced myself, getting ready to hear him yell for the manager to clear the place, but instead, when his eyes fell on me, he smiled and started to snap his fingers and sing, to the tune of "Love and Marriage," the lyric "Christie Brinkley, Christie Brinkley, Christie, Christie, Christie Brinkley" in syncopated rhythm with the song. Soon, everyone in the bar was snapping their fingers, too, and laughing as Frank serenaded me, which was a far better outcome than a buffet dinner in any suite.

A FEW days later, Alexa Ray and I left Australia before Billy did to spend a little time with my parents, who had moved from California to Kona, Hawaii. After Billy wrapped his Oceania tour, he joined us in Honolulu. Because he had been abroad for so many months, I had hoped that our time together in Hawaii would be ours alone as a family, without the stress of travel, constant shows, or other distractions. But life turns on a dime—or, in this instance, on a phone call.

The same night Billy arrived, a friend from Australia called to tell me, slowly and reluctantly, that she'd seen an article in a Melbourne paper with photos of Billy out romantically with an Australian actress. When I heard it, the phone fell from my hand, as I started to feel my heart sink alongside it. I looked at Alexa Ray playing with her dolls on the patio outside our room and felt like dropping to the floor to sob next to my fallen heart, where it lay trampled on the ground.

I can't remember what I said to Billy or how I said it—details always blur when emotions dip and dive faster than a roller coaster— but that same evening, I told him I knew about the Australian actress and that he should find another place to sleep. He left the room outraged, and when he came back later that night, visibly and audibly drunk, I had already locked the doors to both the suite and the outside patio. Billy banged angrily on the front door for some time, then went around to the patio, which was on the ground floor, and banged on the glass patio doors for a while. When I didn't answer, he did something unimaginable: he picked up a chaise longue and threw it right through the doors of the patio, shattering the glass into a million pieces.

In that instant, I felt like the glass door and I were made from the same material, and that I had shattered into a million pieces, too.

I grabbed Alexa Ray and rushed out of the room. While I couldn't quite believe I was literally running away from the man I loved so much, I didn't ever want to see him like that—and I certainly didn't want our daughter to see him like that. I took Alexa Ray down the hall to my parents, who had booked a separate suite at the same hotel, but soon enough, because the breaking glass had caused such a racket, the hotel's manager was outside their room with a team of security guards, demanding to speak with me. Despite everything I felt in the moment—fear, betrayal, anger—I knew what to do: I told the guards that the broken door had been an accident and that they didn't need to report it. Even though I was emotional, I loved Billy and didn't want the incident to become a news story (even though it did anyway, weeks later, with many details incorrectly reported).

The next morning, after Billy had sobered up, the only thing I wanted was to smooth things over, so I chose to believe him once again, telling myself what he had told me, that the Australian actress had only interviewed him for a talk show, that there were no romantic dinners or outings, and that he wanted to be with only me. And just like that, we repaired the fissure in our marriage faster than the hotel could replace that glass door, which remained jagged outside our empty room for hours.

But, then again, incident-and-repair had become our pattern, even if, slowly, things between us were becoming more difficult to mend.

From Honolulu, we flew to Careyes, in Mexico, where Billy was scheduled to resume his tour in the capital city, so that I could show him where I had lived that one summer with Filippo, with whom I'd remained friends. But while Billy adored both Careyes and Filippo, it didn't take long for things to deteriorate again. Our first full day at the resort, Billy excused himself at lunch, saying he wanted to get something from our room, but when he didn't return for some time, a waiter suggested I might find him at a bar that had recently been built down by the beach. So, I paid the bill, gave Alexa Ray to the nanny, and went down to the beach bar, where I found Billy holding a whiskey in one hand while holding court with a coterie of women who'd come from a nearby Club Med. I didn't say a word but watched unseen from a distance as the women fawned over him, constantly touching him, throwing their heads back in laughter, and leaning in again. They were doing all the moves while Billy himself was doing his best album cover poses, eager to please and charm his adoring female fans. I was stunned by how oblivious he was to the fact that he was supposed to be with Alexa Ray and me at lunch, but there he was, and I knew then that I had had enough. I went back to our room alone, where he joined me hours later.

That fall, we stayed in the city to watch the Macy's Thanksgiving Day Parade from our apartment on the Upper West Side, which was so close to the route that you could reach out the window and practically touch the balloons as they floated by, Spiderman almost gliding through our living room at eye level. It was such a unique experience and a happy place to be that we always invited lots of friends over for Thanksgiving breakfast, many of whom ended up staying for dinner as well. But later that day, before I could serve dinner, Billy slipped out, taking the elevator down to find a bar where he could drink, perhaps among his adoring admirers. When my friends gave me that look of surprise and pity, I felt the empty hole inside my stomach spread wider than anything that could ever possibly be sated by a Thanksgiving meal.

WHILE THE issues with Billy worsened, my work still tripped along at the same pace, even though I was in my late thirties—practically geriatric for a model in the early 1990s. But there I was, still doing dozens of magazine shoots and covers, including one for *Ladies' Home Journal* where I appeared in a swimsuit, claiming it would be my last swimsuit cover ever: at age thirty-eight, after eighteen years of doing so, I was tired of sucking in my stomach. (Spoiler alert: It wasn't my last swimsuit cover or last time when I felt like I had to suck in my stomach.)

There were also TV commercials, for CoverGirl and other advertisers, like Prell, MasterCard, and Nissan, and two years before the Honolulu incident, I launched my own version of a Barbie doll, called the Real Model doll, and asked Cheryl Tiegs, Beverly Johnson, and Paulina Porizkova if they would partner on it with me. I wanted little girls to have a toy based on real women—women who had passports, spoke multiple languages, and traveled all the time, as nearly all models do—rather than a doll that lived in the Dreamhouse with Ken. To increase the good intentions, we donated 30 percent of all profits to the Make-A-Wish Foundation, but the toys ended up being casualties of the economic recession sparked by the Gulf War.

In the summer of 1992, CNN asked me to host my own show, called *Living in the '90s with Christie Brinkley*, a lifestyle program that aired weekday mornings, each day of the week dedicated to a different subject in fashion, health, food, travel, or entertainment. At first, I loved working at the same place every day, a consistency that's rare in the modeling world, and I was proud and excited about the show, eager to make it as compelling for viewers as I could. But soon, it became clear that the network was interested mostly in recycling old footage and that I would have little to no creative control or input in the show. While I wanted to do exciting travel segments—for example, on trips to Europe or even closer places in coastal California—the producers liked the idea of repackaging old footage into shiny new segments, such as a travel episode on visiting the prison at Alcatraz, which didn't seem to be a reason anyone would want to tune into a show I was hosting.

To liven the show up, I began editing my own trips—like the one I had taken to Fiji—and doing quick wraparound videos with information that viewers might actually be able to use, like makeup tips and how to do a French twist using only one pin. While viewers loved these quick tips and tricks and even wrote into the station to ask for more, the producers seemed determined to make the show as stale as possible. Three months after the program first launched, when the network asked me to sign a long-term contract, I told them I couldn't work on the show if it remained the same and that I wanted to come up with more creative pieces with the help of a dedicated producer. But they wanted to stick with the status quo, so we mutually agreed—or so I thought—to part ways.

Days later, I was on a shoot in Florida with CoverGirl when the first of several articles appeared reporting that I'd been "fired" from the show by CNN due to poor ratings. I was so stunned and upset that I had to take an early lunch break so I could call my lawyer. While I knew that I had left the show of my own accord and that the network had wanted me to stay, I was still shocked at how the news media were portraying it.

If there was an upside to the incident, it was that Billy, who had always insisted his suspected infidelity was only media spin, may have been right all along: maybe the news media did like to create their own truth from time to time, especially if it made for a more interesting or salacious story.

THE FOLLOWING spring, something beautiful happened between Billy and me that may have been the last meaningful measure of our marriage: I created a painting for the cover of his 1993 album, *River of Dreams*, which would turn out to be the final studio album of his career—the symbolism of which, all these years later, has never been lost on me.

The album cover came about organically, after I was inspired to paint what I was hearing in the studio, telling Billy he was in no way obligated to use my work, recommend it to his record company, or even like it. For the next two weeks, I painted nonstop, working late into the night, just as I had twenty years before, long before I was a model, when I stayed up past midnight drawing in my Paris atelier as my radio hummed softly in the background and the whole world slept outside my windows. Even though I had never worked with oil paints before, I was in heaven. I loved the process, and as it turned out, Billy loved the art—and when he showed it to his record company, they loved it, too, which is how it became the album's cover, later recognized for its design after it made both the best and worst covers list. Alexa Ray and I also appeared in the music video for the title song from *River of Dreams*, and months later, an astronaut sent me a picture of himself holding up my art while Earth floated behind him—the only album cover ever taken into outer space. I felt flattered and hopeful.

Days before he kicked off the *River of Dreams* tour, Billy and the guys from the band were in East Hampton so they could rehearse together, often spending time in our house on Further Lane. One evening, after we had all had dinner out in town, everyone came back to the house, and immediately, Billy went into the kitchen to get a pasta he had made earlier in the week. When he couldn't find it in the refrigerator, he became furious, so I started to search the fridge, too. But it wasn't there, so I told him that either someone had eaten it or the housekeeper had thrown it out. Nothing I said, though, abated his anger, so I decided it was easier just to make him a fresh pot of pasta, which seemed to appease him at first, and he started eating it directly out of the pot as soon as it was finished, when it was still hot on the stove, all while talking with some of the guys, who had gathered in the kitchen as they almost always did. He kept talking and eating, twisting the pasta with a fork and scooping it up over the stove . . . until someone disagreed with something he had said, which made him angry again, although now he was slurring his words.

Then he suddenly looked down at the pot of pasta and realized it was all gone. "Okay," he barked, as all conversation in the kitchen ground to a halt. "Who ate all my pasta?"

Everyone in the room turned to look at him and then at one another, assuming that he was joking. I began to laugh, which prompted a few others to chuckle, too, but that made Billy irate—which was when we realized he wasn't kidding.

"Billy, *you* just ate it," I said as softly as I could.

But Billy went ballistic. "Everyone get the fuck out of my house!" he screamed as he began shoving his bandmates out of the kitchen. "You come here and you eat all my pasta like that? Get out of my house! All of you!"

Suddenly, he was acting delusional in a way I'd never seen before. I was so scared that I couldn't think, and when one of the guys in the band grabbed my arm, pulling me out of the house with the rest of them, I went along.

"You're coming with us," the bandmate said to me. "We're not leaving you alone with him like this."

"But Alexa," I cried. Alexa Ray was asleep upstairs. "I have to get Alexa!"

Despite their pleas that I come with them, I told the guys I had to go back inside the house and stay with my daughter—I didn't want to wake her up and have her see her dad like that. So, I slipped quietly back into the house, tiptoeing upstairs to her room and carrying her to our bedroom, tucking her into bed there before flipping the lock on our bedroom door. But Billy must have heard me, because he rushed over to the bedroom and began pounding on the door, demanding that I let him in.

"I've got Alexa Ray in here," I said as quietly as I could through the door. "Please, you don't want to wake her. You don't want her to see you like this."

Thank goodness Billy, despite how drunk he may have been, knew that I was right: he wouldn't want his little girl to see him like that. And after I said it, he left, retreating into one of the guest rooms where he could sleep it off.

The next day, I asked him for a divorce. It wasn't the first time I had threatened to leave, and even though he was about to go on tour for months, we both knew then that things had reached a breaking point.

To be clear, I never wanted to end things with Billy. I read every self-help book I could find while, together, we went to a see a string of psychiatrists, psychologists, and other medical doctors. I did everything for our marriage, constantly working to make myself, our home, and everything around us into whatever he could possibly want or hope for. I continually told him how much I loved him, making sure he always felt adored and appreciated, because he was. But his drinking was bigger than the both of us—booze was the other woman, and it was beginning to seem that, he preferred to be with "her" rather than with me.

Over time, I also started taking long trips by myself, riding horses with friends along the Oregon Trail the summer of 1993 and taking Alexa Ray alone for three weeks that November to South Africa, where we went on safari after I was invited to judge the Miss Universe competition.

BUT NOTHING worked. Nothing.

That Christmas, Billy and I decided to try one more time by celebrating the holidays together, which have always been a special time for me. But on New Year's Eve, after playing a sold-out show only an hour away on Long Island, Billy didn't come home to our house in East Hampton. I was already sick with worry when someone from his crew called to tell me that, because they couldn't stand the thought of my being up all night on New Year's Eve in a panic, Billy wasn't coming home. He hadn't crashed his car on the Long Island Expressway or wasn't lying dead somewhere else, the crew member said: he was having an affair with a woman who worked as a caterer for the show.

To this day, Billy continues to deny ever having had affairs, and I've always believed him. But on that New Year's Day in 1994, when he did finally straggle home, I asked him to leave.

We didn't tell the press about the divorce for another four more months, and in those intervening weeks, I saw Billy several more times. Once was in February, when I took Alexa Ray to watch him perform in Miami. When he came back to the hotel room that night, he was drunk, unable to piece together a complete sentence, so I pretended to be asleep. The next morning, I realized I couldn't do it anymore—not any of it—and began packing my bags to leave, telling Billy that it was over. But instead of being remorseful, he told me to just go, and later that morning, I learned he had booked a private jet for himself and flown back alone to New York, without, it seemed, a second thought or any concern for where Alex Ray and I were or what we would do.

Then came the helicopter crash. And in the very moment when I needed Billy the most, having come the closest to death I'd ever been—what I thought could be his knight-in-shining-armor moment to come rescue me—what happened instead was that our marriage took its final breath, leaving me with a bruise that would never heal.

PART IV

Telluride

CHAPTER

19

ook!" Ricky shouted over the whirl of the engine, as he pointed through the cockpit to a stretch of red sand below, meandering through the towering buttes like a river rusted into place. "That looks like a flat enough place to land over there!"

Sitting behind him in a seat, I tried to see out my window to where Ricky was pointing as we circled over the red rock canyons and purple-tiered mesas, everything carved by the hand of time, suggesting ghosts of ancient rivers that no longer existed. It was all so majestic and vast, the deserts dotted by a thousand saguaro, their arms stretched out like crosses, punctuating a divine land resting among sacred peaks. As I looked down, it was easy to see why this was the spiritual heart of the Navajo Nation.

It had been Ricky's idea to barnstorm the Wild West in the single-engine plane he owned and piloted, when he suggested the trip the night before, over guacamole and margaritas at a fun Mexican restaurant outside Telluride. After a full day of skiing and a dip in a nearby hot spring, barnstorming had sounded like a great idea, even though small planes and big mountains are usually a combo plate I skip. But there I was nonetheless, wolfing down Ricky's enthusiasm alongside our quesadillas and frijoles refritos.

The following morning, I found myself sitting behind Ricky in the plane with Alexa Ray and a few other friends, with my nose squished against the window like a person in a Picasso painting while scanning a landscape that looked more like a Georgia O'Keeffe as we tried to spot a cactus-free strip to land her. Once we did, I stepped out onto the red dust and into Monument Valley for the first time, which was by then so iconic that I almost expected John Wayne to ride up at any moment and welcome us to the great outdoors.

Instead, there was Ricky, whom I had met just days before but who had thought of everything for the trip, beginning with the hike he had taken Alexa Ray, me, and a few other friends on to the ancient Pueblo dwellings of Bandelier, not too far from Monument Valley, where he had first landed his plane. On the hike, Ricky had regaled us with the ancient history of the tribes who first settled the land, and when Alexa Ray got tired, he had coaxed her to keep going. Soon enough, she was happily skipping along with the rest of us. I couldn't help but take note.

Our next stop: Chimayo, New Mexico, considered by many to be the Lourdes of the United States, where the sick, disabled, and heart-broken go for miracles, considered so holy by the Pueblo Indians that anyone who comes into contact with the dirt inside the ancient *santuario* is instantly healed or protected. Once inside, I was mesmerized by a room full of crutches and braces, discarded by those who had touched the sacred dirt and then walked out fully healed, no longer needing them. Awestruck, I filled up several charms with magic dirt, some to bring home to friends and one to keep for myself.

Later that night, I pinned one of the little charms to Ricky's jean jacket, a token of gratitude for his having taken us to such a special place. Afterward, as we drove back to the plane, singing and laughing along the way, my friend Bonnie, who had had a crush on Ricky, whispered to me, "I don't think he likes me—I think he has a crush on you. And that's okay with me."

As soon as she said it, I started to notice the chemistry. Or was it the enchantment created by the electricity of the adventure?

Yep, that's what it was.

BEFORE MY trip to Telluride, which included that barnstorming ride around the Wild West, I had been feeling a little lonesome at home in the Hamptons. Even before Billy and I separated, he was almost always away on tour, as his phone calls became more and more sporadic, and even when he was home, he was often stressed and drinking, which made me feel lonely despite the fact that he was right there—the worst kind of loneliness there is. I loved him, I was still in love with him, but I wanted him to love me back, and I wanted things the way they used to be.

So, when Bonnie called me in March 1994 to say she was going spring skiing in Telluride and that she would be staying at the home of a man she was interested in, where there was plenty of room for Alexa Ray and me, I thought I'd test the idea that "absence makes the heart grow fonder."

The summer before, Bonnie and I had taken another adventure, riding the Oregon Trail on horseback. We had started in Sundance, where we borrowed horses from Robert Redford, then rode the trail's old wagon wheel tracks through Montana. It had been a breathtaking trip, and when she called me to ask me to go spring skiing, I was already eager for a new adventure. Plus, I had always wanted to go to Telluride, an old mining town surrounded by mountains so steep, rugged, and precarious that miners used to yell, "To hell you ride!" about the journey to get there—one explanation for how the town earned its name.

When Alexa Ray and I arrived in Telluride for the first time, I thought the Victorian-era village, nestled inside a box canyon, looked like a painted backdrop for the movie set of an old Western, with a frozen waterfall at one end of the main street. It was a little town with a lot of history, and even the bank there was pierced by bullet holes from when Butch Cassidy allegedly shot it up during a robbery. Little did I know, as Alexa Ray and I pulled up to the two Victorian houses Bonnie's friend Ricky owned, that one day, I'd become part of Telluride's lore, too.

"Welcome. Make yourself at home," Ricky called over to us as he came bounding out of one house with a group carrying skis. "We're heading out to grab some powder! Heli-skiing! See you later!"

Bonnie, who had arrived a few days earlier, came running over to help us with our luggage. "That was Ricky! Isn't he handsome?" she gushed.

"Yes," I said, smiling at her excitement. "He's ruggedly handsome. Like Al Pacino guest starring on *Little House on the Prairie*!"

"Well, he got lift tickets for us all tomorrow," she said, laughing and bubbling like prosecco as she led us inside the house. "And he's taking us to a theater in town tomorrow night to see *Cabaret*. Here's your room! Unpack and get comfortable now, because as soon as he's back from skiing, he's taking us all out to dinner. Isn't that sweet?"

Bonnie had developed a crush on Ricky when she went to Telluride earlier that year, right around the holidays, and had called me in the Hamptons shortly afterward to tell me all about him.

"Oh, Christie, he's friendly and generous—a philanthropist and a real adventurer!" she'd raved over the phone. "He loves sailing and even raced in the Trans Pac. And he has a ranch in Hawaii, near where your parents live. He's in real estate, but he's also starting his own airline and communication company. He's even getting into cutting!" she said, referring to the sport my friends at the Montauk ranch and I had already fallen in love with.

As I listened to my friend go on, I thought Ricky sounded a little too good to be true. But, as if on cue or as though Bonnie had read my mind, she said Ricky wanted my phone number, so he could ask me about Punk Carter, who trained my cutting horses and whom he wanted to put in touch with his ranch manager in Hawaii.

Well, that sounds pretty dang legit to me, I thought to myself in my best cowgirl accent—I was already getting into character.

At dinner on our first evening in Telluride, it seemed that everyone in the restaurant knew Ricky, and he knew everyone else, as if he were the town's de facto mayor. Before the appetizers even arrived, he had told me about starting a refuge for battered women in town called the Tomboy House and how he'd recently bought a helicopter—the same one they'd used to go heli-skiing—for the town to ensure that children could get safely down the mountain to the hospital in the valley, if needed. It made me think that he was as generous and as kind as Bonnie had told me, and as we left the restaurant, my suspicions had already begun to melt away like the snowflakes I dusted off my jacket.

Ricky had a nice friend named Sandra Carradine, who was going through a friendly divorce from the actor-singer Keith Carradine and who lived right down the street with her daughter Sorel, who was about the same age as Alexa Ray. The two of them became fast friends, and after Alexa Ray skied with us for several days, she asked if she could stay home instead, to play with Sorel. Within seconds of learning I'd be a free agent, Ricky offered to take me up the long chairlift that leaves from town and climbs to the top of the mountain, which was too long and cold to take with kids. But I had wanted to experience the ride, so up we went, and as soon as Ricky had me where he wanted me, alone and without any interruptions, he insisted we have a little tête-à-tête, which quickly turned serious.

"I couldn't help but notice you seem a little sad sometimes," he said gently. "Is anything bothering you? Is everything okay between you and Billy?"

I was surprised he'd even noticed. Over the years, I'd become quite adept at pretending everything was just fine.

"Well, actually," I stammered, "we are having a few issues."

And with that, Ricky was off and running—and running off at the mouth, as he often did—using all sorts of philosophical aphorisms, parables, and sayings that seemed to fit my situation to a tee. I couldn't believe how wise and perceptive he was, although I later learned that many of his expressions were from Alcoholics Anonymous—good stuff, but not original material. But what did I know? Obviously, not much, because I swallowed it all, hook, line, and sinker.

Fast-forward to several days later and to our barnstorming trip around the Wild West with Bonnie, Alexa Ray, me, and a few other friends, where we all ended up hot and sweaty running around the buttes of Monument Valley before Ricky decided we should cool off with a dip in Lake Powell. While I'd never been before, I'd long been fascinated by the beautiful photographs I'd seen of the area, and as we flew over, I thought the reservoir looked like something my favorite artist, Matisse, might have designed, his scissors zigzagging wildly as he cut out the spiny inlets that make up the perimeter of the lake. After a quick aerial tour, we landed, then ran to the edge of the water, where we threw sticks into the lake, making a wish every time. I wished for more days like this one and, of course, peace on earth.

While swimming sounded like a great idea in hot and sunny Monument Valley, we didn't swim once we landed in Lake Powell because the weather immediately started to change. Instead, we raced back to the plane and took off into a darkening sky, where we could feel every bump, and soon enough, it was snowing heavily. Ricky and the co-pilot kept bending forward to look at the wing—a nerve-racking sight, to say the least. What were they looking for? Ice?

After we landed in Durango, a town near Telluride, it was confirmed: ice. But we'd survived, and Ricky had already arranged for a car to take us to a hotel in town, where he'd booked rooms for all of us. But Ricky wasn't staying: he was going right back up in the ice storm to fly to Phoenix to pick up his nine-year-old son, Wyatt, who was coming to visit from Hawaii for Easter break. The next morning, Ricky was back, and I was awakened by a tiny tap on my door, which was Ricky asking me to tiptoe with him into Wyatt's room, so I could see his sweet little boy, who was still asleep. In that moment, I couldn't believe how much like each other Wyatt and Alexa Ray looked, as if they were brother and sister.

Before I knew it, Alexa Ray and I had to go back to New York, and while we'd only stayed a week in Telluride—which had felt more like a month, in a good way—our bags were packed with unforgettable memories. When Ricky dropped us off at the airport, he handed me a pair of fat skis, designed to be used for backcountry skiing, begging me to come back as soon as I could, so we could all go heli-skiing before the season was over.

AFTER TWO weeks alone with Alexa Ray in my big, old empty dream house in the Hamptons, with no Billy in sight, I received a call from Ricky with an official invitation to join a group of friends heli-skiing in Telluride, and in that second, nothing sounded better than the great outdoors and a few margaritas around a crowded table with lots of laughter. So, Alexa Ray and I got back on a flight, and when we showed up at Ricky's, there he was, playing yet another part—this time the Easter Bunny, wearing a rabbit suit and delighting a small huddle of children as all the adults had a party inside. When I met his other friends, I couldn't believe that the group included the likes of billionaire Bill Koch (whose politics I knew nothing about yet), telecom mogul Lynn Forester (who later married a Rothschild), and film producer Kathleen Kennedy. (Later, I would learn that Ricky was also close with the couple who owned the Telluride Ski Resort, along with David Crosby and Graham Nash.) While I've never been impressed by money or prestige, I had wondered many times whether Ricky's stories of great feats told over the dinner table were too good to be true, but the presence of Bill, Lynn, and Kathleen assured me. After all, if these people were friends with him, then he must be the real deal.

The next morning, we all went skiing at the resort, which was breathtaking, but that night at dinner, all anyone could talk about was the heli-skiing trip Ricky had planned for eight of us the next day. I had never been heli-skiing or even used a pair of fat skis on powder, but after listening to the others talk about the unspoiled beauty of the backcountry, my anxiety turned into excitement.

Oh, what a beautiful morning, I hummed to myself the next day as I pulled on my long underwear and glanced out the window, where the sky was so blue that it was hard to believe the forecast called for snow later that day, causing me to question whether we should still go—I had had a bad feeling. But I dressed for spring skiing anyway, in a one-piece red zip-up from Ralph Lauren, thinking, with a little apprehensive smile, *If anything happens, at least I'll go out in style.*

After piling into two cars, we drove crosstown to a snowy hut on the far side of the resort to take a mandatory safety course, and in the icy shadow of the jagged peaks, I listened carefully as the guides explained the importance of buckling up, and if there were ever an avalanche, how to use a transponder, which we all had to wear, strapped to our chests. The course caused my anxiety to come rushing back, and to ease my nerves, I switched on my video camera and began filming, as I did many experiences in life, laughing as I turned my lens on the ski guides and narrated, "Here are the men who will save us later."

Because there were eight of us, we went in two groups of four, with one group taking the helicopter up with a pilot and a ski guide. Ricky had arranged it so that he and I would be in the same helicopter, along with Sandra and her eleven-year-old son, Cade. As we climbed into the helicopter, I pulled out the necklace on which I'd hung my tiny charm of Chimayo dirt and pinched a little around our seats, saying with a smile, "Magic dirt, do your stuff. Protect us all from harm today."

If only I had known . . .

THE CRASH was sudden and traumatic, coming out of nowhere. We had already taken two runs and were circling to land for a third, on the saddle of a faraway peak, when the helicopter just fell from the sky, plunging into a freefall from three hundred feet overhead, with no autorotation. In the time it took for us to smash into the ground, which felt like an eternity, I stared out the glass floor of the cockpit, fixating on the snow and boulders coming up at us rapidly as we spun closer and closer, while a dozen thoughts ran through my mind.

Oh, my god. We're really crashing. This is not a special effect—this is real life.

I thought about how I had written down my parents as my emergency contacts earlier that morning and how Billy used to say that he didn't want to know when he was going to die, but *where*, so he could avoid the place at all costs. These thoughts twisted through my mind like the boulders beneath us, before only one thought remained.

My parents, Alexa Ray, Billy, all my friends and family—I hope everyone knows how much I love them.

Suddenly, it became crystal clear that the only thing that really mattered in life and at death was the same: love.

Love.

I focused on Alexa Ray, holding her pure in my thoughts and hoping to project all my heart and soul to her so she would feel it at the very moment of impact. And then we hit.

The helicopter smacked into the granite mountain with such terrible speed and force that it split in two, the pontoons and tail rotor snapping like twigs off a dead branch. Trapped inside the shattered cabin, the six of us began to bounce violently across the saddle, glass, metal, and other debris flying everywhere, as we tumbled like bodies in a washing machine set to the spin cycle, with such centrifugal force that it sucked off my watch. Through all the noise and the sickening smell of engine fuel and grease, I suddenly realized I was still alive—I hadn't died on impact—as I kept repeating Alexa Ray's name like a mantra, praying that I wouldn't feel the helicopter blades when they sliced through my neck.

I'm not sure how much longer we walloped, whacked, twisted, and ricocheted across the saddle of that mountain in that terrible Tilt-A-Whirl of a helicopter cabin, but suddenly, we were no longer bouncing but rolling—because we had bounced right over the edge of the saddle. For a moment, I was vaguely aware of Ricky's leg against mine before it lifted and disappeared, as everything else around me went airborne. I tried to grab on to something—a seat, a railing, anything—but my entire body felt pinned down, restrained by a force I couldn't see or stop. Overwhelmed, I closed my eyes and waited to faint, still hoping I wouldn't feel the blades when they cut into my neck. But then the rolling stopped, the wrecked tips of the rotor blades digging into the mountain as we started to slide.

Flash, click, frame change.

LIGHT ON my face. *I must be outside the helicopter.*

After squeezing my eyes shut for so long, I finally opened them and saw that it was true—I was outside the helicopter. I was safe. But then, suddenly, I felt a tug on my leg, and looking down the mountain, I realized with horror that my seat belt strap had somehow wrapped itself around my ski boot, even though it was still attached to the wreckage, which was sliding—and dragging me—down the mountain toward a sheer granite cliff. If the wrecked helicopter tumbled over that cliff, I would be going with it.

So, that's what's going to kill me? A seat belt strap tangled around my boot?

But then, only feet away from the cliff, the helicopter stopped sliding, immobilized by a white wall of snow that had mythically, magically, and wonderfully piled up underneath it. In that moment, everything I had learned in our safety course that morning clicked back into my mind, and I hit the transponder strapped to my chest, hoping the signal would be picked up miles away, thousands of feet below, by someone who knew we had crashed and was monitoring the radio frequencies.

After managing to free my leg from the tangled debris, I scanned the steep terrain rising behind me, half-expecting to see an avalanche spinning down the mountain. *Am I the only one alive?* I thought in a moment of panic. All I could see behind me was a trail of metal, clothing, and other debris marking the path where the helicopter had careened down the mountain, the white snow streaked black by engine oil and grease.

Then a piece of debris moved. I refocused my eyes in disbelief and realized it wasn't debris, but Sandra Carradine's son, Cade, who, like me, had been thrown out of the helicopter and covered in snow. But now he was sitting up, and I could see there was blood on his face, and after he saw me too, he cried out, "Hug me." He tried to stand, but his legs just buckled under him, and he started to slide down the mountain instead. Intuitively, I wedged my boots into the snow to give myself the leverage to block his slide, and after I had pulled him into me, the two of us slid down a few more feet together, stopping in the snow closer to the wreckage.

At first, it was just Cade and me, alone for I don't know how long. I tried to stay positive and keep him warm while the sun disappeared, the temperature dropped, and the wind picked up. When he asked me where his mom was, I told him she was probably just on the other side of the helicopter and would be okay. When he complained that he couldn't feel his legs, I smiled and told him not to worry, even though *I* was worried, as we sat in the cold under the gathering clouds. I knew we'd be in trouble if we didn't conserve our warmth, so I grabbed whatever clothing had been thrown from the helicopter that I could reach, zipping a jacket over Cade and pulling on someone's vest that clashed horribly with my Ralph Lauren suit. But by this point, it was no longer fashion "to die for," but rather fashion to keep us from dying.

When I found a disposable camera in one of the vest pockets, I held it up for Cade to see. "Look, we're going to get you off this mountain, and then you'll have the best show-and-tell for school on Monday," I said, pulling him in to take a picture. "You can tell everyone that you were in a helicopter crash with that model Christie, and now you'll have the photos to prove it!"

I was desperately trying to keep Cade engaged when his mother suddenly appeared from behind the wreckage, her face covered in blood. She dragged herself to where we were sitting, using the sides of the smashed cabin to hold herself up. She looked dazed, as though she didn't know what had happened—as it turned out, she had been unconscious until that moment. When she saw Cade, though, her face lit up, and the three of us immediately hugged and huddled together, trying to create more warmth as snowflakes started to close around us and I began to wonder if anyone off the mountain knew we had crashed. Was help on the way? Then, when Cade started repeating, "We're going to die, we're going to die," I suggested we sing, hoping it would help distract and relax him and lift all our spirits.

I'm not sure if the pilot heard our songs, but soon enough, he pulled himself around the side of the helicopter as Sandra had, and I instantly saw that his face was cut by tiny gashes.

"I think Ricky's dying," the pilot said right away. "He's on the other side of the helicopter with the ski guide, who's okay, but I think Ricky has a punctured lung, maybe a broken collarbone. And the whites of his eyes are filled with blood."

I felt my breath catch at the back of my throat as the pilot spoke. He said Ricky must have been flung from the helicopter, then crushed by it, and that he would die soon if we didn't get help. The ski guide then appeared, saying he'd found a radio that he had used to call into town—Sandra and I exchanged a brief look of relief—before adding that he wasn't sure anyone had heard him. I told him and the pilot that Cade couldn't feel his legs and needed help, too.

In the next instant, we saw it, through all the spinning snow: little pinpoints of red and blue flashing lights in the distance, so small and remote that they looked like tiny flickers inside a toy train village at Christmastime.

Next, we heard the helicopters before we saw them, chop-chopping up the side of the mountain through the snow and wind—which was now gusting up to seventy miles per hour, I later learned—but one after another, the choppers turned around, battered by the storm and the lack of visibility. Not even a Chinook sent by the National Guard to aid in the search and rescue could make it all the way up the mountain. As we waved our arms wildly and yelled, "Over here!" I began to wonder if anyone would be able to save us before we froze to death on that icy perch.

But then, one helicopter broke the pattern, making it up the side of the mountain to drop wool blankets over us—one of which I was able to grab and tuck around Cade, even though the wind continually untucked it. Soon, another helicopter approached, this one with a rescue basket swinging at the bottom of a long line so uncontrollably that I thought the basket would hit us. The scene felt precarious, with the racket of the rotors and the vibrations of the helicopter reverberating through my body, and as I caught the same sickening smell of engine oil, I suddenly thought the helicopter would smash into us. But the aircraft kept fighting the gale force winds, and watching the basket swing violently down to the ground, I wondered how Ricky would ever get into it. I hadn't seen him yet—unable to move, he had remained on the other side of the wreckage, and the mountain was too steep and perilous for me to walk toward him—but I finally did when he and the guide were lifted into the sky, twisting back down the mountain in the tiny rescue basket through the blizzard-like conditions.

After Ricky and the guide spun away, we heard on the radio that a rescue team had hiked up the backside of the mountain and somehow made it to the saddle, where crews were going to scale down the face of the cliff on ropes so they could fasten Cade inside a rescue sled, then pull him back up to the saddle, where a helicopter would take him down. The boy was terrified of being hoisted in a sled up the side of the mountain, but it was better than twirling through the wind and snow in a basket below a helicopter, I told him.

After the rescue crew brought Cade to the top of the saddle, they came back with ropes for Sandra and me, telling us that they had been able to hike up with only one sled and that if we didn't think we had any broken bones, we'd have to hike up to the saddle using the ropes and our own feet. While I wasn't sure if anything was broken, when I initially tried to move, I realized for the first time since the crash just how battered my body was, everything stiff, sore, and bruised. It was difficult to walk, let alone hike, but both Sanda and I did so, one of us at a time, making our way up to the saddle like mountaineers climbing Everest, jamming each foot slowly and decisively into the steep, icy snow.

When we got to the top of the saddle, we both collapsed, which was when, while lying there in the snow, I realized that there was a toylike bubble of a helicopter waiting there to take each of us down separately, since it was so tiny. I insisted that Sandra go first: she had been unconscious, and Cade needed her. After the world's smallest helicopter spun off into the blizzard with one pilot and Sandra inside, I wondered where the miniature aircraft had come from, who the mysterious pilot was, and how on earth he had ever made up to the saddle in the first place.

The answers to these questions make for quite a story.

HOURS EARLIER, while we were all stranded on the mountain, something else was happening outside of town that I learned about days later. As soon as the networks got wind of the accident, a special report went out on televisions nationwide, interrupting regularly scheduled programming to report that model Christie Brinkley, the wife of Billy Joel, had been in a helicopter crash near Telluride and that her condition was unknown. A rescue mission was under way, but the team hadn't been able to reach Brinkley's group, and the special coverage would continue until she was found, no matter her condition.

Meanwhile, at a ranch outside Telluride, two cowboys saw the same report, and when they heard that rescue teams had been unable to reach us, they exchanged looks of concern.

"Well, she's going to freeze to death if we don't get her off that mountain," one of the cowboys, whose name was Richard Dick, said calmly to his friend. "I think I should do it."

"Yeah, I'd say give it a try," the friend agreed coolly, and minutes later, Richard had climbed into his bubble helicopter with only two seats, and taken off to fly into the biggest danger zone anywhere in the San Juans that day.

When he learned by radio that not even a Chinook had been able to make it up the mountain, he decided to let the gale force winds blow his helicopter up the mountain's backside, and after several failed attempts, he was finally able to land on the saddle, near where we had crashed. After whisking Sandra off the summit and flying her to safety, Richard bravely turned around and flew back in his bubble through the ever-worsening conditions to get me.

When I first climbed into the bubble, wave after wave of fear and relief broke over my body, and for the first time since the crash, I started to cry. As we took off into the wind and snow, Richard looked back at me and said simply, "It's okay now, honey. Just let it all out."

And if it hadn't been for that kind and courageous cowboy, I wouldn't be alive today.

Richard wasn't the only one prompted into action by the special news report blaring on TVs nationwide. Mindy Moak, an art dealer in New York City and my faithful friend of thirty years through thick and thin (and the godmother of all my three children), saw the same news bulletin, and in an instant, she knew she had to call my parents before they saw it, too. She instinctively knew I would want her to do what I had written down in the waiver that morning, when I listed my parents as my emergency contacts: "Break the news gently." Mindy, with all the sweetness of her soul, did just that, staying on the line with them for hours, until the newscasters finally announced that I had been rescued and taken to a hospital.

When Richard landed me safely in his bubble back in town, a team of paramedics was waiting there to pull me out, strap me onto a stretcher, and wheel me into an ambulance, which could only drive slowly due to the heavy snow. As soon as I got to the hospital, doctors cut off my Ralph Lauren suit and discovered severe contusions all over my body, my kneecaps appearing so black and blue that, at first, they thought I had broken the bones. That's when the shock of what had happened hit me, and I began to shake as though I were still stranded on the side of the frigid mountain, every part of my body now throbbing in pain. My hip in particular felt like it was on fire, as the doctors wheeled me down for immediate X-rays.

Alexa Ray, who had stayed back in Telluride to play with Sorel for the day, was already at the hospital, waiting for me, and as soon as we saw each other, we both started to sob. She hugged me tenderly, knowing that I had sore spots, but then didn't want to leave my side for hours, telling me over and over how much she loved me, as I said the same thing, so grateful to be able to experience that moment.

When I first got to the hospital, someone else was waiting for me, too: a man named Don. He introduced himself as a friend of Ricky's and then told me that Ricky's injuries were so severe, he had been airlifted to a hospital hours away, in Grand Junction, where his first words, despite a punctured lung, had been "Christie, Christie." From his potential deathbed, Ricky had called Don to ask him in a whisper if he could find me at the hospital in Telluride and let me know he was thinking about me. By that time, the doctors had already given me morphine for the pain, and in a drug-induced haze, I began to think that if Ricky survived, I had to do everything possible to see him, even if it meant flying from Telluride to Grand Junction after I was released.

BUT I didn't go to Grand Junction, at least not yet. What happened instead was something I had always longed for—because, suddenly, Billy was there, and just like a knight in shining armor, he was lifting me up out of my hospital bed and carrying me to a private plane to fly me back to Long Island. In that moment, I thought my prince had finally come to rescue me, and I waited for Billy to say the words I so badly wanted to hear: "I almost lost you, I can't live without you, I love you."

On the plane, Billy and a stewardess settled me onto a couch, where I took another pill for the pain, as ordered by the doctor, and then drifted in and out of sleep. I think Billy must have thought I was asleep when he made a phone call from the plane, but I was very much awake when I heard him say the words I didn't ever want to hear: "No, don't worry. I'm not going back to her. I just need to see her through this." And just like that, the dream broke apart like debris. I knew then that our separation was real and that while I had wanted to believe he couldn't live without me, apparently he could. And I was going to have to learn to live without him. Later, I asked my assistant, Margo, who had also been on the plane with us, if she had heard Billy say the same thing, and she told me, unfortunately, that she had.

Less than two weeks later, Billy and I announced to the press that we had separated months before and were now getting a divorce. The pain was real, but I couldn't let it be all-consuming, and days afterward, when headlines appeared that the crash investigators had found my watch, video camera, and necklace with the Chimayo charm amid the wreckage, I found some consolation when others said it was the magic and the miracle of Chimayo that had saved us that day.

Was it? All I know is that I try to find magic and miracles every day I'm lucky enough to be alive.

20

We hadn't even kissed yet. But suddenly, there I was, making love to a man in a hospital bed as he lay hooked up to all kinds of machines, as tubes and IVs twisted around and over us like a canopy of plastic trees. That he had punctured a lung and fractured several ribs? He acted like those were only inconveniences compared to the passion we were both beginning to feel.

Not even Nora Roberts could have made it up—not the story of the first night I spent with Ricky, in that hospital bed in Grand Junction, Colorado, nor all the days and nights that followed in what became one of the most bizarre, upsetting, and turbulent relationships I've ever heard or read about, let alone experienced personally.

Maybe it was the intense gratitude I felt to be alive after the crash. Or some romantic sense of destiny I thought I shared with Ricky after surviving a death-defying experience together. I'm not sure what led me into such a whirlwind relationship with him, and while a psychologist later diagnosed me with post-traumatic stress disorder, which often causes people to make impulsive, irrational decisions, I also think the lure of experiencing a majestic western landscape with a can-do cowboy who was constantly conjuring up outdoor adventures was difficult to resist. I also think Ricky saw me as a meal ticket the moment I showed up in Telluride, when he proceeded to work his magic on me until I became just that.

Days before I went to Grand Junction, after Billy flew me back to Long Island, I spent a lot of hazy hours alone in the East Hampton house, propped up on painkillers for both a wrist injury and hip pain while navigating a succession of hospital visits for scans and follow-ups. There was also the phone, which started ringing off the hook the moment I got back, with calls from every talk show and celebrity magazine, all begging for an inside scoop on what had really happened high up in the San Juans. But I didn't want to do any interviews: there had already been bad breakup rumors about Billy and me, and I knew the press smelled blood when they learned that I'd gone to Colorado alone.

Then I remembered the photos Cade and I had taken with the disposable camera. Knowing that *People* would pay top dollar, I told the magazine I'd give them an exclusive if they didn't ask me about my marriage, with the plan to donate all the money from the photo payment to the Telluride ski patrol as a gesture of gratitude. I was thrilled when the *People* payout ended up covering the entire cost of our rescue, with enough money left over to help the patrol buy a new ambulance.

But being alone out in East Hampton, now that my marriage was definitively and indisputably over, was tough, worsened by the fact it was early April, when all my friends were still in the city. At the same time, I felt this strange euphoria, like I couldn't believe I was still alive, and every morning when I woke up and saw a pretty cloud sailing across the sky or dappled light dancing on the lawn that overlooked the sea, I was struck by how beautiful it looked and amazed that I had almost missed it. Similarly, every time Alexa Ray gave me a hug, I felt like crying, knowing how close I'd come to never holding her again.

And then there was Ricky, who started calling me several times a day from the hospital. I started to look forward to his calls, when we shared what we could remember about the crash and relived the terrifying moments together, which only deepened the trauma bond between us (a term I only later learned). When he said the words that I had wanted to hear from Billy following the crash—things like, "I thought you might have died, and I realized I couldn't let you die because I needed to see you and be with you"—I felt validated, bolstered, and carried up by a wave of emotion after everything I'd been through in less than a week's time.

While my dad always said, "Christie, baby, you write your own script," at that moment, I felt my script was being written by destiny and that it was a real page-turning adventure in which I had to see what the next chapter would bring. So, I gathered up all my cowgirl things and rode off into the sunset—or, to be more precise, I rode off to Grand Junction, Colorado, where Ricky was in the hospital.

When I first saw him lying there, attached to an oxygen machine just so he could breathe, the whites of his eyes still bright red with blood, I felt even more stunned by all that had happened, and that he, I, and all of us had almost died. I pulled a chair up next to him, and when he let his hand dangle off the bed, searching for mine, I grabbed it, and we held hands there for hours, Ricky wordlessly squeezing mine at times in a silent exchange of empathy and affection. Later that night, despite all his injuries, we made love in the hospital bed, and afterward, as I lay next to him listening to the sighing ventilator, I thought I had found my kindred spirit at last.

Eleven days after the crash, Ricky was finally released from the hospital. Because it was Billy's turn to have Alexa Ray, I decided to go back to Telluride with Ricky to see if there was anything between us. Either way, it was a beautiful drive south from Grand Junction, where we wove through the Badlands, and just as we were entering the San

Juans, we saw a flatbed carrying a demolished helicopter, the same one in which we had almost died. Ricky and I looked at each other in amazement, both of us wondering how we had ever escaped from that wreckage alive—it must have been a miracle; it was meant to be; *we* were meant to be—and I felt a kind of cosmic kismet as the symbol of our near death left the mountains the same moment we entered them, as though the wreckage were making way for new life within.

NO MORE than a day or two after we arrived back in Telluride, Ricky suggested a trip to nearby Dunton, an old ghost town huddled up on a river under the San Juans and dotted with natural hot springs. The town wasn't really a town anymore, but a string of old, abandoned cabins, one in which we spent the night, and after spreading our sleeping bags out on an old, dusty box spring, we fell asleep listening to the tinkle of a nearby waterfall. That night, I dreamt that something was crawling on my arm, and when I swatted it away in my sleep, the thud of a rat hitting the opposite wall woke me up. *Yep, this truly is the Wild West*, I thought, and having just finished *Cowboys Are My Weakness*, a collection of short stories about smart women looking for love out west, I felt like I had finally found my own dashing, thrill-seeking cowboy—and there we were, already off on another adventure.

After a week or so in Telluride, I was so swept up by Ricky, the Wild West, and our sense of a shared destiny that I decided to stay out west, flying east only to get Alexa Ray and more of my things. A little more than one month after the crash, Ricky proposed to me in a high alpine meadow amid waist-high wisps of wildflowers just beginning to bloom—and in the shadow of the same peaks that had nearly killed us, I said yes. It felt confusing and exciting all at once, and believing that fate had brought us together in an incredible way, I thought it made sense that our relationship would continue to unfold in incredible ways.

Boy, did I have no idea.

Within weeks, I had enrolled Alexa Ray in school just a few doors down from Ricky's house and had moved both Goodbar Miss and Blue Jean to a ranch on the outskirts of town. Soon enough, I flew back to New York and packed up all my things from the home on Further Lane in East Hampton, dismantling in three days the dream that had taken Billy and me more than five years to build. I made sure to take only the things that belonged to me, rearranging each room after I had moved my stuff so that the house would still look pretty and well appointed for Billy.

I'd never spent an entire summer in the Southwest before, and the months of June, July, and August were magical, marked by fields of wildflowers; long, meandering hikes to hidden waterfalls; beautiful horseback rides across stunning mesas; and big, brilliant rainbows that spread across the sky nearly every afternoon, after fast-moving rain showers brought the sun back out. Ricky also continued to suggest a string of fun little adventures, and that summer we went to Hawaii, where we stayed in Graham Nash's house on Hanalei Bay and where Mindy visited us for a week. We also sailed the Sea of Cortez, where I swam with a whale shark and saw so many spinner dolphins leaping and diving back into the water that the flat sea looked like whitewater. Back in Telluride, whenever friends came to visit, we'd drive over the peaks to catch the narrow-gauge railroad to Silverton, an old mining town where they sold turquoise jewelry the same color as the nearby alpine lakes.

But not everything that summer was adventure and rainbows. While Billy adjusted to the extreme inconvenience of picking up Alexa Ray in Telluride whenever it was his turn on our visitation schedule, he didn't like that I had moved to Colorado so quickly and abruptly after the crash. Neither did my parents, who were skeptical of Ricky, continually asking if his fantastical stories were true and how he actually made a living. They also didn't like that he kept proposing dangerous activities even after the crash, one of which included kayaking down a "gentle" river that turned out to be whitewater: I ended up pinned underwater against a boulder by a heavy torrent that not even a strong swimmer like me could have escaped. Luckily, I held tight to the rope still attached to the kayak, which finally broke free and pulled me out just as I was about to lose my breath.

But soon enough, like my parents and even Mindy, I also began to wonder what Ricky actually did for a living—especially when, days after we were engaged, he asked to "borrow" money, something he continued to do throughout our relationship. (I soon realized that "borrow" was likely only a euphemism because I don't think he had any intention of ever paying me back.) The first time, he wanted $75,000, explaining that he'd just hit a rough spot and needed a little help, because nothing he owned was liquid at the time. I was surprised, but I believed the story that he was a super-successful guy who had just fallen on tough times, which could happen to anyone. But Ricky *kept* asking to borrow money, over and over again, and I kept lending it to him, with the understanding that he'd pay me back, which I believed he would: he'd just hit rough seas, I told myself, but he'd soon right his own ship. Ricky was also my soon-to-be husband (and eventually, husband), and as our lives became more entangled, I think he felt more empowered or entitled to ask for larger and larger sums. By the time our tumultuous relationship ended less than a year later, I had lent him nearly two million dollars.

WHILE ALL Ricky's talk of money made me uncomfortable, I had other things to focus on that summer, primarily planning a major charity event called Wild West Weekend, which we held in Telluride in September to raise money for the Southern Ute Indian Tribe and other area nonprofits. For weeks, I worked around the clock to organize a rodeo, a cutting competition, an outdoor concert, and a tribal dance, all while getting cattle ropers, belt toolers, boot makers, jewelers, and other tradespeople to come teach their crafts to those who attended the event. Through Ricky's connections, we got chiefs from various Native American tribes to come set up teepees and sweat lodges, and we arranged for covered wagons, an old-time saloon, a Ferris wheel, and pony rides for kids, the latter two of which were donated by Tom Cruise and Nicole Kidman, who owned a house in Telluride. I also got CoverGirl and my eyewear and jewelry lines to donate product and money. In the end, the weekend was a huge hit, covered by all the major talk shows and celebrity magazines, including the *Today Show*, *Good Morning America*, *Entertainment Tonight*, *Extra*, *In Style*, and *People*.

For me, Wild West Weekend was the epitome of summer in the Southwest, the fulfillment of my childhood dreams, and an experience I'll never forget. (I was once in the play *Annie Get Your Gun* when I was in high school, even though it was a little community production, and that weekend in Telluride gave me the chance to feel like a real Annie Oakley come to life.) And after the weekend was over and everyone had packed up their teepees, trailers, saloons, and sweat lodges, I experienced another moment of magic.

The day before, even though I had a feeling that I might be pregnant, I had ridden in the cutting competition, deciding to let fate take the reins, literally. But after the dust from the weekend had settled, I went immediately to the pharmacy in town and bought a pregnancy test. When the little window on the stick read positive, I was thrilled. For years, I had wanted another child, and even though I was starting to have doubts about Ricky, it seemed that destiny was already writing the next chapter.

On December 22, 1994, just nine months after the helicopter crash, Ricky and I were married at the summit of the ski resort in Telluride, at 12,000 feet, outside a restaurant he called Top of the World. I invited all my close friends, but many, like Mindy, Simon, and Rupert, refused to come, saying they loved me so much that they couldn't condone or bear witness to a union they knew might be harmful. And while my parents came, they weren't exactly happy, especially when they realized that, though we had agreed beforehand to have a small wedding, Ricky had invited the entire town.

That afternoon, I rode the chairlift with Ricky to the Top of the World in my white satin wedding dress, over which I wore a fuzzy cream-colored jacket I already owned. There, on the summit, we were married under an archway of red-ribboned ski poles in front of all the people who did come, and I accepted the inexpensive silver band Ricky had bought me only days before in a trinket shop in town.

While there were many aspects of the wedding I did not like— Ricky had a field day, for example, booking snowcats and horse-drawn sleds to take his friends up and around the mountain—we had a fun moment when we pulled off a visual gag for our wedding guests with the help of a professional skier named Suzy Chaffee (better known by her nickname, "Suzy Chapstick"), who had a similar look to mine. I skied partway down the mountain in my wedding dress before Suzy and I secretly switched places in a bend in the run, and she skied down the rest of the way with Ricky, in what looked like the same dress, doing backflips, somersaults, and other tricks, much to the delight of all our friends. Eventually, when I skied down with Ricky afterward, everyone burst into applause, doing so again later when we announced that we were expecting a baby boy. While my parents were thrilled for me, they were appalled by Ricky, and the day after the wedding, my mom asked me to have the marriage annulled immediately.

If only I had listened. (And why wasn't I listening? What was wrong with me?)

Things didn't improve with a honeymoon. Before we were married, Ricky had pulled out a brochure for a glitzy party boat in front of our friends, saying he'd already booked it for our honeymoon and needed me to send a deposit ASAP. The boat wasn't what I would have imagined for a honeymoon—I've always preferred a simple, classic wooden sailboat—but Ricky was adamant, saying we *had* to do it, that it had a bunch of bells and whistles for the kids, which was when and how I learned we were taking both our kids on our honeymoon. Because the boat was in Florida, I suggested we take Alexa Ray and Wyatt first to Disney World, which we did. But while there, amid all the resort's wonder and magic, Ricky somehow managed to pick a fight with me and started sulking, which made me question how I could have married a man who could be miserable in the happiest place on earth.

OVER THE months, Ricky's disposition remained mercurial, and after more misery, more loans, and what felt like more emotional manipulation, I realized that life with him wasn't what I wanted, nor would I likely ever be able to have the one big, happy family with him that I had always dreamed of. By late spring 1995, I knew I needed space and time to think things over, away from Ricky's emotional artistry, so I decided to leave Telluride and go back to New York. Months before, I had already decided to have the baby in New York because my doctors said having a baby at high altitude wasn't safe. Plus, my parents were spending the summer in the Hamptons, so it made sense to go back east, even if my apartment in the city didn't have even a single lightbulb left—that's how completely and thoroughly I had moved to Telluride. I stayed with my parents for a bit, but as the baby's due date approached, I wanted to be closer to the city, so I got a room at the St. Regis in Manhattan—the "St. Regis and Kathie Lee," as Alexa Ray called it—and began seeing a therapist to try to figure out why I was so hypnotized by a man I knew wasn't good for me.

When it became clear that I wasn't coming back to Colorado, Ricky started calling me all the time, eventually flying to New York and begging me to meet him for lunch—he knew as I well as I did that I was his best and only meal ticket. He didn't have much to say at lunch, but as we were walking up Madison Avenue, he suddenly and casually dropped that he had tracked down my biological father, Herb Hudson, and had even spoken with him by phone. I hadn't seen or talked with Herb Hudson since I was eight years old, when he gave me up in a Los Angeles courtroom, and yet Ricky had gone ahead and established a connection to my past—the most painful part of my past—that he had no reason or right to make. I was so shocked and outraged, I couldn't see straight as tears of anger welled up in my eyes. How could Ricky have done this? I was so angry that I didn't care whether paparazzi were nearby when I told him on the street to get out of my life before running away and hailing a cab back to the hotel.

BUT RICKY didn't get out of my life. He stayed in New York instead, where he continued to work his emotional voodoo on me. At the same time, I was just days away from having our baby, and while I was angry, I felt it would be unfair to deny Ricky the opportunity to be there for his birth.

On June 2, 1995, I went into labor, and by the time I arrived at the hospital, Ricky, Alexa Ray, Margo, and Mindy were already there. Alexa Ray was so excited to be a big sister that she immediately called Billy to share the news, and several hours later, while we were all waiting for the baby to arrive, a nurse came into the room to say that Billy had called back on the line. For no apparent reason, that caused Ricky to explode, as he demanded to know why Billy had to interrupt our private time before he stormed out and raged down the hospital halls.

But while he raged, I labored, turning up the music I had brought into the hospital and focusing on the miracle of my son's birth. I decided then that I'd name the baby August River, but the next morning, when anchor Bryant Gumbel announced my son's name on the *Today Show* with a little pause and then a snicker, I felt so much self-doubt that I immediately withdrew the name, and my newborn remained nameless for weeks. Eventually, I decided on "Jack," which I thought was a good, solid, playground-proof name, with the middle name of "Paris," for a little romance.

The evening Jack was born, I stayed awake nearly all night, gazing at his face with such awe and affection. He had a perfect, little round head and the most soulful eyes, and from that day forward, he was the happiest and sweetest son I could ever imagine. I was so excited that I called everyone I knew, leaving messages on answering machines for those who weren't awake.

After Jack was born, I had a long session with my therapist and decided that, for my son's sake, I should give my marriage one more try. If this was really the end, I wanted to be able to say to Jack one day, "I did everything possible to make it work with your dad. I never gave up on him." So, I bought a one-way ticket to Telluride for the two of us, hopeful that spending time together as a family would erase the mania of the last several months. And while I found the West as captivating as ever, just hours after we arrived, Ricky asked me for more money. That's when I knew that this was not nor could it ever be love or even a real relationship: it was usership, manipulation, and at its worst, emotional torture. I booked a flight back to New York.

When I got back to the city, Ricky called me at the St. Regis. "We're going to make a deal," he said squarely, without any pleasantries. "I'm going to walk away from you and the baby just like Herb Hudson did."

In that second, the room collapsed around me, as Ricky's words hung in the air like dark, dirty soot, choking me with so much shock and outrage that I felt breathless. It was the same feeling I had had when I was eight years old and Herb Hudson told a crowded court-room that he didn't want to be my father anymore.

Sometimes, history has a horrible way of repeating itself.

While what Ricky had said was disgusting, I wanted it to stay etched in my mind forever, so I could use it to break his spell: I could never remain hypnotized by a man who would do what Herb Hudson had done to me.

After Ricky and I hung up, I called my parents, and then my at-torney, whom I told I wanted a divorce, asking the lawyer to start the paperwork immediately.

WHEN THE press learned I had filed for divorce, they stormed the St. Regis, camping out on the sidewalk on Fifty-fifth Street for days, from morning to midnight. I hid in my room for the first week, but it wasn't a tenable or a long-term solution, and when my friend Simon called to offer his sailboat, which was sitting docked and idle at the Sag Harbor marina, I thanked him profusely and decided to head out onto the open sea, where I figured no one would find us.

In the wee hours of the morning, I snuck out the St. Regis's ser-vice entrance with Alexa Ray and Jack and took a car to Sag Harbor, where later that afternoon, we met Billy, who was picking up Alexa Ray for a visit. He had never met Jack before, and very sweetly, he began cuddling him, oohing and aahing over how cute he was. When Billy saw all our luggage, which included strollers, car seats, and di-aper changing bags, he offered to help carry it, and soon enough, the four of us were walking together past the restaurant that used to do a booming business across from the marina. This launched a hundred rumors that Billy and I were getting back together, whispers that only intensified after Billy helped me secure a mooring in Martha's Vineyard, an often-impossible feat during the busy summer season.

The buzz that Billy and I were reuniting and on our way to Martha's Vineyard stoked the media fire around my divorce from Ricky. After Jack and I spent a few days with friends on island, there was so much press that I knew we had to leave again. This time, I decided to go farther away, sailing to Nantucket, where Alexa Ray joined us. But the island, while smaller and more exclusive, proved to be no less frenetic, and soon after we moored there, the harbormaster told me there was press at the end of every dock. Realizing Simon's boat had become a floating target, I called my friend Ben Krupinski, who had built Billy's and my house in East Hampton and who owned a small private airline on Long Island. Generously, Ben arranged for one of his planes to pick us up in Nantucket the next day and fly us to East Hampton.

That morning, we were getting ready to leave for the flight when a splotch of poop from Jack's diaper slipped out and ran down my blouse, staining the entire outfit. That wouldn't have been such a problem if all my other clothes weren't already packed and on the plane, which was waiting for us. Ben had filed the flight as though we were going to New Jersey, to throw the press off our scent—although now our scent was going to smell a bit like baby poo—and just when I felt I'd hit my breaking point, the harbormaster said he had a spare polo shirt and a pair of men's shorts I could wear. I thanked him, and with no other option, I put on his clothes, which caused Alexa Ray to clap her hands together and tell me I looked just like Paddington Bear. Her excitement was infectious—and also inspiring. What if Alexa Ray, Margo, and I all wore polo shirts and men's shorts? That way, we'd look like dockhands, and the press would never know the difference.

It worked like a charm.

After we arrived in the Hamptons, I felt relieved: we had finally shaken the paparazzi. But I now had other problems because I had nowhere to live. While we were in Nantucket, Ben had told me about two houses for rent that he thought would be perfect for me, and after I saw the first one—a contemporary white home in Bridgehampton surrounded by fields, with a barn, horse paddocks, a basketball/tennis court, and even its own cow—I told him I'd take it without looking at the other.

That week, I moved the kids into the house with the help of my closest girlfriends, Mindy, Jill, and Lisa, who came bearing good, uplifting energy—and several bottles of wine. In short order, they helped me see that I had never taken the time to mourn the end of my marriage with Billy, and little by little, I began to feel stronger and more like myself again, unwinding Ricky's brainwashing effects while remembering that you can never underestimate the power of female friendship. I don't know where I'd be without them.

In December 1995, Ricky agreed before a judge to relinquish his paternity rights to Jack. After he left the courtroom—and my life—I felt numb, but I also felt a sense of relief, and afterward, when I went back to my apartment, where Mindy had been watching the baby all day, and I saw Jack's sweet face light up when he saw me, I knew everything was going to be okay, just as it had been for me when I was a child and ended up with the greatest dad ever, Don Brinkley. While I didn't know what the future would hold for Jack, I knew one thing: he already had Alexa Ray and me, along with my parents and Billy, who officially became his godfather, in addition to all our close friends, and together, we made one loving family. So, if history was repeating itself, so be it.

They say Telluride means "to hell you ride," and I sure did. But I also came out of it with an angel.

PART V

Home

Christie Brinkley '17

Top down, sun up, wind back, hands on nine and three, and a little white dress with a deep and dashing décolleté.

It felt fantastic to be back behind the wheel of the little red Ferrari, speeding across the desert on the interstate while giving Chevy Chase a wink and a smile as he mouthed sweet nothings at me and made his iconic funny faces.

Because sometimes when history repeats itself, it's a ton of fun.

Fourteen years after my big-screen debut in *National Lampoon's Vacation*, there I was again, playing "the Girl in the Red Ferrari" in *Vegas Vacation*, which is part of the National Lampoon franchise, and even though I was forty-two, not twenty-eight, the crew thought I looked better in the sequel. This may have been due in part to a whole new feeling of freedom I had after Ricky, but I think it was mostly thanks to a superbly talented hair and makeup team.

It wasn't the first time I had been asked to be in a National Lampoon sequel, but only bad advice I ever got from my dad was to turn down the offer to appear in *Christmas Vacation* because he was worried I'd be typecast as the ingenue. But the *Vacation* sequels were hugely successful, one of the most successful film series ever, so when the directors asked me in 1996 to do *Vegas*, I said yes—on the condition that I have a speaking role. This led them to write a neat little part for me as a slick and sexy card counter in the casinos.

If only Mother Nature hadn't intervened . . .

Filming began auspiciously enough, as I drove my flashy red Ferrari up to Chevy's old station wagon, flirting with him just as I had in the original movie. But in the sequel, we orchestrated this great sight gag, and right as I sped away, you can see that I have a baby in the back seat—totally fitting, I thought, since I had my own baby around the same age at home, in addition to sweet Alexa Ray, now ten.

Afterward, in a makeshift trailer on the side of the interstate in the middle of the Nevada desert, the hair and makeup team worked their magic on me again, making me look as sexy as they could for my big speaking scene with Chevy. The directors had written the scene to take place in the Ferrari on the side of the highway, where Chevy's character and mine would meet at last, but the very moment I stepped outside the trailer, a dust devil flared up from out of nowhere and smacked right into me, whipping me up in an orange tornado of dirt and debris that left my hair, makeup, and little white dress dusted in a thick layer of carroty chalk. By the time the team was able to clean me up and work their wonders again, we'd lost the light for the day, and while we tried to shoot the scene anyway, it looked inconsistent with the earlier ones we'd already done. I was disappointed, but at the same time, I was thrilled to be working again with Chevy, Beverly D'Angelo, and the rest of the *Vacation* gang.

AT AGE forty-two, I was also thrilled to be working as much as I was in general, appearing on the covers of magazines, doing print and TV commercials, overseeing my eyewear and jewelry lines, and hosting

TV special after TV special, even making a cameo on an episode of the NBC sitcom *Mad About You* that aired the night of the Superbowl XXVIII in 1994. Six weeks after Jack was born, he, Alexa, and I also appeared in a "Got Milk?" ad, the three of us proudly wearing our milk mustaches in the cutest commercial for a dairy product this lifelong vegetarian (now vegan) had ever seen.

That summer, I also started doing some of the first-ever infomercials, in this case for the all-in-one fitness equipment Total Gym, which I continued to represent until 2024, despite that, when I began, the idea of a celebrity doing any infomercial was frowned upon. But by that time, Cher had already done a few, and I figured that if they were good enough for the Queen of Comebacks, they were good enough for me—but only if I believed in the product, which I did in the instance of Total Gym (as did Chuck Norris). Plus, in 1996, I was just like Cher in that I was all about making a comeback, excited and eager to begin my new life in New York as a single mom of two beautiful children. While I was representing the company, Total Gym became the bestselling total body fitness equipment ever, the company making over two billion dollars.

That winter, I finished refurnishing my apartment on the Upper West Side, and we moved back to the city so Alexa Ray could attend one of the best elementary schools in the country. I still took the kids out to the Hamptons on the weekends, so they could run around outside and play on the beach, and one April weekend, my friend Jill Rappaport, a *Today Show* entertainment reporter whom I'd known for years, asked me to look at a barn she was building outside her house so she could get my advice on its interior design—one of my favorite hobbies. Plus, she added, she had a good-looking architect whom she wanted me to meet, and while dating was the farthest thing from my mind—after Ricky, I felt so whittled down that I didn't trust my instincts anymore—I went to check out the barn anyway.

When I first saw Jill's architect, a man named Peter Cook, I didn't remember him as the Ford model who'd introduced himself in Studio 54 the night of my *Sports Illustrated* swimsuit calendar party, where I met Olivier. Peter wasn't my type: he seemed too groomed, too slick. At the same time, my "type" obviously wasn't working for me, so when he asked me out later that week, I agreed to go on a date.

Things happened quickly after that, and for a number of reasons, primarily because I felt both a sense of urgency to find Jack a father figure and terror at the thought that Ricky might swoop back in if I didn't, I said yes when Peter asked me to marry him later that year.

On September 21, 1996, the last day of summer, we were wed in the backyard of my Bridgehampton home, with Alexa Ray as our flower girl and Jack our ring bearer. Billy came, too, which delighted both Alexa Ray and me, and I couldn't have been happier that our friendship survived our divorce.

Later that fall, I said goodbye to another relationship, one of the longest of my life: after twenty years together, CoverGirl and I amicably parted ways because the brand, I believed, thought I had aged out of being able to sell cosmetics. But women don't have an expiration date; we don't disappear as we get older, and even though there were very few mature models at the time or even cosmetic lines targeted to older women, I landed a new role almost immediately, signing a contract with Nu Skin, a multilevel marketing company with a skin care line. I loved working for Nu Skin because anyone could sell its products, and when I traveled around the world to give speeches to its sales reps, I was emboldened to see auditoriums full of thousands of enthusiastic female entrepreneurs. With Nu Skin, I also launched my first signature perfume, calling it Believe because, even after all I'd been through, I still believed in love.

BY THE time my perfume hit stores in 1998, I had even more love to believe in: at age forty-four, I was pregnant again. Peter, the kids, and I were in Hawaii visiting my parents at their home on the island once discovered by Captain Cook when I got the call from my doctor with the news. Immediately, I began thinking of a name for the baby that would embody my love of the sea, and because we were in Hawaii, I thought "Captain Cook" might be nice for a boy and "Sailor Cook" if the baby was a girl. Either way, I wanted a name that rang with adventure, independence, and what it's like to harness Mother Nature while gliding silently on her breathy wind.

At age forty-four, I hadn't found it easy to get pregnant after Peter told me he wanted a baby, even though, as soon as it was legally possible, he adopted Jack. Following the wedding, I had had two upsetting miscarriages, one that required a D and C. At the time, I took for granted my access to the lifesaving procedure, but today, I know many women don't have that same right. (And I think everyone should be able to receive the health care they need without doctors fearing they'll be thrown into prison for supplying it.)

After my miscarriages, I turned to IVF for help, and while the process didn't work, it did seem to relax me enough that I was able to get pregnant naturally immediately afterward. (I also believe that IVF should be available to all families who ever dream of having children.)

Now that I was about to be a mother of three, I wanted a real house, not just a rental, and after looking at various properties around the Hamptons, I eventually found Tower Hill, a magical place high up on a hill that, over the years, I've made into my dream home, one filled with light, laughter, and love. Built in 1891 by the Gardiner family, who founded the first-ever English settlement in New York, on a nearby island by the same name that was a gift from the King of England, Tower Hill was an old country estate. When I first saw it, I knew immediately it would be a paradise for children, one where they could go sledding and snowboarding in the winter and throw balls and chase butterflies in the summer, with acres of woods perfect for running, picking mushrooms, and catching tadpoles in the little sun-dappled pond that lay nestled at the bottom of the grassy knoll.

While the house had other names over the years, I called it Tower Hill after the crenellated observation tower that still tops the old home, where you can see the sea, the first family's Gardiners Island, the Montauk Point Lighthouse, and even the coast of Connecticut. Today, Tower Hill has become such an integral part of my life that I named the clothing line I launched in 2024 TWRHLL.

We didn't move into Tower Hill until after the baby was born, though, staying instead in a charming old house in Sag Harbor that had once belonged to President Chester A. Arthur. For the last few weeks of my pregnancy, I remained there overseeing renovations on Tower Hill, going into the city only right before my due date—which was when I learned, much to my dismay, that the baby was in breech. The doctors said I would probably need a caesarean, but I didn't want to have major surgery for a number of reasons, so I hired a midwife— who, coincidentally, was supermodel Paulina Porizkova's mom.

On July 2, 1998, I went into labor a week early, causing the midwife and everyone else to scramble over to the hospital. There, doctors hovered above me as I crawled around the delivery room on my hands and knees, a technique that can flip a breech baby, while Paulina's mom applied ice packs and blasted a little transistor radio over my belly, both which can encourage a baby to move. When the baby finally shifted into the right position, it felt like an earthquake inside me. The doctors started shouting for me to push as hard as I could while the nurses frantically pressed down on my stomach, trying to hold the back of the baby's neck so that she wouldn't flip back into breech position. It all felt like a high-drama outtake from some medical thriller, and in between the pushing, shouting, ice packs, and loud music, my blood pressure dipped so dangerously low on two separate occasions that the doctors gave me shots of norepinephrine.

Finally, I gave birth to a beautiful baby girl, and seconds after the nurses handed her to me and I saw her sparkling blue eyes, sculpted nose, and pointed little lips, the legs of the hospital bed broke underneath us, causing us to slide down together and into the arms of the stunned doctors.

Welcome to the world, Sailor, I thought with a smile. *Never a dull moment with this crew.*

DAYS AFTER Sailor was born, Alec Baldwin and Kim Basinger invited me to a fund-raiser in the Hamptons for President Clinton. While I desperately wanted to go—I've always been a huge supporter of the Democratic Party—I hadn't gotten into a good rhythm with nursing yet and decided to stay home (in another president's house, Chester A. Arthur's). That afternoon, I was there with my mom and Sailor when we heard sirens wail slowly by—I knew immediately it was the presidential motorcade. Holding Sailor in my arms, I rushed outside to see if I could catch a glimpse of the president, but all I saw at first were six motorcycles leading a long line of black cars snaking slowly through the small-town streets. But then I caught the white of President Clinton's smile through the tinted glass, and in the next moment, I read his lips as he said, "Stop! There's Christie Brinkley!" and the motorcade came screeching to a halt. The president then climbed out of the car himself, as his security detail scrambled.

"This must be the new baby," he said to me with a chuckle. "Is this why you weren't at Alec and Kim's?"

"Yes!" I said, as I returned his hug. "I really wanted to go, but I couldn't make it with Sailor."

The president then took Sailor in his arms and held her while my mom came out to introduce herself, even though she'd met Clinton once before. By then, dozens of onlookers had also stopped to watch, which was when a journalist following the motorcade snapped a picture of Sailor with the president that made it into the *Sag Harbor Express* the following day. And that was Sailor's very first public appearance, cuddled up in the arms of our sitting president.

Never a dull moment, for sure.

Before the next presidential election, I was back again in politics in full swing, attending fund-raisers for Clinton and then campaigning for Vice President Al Gore, who named me to his New York delegate slate in 1999, when he announced his own presidential run. To me, being political is what it means to be American—you want to make your country the best it can be. Plus, I've always been an activist since I was young, marching against the war in Vietnam and stumping for Democratic presidential candidate George McGovern when I was only sixteen. Since then, I've met nearly every president, including Jimmy Carter, George Bush, Sr., Geoge Bush, Jr., and Barack Obama, among others.

I've also been a die-hard environmentalist for as long as I can remember—one reason I became a vegetarian at age fourteen—but after attending a talk with Alec Baldwin given by renowned pediatrician Dr. Helen Caldicott, where I learned all about the dangerous health effects nuclear power plants can have on children, I became passionate about fighting radiation. Soon enough, I was participating in protests across the Tri-State area and, within months, had joined the board of directors of the STAR (Standing for Truth About Radiation) Foundation. (Today, I continue my advocacy as vice president of the Radiation and Public Health Project.)

For me, the issue was personal as well as universal: Long Island has long been surrounded by leaky old reactors, which not only emit radiation but also pose a catastrophic threat if there were ever an accident necessitating a mass evacuation off the island. I had moved my kids to the country to protect their health, not to expose them to additional hazards.

In 1999, I chartered a plane to Washington, DC, with other STAR members to try to convince then–Secretary of Energy Bill Richardson to close the high flux beam reactor in Brookhaven, a particularly leaky Long Island reactor. After we arrived five minutes late, Richardson canceled our meeting, so I marched over to the White House and asked to see Clinton. The president then called Richardson and got our meeting back on the books that same day, which was when we convinced Richardson to shutter the high flux beam reactor for good.

Later that year, the USO asked me to go on tour with then–Secretary of Defense William Cohen (who has always been immensely kind) to help boost morale among American troops stationed in Italy, Kosovo, Bosnia, and Macedonia. Even though it was Christmastime and I had three young children at home, I agreed to go—and loved every second. We flew overseas on the secretary of defense's fully militarized plane, where I sat behind an intelligence desk comprised of a wall of computers, and while we were airborne, the plane received a midair refueling during a snowstorm. It was an incredible sight to see, especially when the pilots invited me to sit in the cockpit to watch it all, as another giant plane precariously attached a hose to our plane thousands of feet over earth, sending us into a tremor of turbulence.

Once we were in Europe, I got back on another plane, this time a transport jet, to play football with Terry Bradshaw as the Dallas Cowboys Cheerleaders danced behind us—another surreal experience, since the plane was so grand and cavernous, practically the size of a full football field itself. I also lip-synched to Mary Chapin

Carpenter while she sang offstage, inserting little gags to get the troops laughing. And in the mess halls, I table-hopped as much as I could, trying to make the troops smile and feel the deep gratitude I had for their service.

THEN, SEPTEMBER 11 happened. That morning, I was in my house with two dozen other people, preparing to film an infomercial for Total Gym, when Mindy called from the city to say she had just seen a plane flying dangerously low past her apartment. Moments later, after the first plane careened into the Twin Towers, everyone gathered around the small television in my kitchen and watched in horror as the second plane hit, which was when we started to realize the United States was under attack. From that moment onward, no one took a step outside my kitchen, as we remained huddled around the TV, staring in disbelief as people jumped out of the burning towers to their deaths or ran through the city streets trying to escape the destruction while emergency crews ran in the opposite direction, toward danger. Jack and Sailor were already home with me, but Alexa Ray wasn't, and immediately I raced to pick her up—it was all too frightening not to have all my babies safe at home with me. No one knew what might happen next.

Nearly everyone who was in my house that day knew someone in Manhattan, but none of us could get through—all the phone lines were jammed. So, we stayed in my kitchen, dealing in our own ways with all the shock, fear, and grief, and throughout the afternoon into the evening, I felt so much emotion ricocheting around the room that all I could do was sob and hug my kids over and over.

A few days later, I got another call from the USO, this time asking if I'd visit Ground Zero to see the emergency personnel there, who were exhausted after sifting through the rubble for last remnants of life, in any form they could find them. I didn't hesitate: like many Americans, I felt intensely patriotic and wanted to do my part. The next day, a fireboat picked me up on the Upper East Side and brought me down around the tip of Lower Manhattan to dock at a tiny marina outside Ground Zero. To see New York City from a boat so soon after the attack was shocking, the city's iconic skyline now unrecognizable, with an entire neighborhood just gone, wiped off earth forever, leaving behind only an apocalyptic jumble of ash and debris.

At first, the USO asked me only to serve meals from the boat, but when they told me that many of the first responders had heard I was there and had asked if I could come into the site, I wanted to support our heroes. What happened next I'll never forget, as I walked to the edge of "the Pile" and saw a long line of mostly men, who simply wanted, even *needed*, someone to talk with or a shoulder to cry on— and I was happy to provide both. I was so indebted to the men and women who rushed to Ground Zero after the attack, and to this day, I remain grateful that I was able to do something for our country in the wake of one of its greatest tragedies.

THE FOLLOWING summer, my mom suffered her first stroke. None of us could believe it: she was only seventy-two and incredibly young and active for her age, routinely playing tennis and always running around after her grandchildren whenever we came to visit. But it was a bad episode, and I rushed to Hawaii to be by her side and help her in any way I could. No sooner did I return home, though, than she had another stroke, this one so severe that she had to be evacuated from Hawaii to Los Angeles to receive more advanced care. While doctors were checking her into the hospital, my dad, who had made the trip with her, collapsed from pneumonia, and suddenly, I had two parents with serious illnesses on different floors of the same hospital. At the same time, I also had three young children and a husband who was not as supportive as anyone would have expected.

Once I returned to New York, my life in the Hamptons as a self-proclaimed "soccer mom" continued, though, which I welcomed. I loved having three young kids at home and being involved in every aspect of their lives—taking them to school; going to their games, dances, and piano recitals; and volunteering with the other moms to work the bake sales and do the students' hair and makeup before school plays. I never missed an important event, and when Jack became obsessed with Little League, I even learned how to work with him on his windup and grounders so I could be the best boy mom that I could.

ON FEBRUARY 2, 2004, I turned fifty, which is monumental for anyone, of course, but felt like a massive milestone for me as a model, especially because most other women I knew in the industry had retired by age thirty-five, if not on the eve of their thirtieth birthday. But I felt good and wanted to embrace my age, so I decided to splurge and charter a private plane that could fly my entire family and a few close friends to my two favorite destinations, Paris and Morocco, for one big birthday party. (Otherwise, I almost always flew commercial—I am a die-hard environmentalist, after all.) The flight alone was worth every penny, and as we swooped around the Eiffel Tower before landing in Paris, I remember looking out my window with delight, knowing that we'd all be atop the tower the next day for lunch. The following afternoon, Simon and Rupert joined us there for an unforgettable meal, made more extraordinary by the dazzling views of the Seine and the City of Love.

Maybe it was the *esprit de vie* I felt after turning fifty or that I never cared if I looked or acted a certain age, but CoverGirl came back to me the following year, when I was fifty-one, asking me to re-sign with the brand so that I could rep its new line of cosmetics for women over thirty. While I couldn't understand how anyone would be considered old at thirty—or forty, fifty, or sixty, for that matter—I was excited to show other women that we could redefine the numbers and make age into whatever we wanted it to be. And because being a mom was the most important job I'd ever had, I wanted to show other working moms that it was possible to find balance, so in one of my first commercials back with the brand, I ran through the waves with Jack, Sailor, Goodbar Miss, and our dog Maple Sugar—Alexa Ray, who has always been shy, politely demurred—hoping it would show others that family makes a woman beautiful, both on the inside and out. For me, the commercial was the culmination of my greatest dream: I finally had the big happy family I'd always wanted, a feeling strengthened by the fact that Alexa Ray and I had both just attended Billy's wedding to his third wife, Katie Lee. My world felt happy and homey—or, as I said in all my CoverGirl commercials, easy, breezy, beautiful.

BUT THEN, life turned on a dime. As it always does.

Years later, in 2012, after a tumultuous six-year divorce and custody battle with Peter, he called me a liar on national television. I never defended myself, and while I'm not interested in talking about him now, I do want to share a little story.

In June 2006, Southampton High School invited me to be the first woman ever to give a commencement address in the institution's two-hundred-year history. I was honored, and for weeks, I worked on my speech, which I decided to make about environmentalism—an integral ideology for anyone who grew up in the Hamptons, where so much of our life is influenced by the ocean, wetlands, and beliefs of our Native American neighbors, the Shinnecocks, who have reservation land in Southampton and send many children to the same high school. In my speech, I wanted to emphasize to students that they had a right to inherit a healthy environment and a happier future— and the responsibility to pass both on to succeeding generations. For the commencement, I asked Al Gore to autograph copies of his new groundbreaking book on global warming, *An Inconvenient Truth*, which I presented to each graduating senior.

When the day of graduation arrived, it was one of the hottest and most humid on record, even inside the high school, and while I knew it was going to be a flat-hair day, at least my speech would hold up, I thought with a chuckle. When it came time to give the address, the auditorium was so hot and muggy that the air-conditioners were sputtering and chugging on overdrive—and one minute into my speech, the power cut out, everything suddenly going dark and quiet, due to a temporary outage in town. I didn't miss a beat, though, using the incident as an example of what our future would look like if we didn't get a grip on global warming and embrace renewable energy ASAP.

Soon enough, the power came back on, and after I finished my speech, the auditorium erupted in cheers and applause. Smiling out at the sea of clapping hands, I felt flattered as I stepped to the side of the stage, joining a line of other officials standing in front of a folded crimson curtain as the program continued. At someone's signal, the graduates tossed their caps up into the air, one soaring haphazardly across the stage and clipping me so hard across the nose that my eyes began to tear.

Minutes later, I was grateful to have an apparent reason to cry.

That's when it happened. I don't remember who was speaking or what they were saying when, out of nowhere, I felt a startling tap on my shoulder. When I turned, I saw an arm—only an arm—reaching mysteriously through the curtains, and then, after they parted slightly, a man who wasn't part of the ceremony was standing there on the stage, right behind me, trying to remain concealed from the audience.

"Excuse me," he said softly, leaning toward me so I could hear precisely what he was about to say. "I need to tell you that that arrogant husband of yours has been having an affair with my teenage daughter, and he won't knock it off."

I was so stunned that I froze. Immediately, I glanced into the audience, scanning the front row for Peter, who was sitting there with Jack, and as soon as I saw him, Peter's eyes were already trained on my face, as he began shaking his head "no" and mouthing the word silently at the same time.

He knew. Peter knew.

I turned back to the man. "I'm sorry," I said faintly. "Could you repeat that?"

"I said your arrogant husband has been carrying on with my eighteen-year-old daughter, and he won't knock it off."

I knew from Peter's face that he was guilty, and in that moment, I thought I was going to pass out onstage, in front of hundreds of people. I also felt tears begin to well in my eyes, and I bent down to pretend to retie the ribbons of my espadrilles around my ankles so I wouldn't faint or start sobbing onstage. When I stood back up, I asked the man for his card, but he told me he didn't have one and that he was a police officer in town, so all I had to do was to go into the station if I wanted the full story.

I knew the graduation had ended, but I couldn't hear the applause. The room had become like a vacuum, noiseless and airless, and everything around me started to spin as I tried to walk off the stage

371

without collapsing. Somehow, eventually, I made it home, where, out of earshot of the kids, I told Peter to pack a bag and leave. I then went to the police station to learn more.

When your whole world falls apart and you realize in a heartbeat you've suddenly become the cliché middle-aged woman whose husband is having an affair with a much (*much*) younger woman, what do you do?

You call your best friends.

Peter was gone by the time my friends Jill and Mindy made it over, when I was so upset that I couldn't see straight. But I knew that before I did anything else, I had to find out if what the police officer had told me was true. So, the three of us decided to go on a mission, and like the three female detectives of *Charlie's Angels*, we immediately went undercover—which, as I learned from my friends that night, meant searching the computer.

After making sure the kids were absorbed in a movie, the three of us crept upstairs to the study and switched on the family computer, which immediately cast a blue light around the room, illuminating our faces in an eerie electric glow as we clicked and moused our way into a creepy labyrinth of files and photos I never knew existed. While Jill and Mindy had used computers at work, I had never been on one before, but turns out, I was good at guessing passwords, and soon enough, a panoply of frightening email exchanges, incriminating photos, and porn accounts populated the screen like fireworks, and before I knew it, my printer was shooting beaver shots out into the room. It was so insane that it was almost funny, and soon enough, the three of us were doubled over in laughter, as printouts of girls in X-rated poses began piling up on the floor faster than trash outside a greasy takeaway.

One thing I've learned in life is that you always have to be able to laugh, no matter how bad things become.

For the next several weeks, Peter stayed away at my insistence while I told everyone, including the kids, that he was away on a business trip. I wanted time to collect evidence and play it smart, although after two weeks, I had found so much evidence that I knew I had to file for divorce. In early July, I called my attorneys and asked them to quietly initiate the paperwork.

But my gumshoe days weren't over—not yet. I still had to recover my things from the building where Peter and I both had offices, inside a restored train station in Southampton, where I figured I might find a few more clues to what had been happening behind my back for years. First, though, I had to make sure Peter wouldn't be at work, so I bought two tickets to a Yankees game in the city and told him to take Jack. The stratagem worked, and by the time they were hours away on the Long Island Expressway, I was only feet outside the office door with two detectives my personal accountants had insisted I hire. But as soon as I thrust my key into the lock, I could tell it wouldn't work; the lock had been changed. While the detectives acted as though we'd been foiled, I wasn't about to give up—smooth seas don't make for skillful sailors—so I told one of them to give me a hand and shimmied up the building to the first-floor window, where I attached a rope around the AC unit, then to the trailer hitch of my old red pickup truck before pulling the unit out of the wall completely. Afterward, I scaled back up the building and dropped in through the open window as quickly and nimbly as a cat, landing on the office floor and rolling up onto my feet as though I had been born to do detective work. Once inside, I discovered more evidence, which, while upsetting, also corroborated that I needed to end my marriage.

Then, suddenly, my cellphone rang: It was Mindy, who knew all about the caper and was calling to report that the Yankees game had been rained out hours before and that Peter could come walking into the office at any minute.

"Slim," she said emphatically, using her favorite nickname for me, "you gotta get out of there now! Abort, abort!"

I didn't wait. Grabbing my things, I sprinted outside, jumped into my pickup truck, and peeled out of the parking lot like a bat out of hell—my personal hell, that is.

But risk averted. And mission accomplished.

Even though my life was unraveling before my eyes, I knew I had to pull off the greatest acting job of my career yet, pretending to be the happy housewife when I threw Sailor a big party for her eighth birthday that July—to which she had invited the entire school and their parents. On the inside, I felt shattered, but on the outside, I still wore a pretty party dress and smiled so widely it hurt, greeting all our guests and telling everyone, including my kids, that Peter was still away on business.

THEN THE paparazzi came. And they never left.

Someone who knew that my marriage was crumbling and who cared deeply about how it might be portrayed by the press must have started feeding them stories, because suddenly, out of nowhere, the articles began to appear: I was impossible to live with, I was washed up, I was unhappy with my looks, I was desperate to keep my "younger" man. Either way, there was trouble in paradise, the press concluded, speculating that it might be my fourth divorce, which was somehow besmirching for a woman (even though many men, including plenty of famous ones, have been divorced four or even five times without anyone batting an eye).

The narrative changed, however, after the paparazzi discovered that Peter had been carrying on with a teenager, and suddenly, the gossip around our alleged divorce turned into the scandal of the decade, with the names and photos of Peter's girls splashed across the page with our own. It was all so juicy, and the paparazzi couldn't resist descending in droves on Tower Hill, camping at the end of my driveway and even flying planes over the house, photographers dangling out the windows to snap photos of the kids and me in our most private moments and in our most sacred space.

Whenever I left the house, even if only to go to the grocery store, the paparazzi followed me around like a wagon train, and after a day or two, I realized I had become a prisoner in my own home yet again. But this time, there was no way out, and making matters worse, my brother, Greg, and his kids were coming to visit in August, when we wouldn't be able to go to the beach or even out for ice cream without a crowd. At the same time, I wanted my kids to have one last summer before their world exploded. I knew we had to escape, but where could we go where no one would find us?

In my mind, I pictured a dude ranch out west, ringed by thick forests, impassable mountains, and babbling brooks, that was so far removed from any airport or even a paved road that it would be impossible for anyone to trail us. Once there, we'd sleep in teepees or log cabins and go horseback riding by day, then catch fish at night to fry over a dancing campfire. Because I knew my accountants had high-profile clients who probably frequented these types of high-privacy places, I phoned them, telling them exactly what I wanted and asking if they could arrange it because I couldn't use my name or credit cards without tipping someone off.

There was still the problem of leaving the house without being seen by the press. But like Cinderella, the paparazzi always left my driveway by midnight, so in the overnight hours, the kids and I snuck out, hamming it up by pretending to be outlaws in a black car that took us to the nearest airport, where we boarded a private plane for Colorado. When we landed at a tiny airport in the southern part of the state, I was so sure we'd be met by cowboys standing in boots and Stetson hats outside a beat-up old pickup truck that I was shocked when two men wearing suits and earpieces approached us, one who introduced himself as "Rock" before wordlessly grabbing our luggage and escorting us to two blacked-out SUVs in the parking lot.

"Rock to base, suitcases are loaded, subjects are in the car," Rock reported into his earpiece after we had climbed into the cars.

When I told Rock that suits and SUVs weren't exactly what I had had in mind, he didn't respond, as if acknowledging my statement would somehow disrupt the solemnity of our security. But I tried to stay positive as he drove us several hours to a long, low building in the middle of nowhere that looked exactly like a strip mall, without windows, wooden fixtures, or green bushes to suggest otherwise. There were also no woods, streams, or even a pool where the kids could play—at least not without an escort, Rock noted—and just when I thought things couldn't get worse, he showed us to a separate building that housed our room, which looked like the shellacked interior of the same bad shopping mall. On the verge of tears, I told the kids not to step outside the room or unpack anything while Greg and I checked out the rest of the "ranch."

Rock escorted us back to the strip mall building, where the front doors opened with the scream of an alarm, which he explained was "a security precaution." It didn't take me long to realize why that security was necessary: the walls of the room we had just entered were covered with framed photos of politicians like Dick Cheney and other GOP members brandishing massive guns.

We weren't alone with Rock for long before a man with a neck the size of a sequoia walked into the room and introduced himself as the owner of the place. After I told him his "ranch" wasn't quite what I was expecting, especially because I had young children, he insisted on giving us a full tour of the place, promptly leading us through another set of doors that opened with the same screeching alarm.

"Do you have to live with that noise all day long?" I asked, trying to find a point of shared humanity.

"Yes, ma'am," the sequoia answered humorlessly. "Live ammo."

Live ammo? And in the next second, I understood what he meant: we were inside a shooting range, with targets that looked like bodies hanging from a giant conveyer in the darkened distance, which dropped down and rotated whenever the sequoia pushed a button. Each faceless target had a bull's-eye stamped across its head or heart, and before I could say a thing, the sequoia pulled a gun from his belt and shot one of the targets right between the eyes. When I told him that this wasn't what I had in my mind, he simply said not to worry: he'd train me to think otherwise.

The next room we entered on our tour was even creepier and more dystopian, built to look like an old saloon, with bodies slumped over a bar. But this room, much to my dismay, was interactive: the moment we walked in, one of the bodies mechanically spun around on its stool and held up a gun, and after the sequoia shot it "dead," other targets jumped out with more guns, giving any real humans in the room the bleak opportunity to play-act at being active shooters. The last room, however, was the worst of all, designed to look like the cabin of a 747 taken over by terrorists, whom, as the sniper, you were supposed to shoot dead.

Don't get me wrong. I believe that having good aim is worthwhile, and when I lived in Mexico, I used to shoot coconuts off the trees for fun. And I've always loved practicing my sharpshooting skills at state fairs and local carnivals. But using guns as weapons and endorsing violence in any situation, whether real or created, is opposite to everything I've ever believed in, not to mention not what I would ever want for my children during some of our most trying times.

When I told the sequoia we wanted to leave, he said they guaranteed the satisfaction of everyone's stay and that checking out early wasn't a good idea. There were no phones in our room, and no other guests we saw who could help us, and beginning to panic, I finally threatened to march out to the main road unless the sequoia let us go. Finally, he relented, allowing Rock to drive us to a rental car agency many miles away, where we hired the last vehicle in the lot. When I asked the agent where the nearest town was, I almost fell over backward when he said simply, "Telluride."

This is the universe having a moment, I thought. And then, in the next synapse: *So I'll use this moment to my advantage.*

On the drive to Telluride, I told the kids that life doesn't always work out the way you want, and that's why it's so important to learn how to be flexible, roll with the punches, and make the most of your circumstances, whatever they might be. We were now on a great adventure, I added, and while we had no idea where we were headed, it sure was going to be exciting to see what the universe had in store.

While it wasn't easy finding a place to stay in Telluride in the high-summer season, I managed to rent us a little ski chalet in a part of town I'd never been to before. The next morning, I woke up early and excited, rallying the kids to come with me to buy cowboy hats so that we'd be protected from the sun when we went horseback riding later in the day. In the hat store in town, the man behind the counter recognized me the moment we walked in, coming around to hug Alexa Ray and get a better look at Jack, whom he remembered as a baby. The store felt incredibly cozy with the kind man, as he showed us his hats among the faint smell of leather—cozy, that is, until the kind man pulled me aside and said that a reporter had just been in the store asking if he'd seen me, and I knew in a heartbeat that paparazzi had found us. Seeing my sudden panic, the man assured me that our secret was safe with him while adding that we better skedaddle out of town as soon as possible.

"Where do you think we should go?" I asked, trusting him more than my unctuous accountants.

"I know," he said after giving it a moment of thought. "There's a place called Tall Timbers, not too far from here, that you can get to only by helicopter or the narrow-gauge railroad, so not many folks will be able to follow you. It's quiet and remote, and they have a lot of activities for the kids, too."

"Really?" I said eagerly, as I lifted a pile of cowboy hats onto the counter. "That's what we'll do, then."

"All right. I'll call ahead and get you settled," the man said warmly. "And good luck, Christie."

Before we hightailed it out of town, I took Jack up the hill behind the little ski chalet, so I could show him the mountains that made him.

"That's what I was looking at when you were made," I said softly, leaning down to him as I pointed up toward the rugged peaks. "I was constantly seeing all this beauty and drinking this mountain water and breathing in this fresh air when you were made. So, all this is part of you and who you are. Isn't that cool?"

Jack just nodded in awe—he liked knowing he was part-ocean, part-mountain—and we stood there holding hands for a moment before we both saw them at the same time: a group of paparazzi, cameras jostling and jangling around their necks, running up the hill toward us. I grabbed Jack's hand, and the two us sprinted off toward the car, giggling as we jumped in next to the others, then tore off to our next adventure.

The decision was easy with this crowd: everyone wanted to take the narrow-gauge railroad to Tall Timbers, which was a ride to remember. But if we had taken a helicopter, in an extraordinary twist of fate, I would have been right back beside Richard Dick, the pilot who plucked me off the mountain after the helicopter crash.

BY THE time we boarded the railroad, it was night, and as we threaded up the side of shadowy canyons, under snow-capped peaks, and over deep ravines sliced by a single, slender river, we all stared out the open windows, where the moon illuminated everything in a ghostly white, the train clicking skyward toward a place we'd never seen. We were all wondering where we would end up next on our magical mystery tour.

Suddenly, a white horse leaped out onto the train tracks in front of us, followed in the next second by a black horse, the two galloping and dancing in between the railroad ties in a way I never knew horses could, leading us as if they were pulling our car like Santa's sleigh. The kids were ecstatic, and I felt so much magic in the moment, as the horses guided us up those tracks, that I knew in an instant we had made the right decision to do what we were doing, whatever that was.

When the train pulled into Tall Timbers, the place was ringed by so many miles of forest that I knew instantly the kind man from the hat store had been right: few reporters would be able to find us here. Some friendly people were waiting outside to meet us and show us to our room, where they had turned the couches into beds so we could all fit into a single suite. We hadn't eaten all day, and even though it was late and this wasn't the kind of place with room service, the friendly people made us plates of food, all vegetarian, which they wheeled into the suite after we were already in our pajamas, turning the night into a fun family feast.

The next morning, the friendly people asked if we wanted to go "soaring," and within an hour, we were all zooming above the forest on zip lines, riding high over the treetops and the single, slender river, zipping and zooming on one of the longest lines in the country. None of the kids had ever been zip-lining before, and after everything we'd been through, it felt like absolute freedom to them to glide high over the world, their adrenaline mixing with a sense of both fear and fun that left them feeling exhilarated and proud. And I found it remarkable that we had ended up in a place that teaches trust, as Tall Timbers used their zip lines in part to help people on employee retreats or other group trips learn to trust one another unconditionally.

FOR THE next week, we stayed at Tall Timbers and swam in the slender river, hiked to nearby waterfalls, had more zip-lining adventures, and rode our horses up and down the mountains, discovering fresh bear tracks and markings on trees where the big animals liked to scratch their backs. Every day, a weathered old man in the stables helped the kids saddle up their horses, and one afternoon, he even showed them how to hammer railroad spikes so the spikes could be used as picks to clean the horses' hooves. The kids were fascinated by how much the old man knew, and after they ran off to try to hammer their own railroad spikes, the man turned to me and asked if I knew the name of the slender river that circled Tall Timbers and ran through the mountains.

"It's called Animas," the old man said. "The 'River of Lost Souls.' It always pulls people here when they're the most lost in life and need to find their way home again." He paused for a moment, then looked up at me again. "I know you're lost right now," he said slowly. "But you've got your family, and you're such a great little family that I know you'll find your footing, just like those horses do out on the trail." He then handed me a pick and an old iron horseshoe, both rusted from time and good use. "This horseshoe is for good luck," he said, "and this pick is to remind you that you can always find your footing again."

I was so touched that I couldn't speak at first, but the old man, wise in his ways, still had another gift to give.

"Now, listen, little lady, it's time for you to move on," the old man said. "The conductor told me that reporters boarded his train this morning and that they'll be here soon. But I know a place where no one will disturb you, where you can stay out on the trail all day and night, riding and camping with a man whom they call the 'last real cowboy of Colorado.' And it's pure magic."

I was ready for more pure magic, that's for sure. The entire time we'd been away, I'd been calling home to my friends and attorneys, who told me that the press had erupted into chaos, printing nonstop articles about my developing divorce and airing TV shows about it, too, to the point that Judge Judy Shapiro and Raoul Felder were talking about my "character" on the news networks. But I had held up a brave face for the kids so far and was determined to continue to do so.

The next morning, we woke up before the sun rose and started the several-hour drive through the mountains, singing songs together while following the old man's directions until we came to a stable nestled into the bottom of a hill surrounded by an open field of tall grass and wildflowers. Standing next to the horse fence, sure enough, was the cowboy the old man had mentioned, looking like the actor Sam Elliott himself. He held out his hand for each of us to shake before helping us find the right horses to ride and adjusting our saddlebags so we could carry the tents, sleeping bags, cookware, and everything else we needed to spend a few nights out on the trail. Like the old man at Tall Timbers had promised, it seemed like the beginning of a great adventure.

Simply being on horseback and trusting the footing of the majestic animals as they stepped up the rocky trail felt fearless and exhilarating. But what really contributed to the sense of the adventure was the landscape itself, as essentially Coloradan as the last living cowboy who had led us there, under tall peaks laced by deep canyons, through thickets of fragrant pines, and around vast fields of wildflowers. It was all so beautiful . . . until we came around one corner and, suddenly, saw a gulch that was black, burned out, dark, and dead.

"Yep, we had a forest fire here a while ago," the cowboy said with a nod after seeing the expressions on our faces. "It looks pretty bleak right now, doesn't it?" He stopped talking for a moment, and the only sound in the canyon was that of the horses' hooves clacking over rock. "But it's a lot like life," the cowboy started again, patting his horse's big neck as he spoke. "Things can happen that are devasting, rip your heart out, and tear you down to the ground raw. But then you remember that what doesn't kill you makes you stronger. Because just wait until you see what's on that mountain over there."

No one said a word as we followed the cowboy around the curve of the canyon, and as soon as we were on the other side, we saw it immediately: an entire gulch full of gorgeous regrowth, with the thickest, healthiest-looking trees I'd ever seen carpeting the landscape in deep greens and rich browns. And as we kept riding, the canyons looked stronger, healthier, and more resilient around every twist and turn.

"You would never know that we had a fire here that burned this entire mountain down to the ground, just like that other canyon we already rode through," the cowboy said, looking each of us in the eye as though to drive home the resilience and rebirth that was all around us.

I knew it was a great life lesson for the kids, and as I started talking about how hardship can only you make stronger, I felt the weight of that lesson seeping into my own blood and bones, kindling a fire I'd always carried inside.

What doesn't kill you makes you stronger. A phoenix always rises from the ashes. Bloom where you're planted. Christie, baby, you write your own script.

And just like that, I knew my script was far from over. In fact, it was just beginning.

CHAPTER

22

What doesn't kill you makes you stronger, but boy, oh boy, did I get clobbered over and over for a number of years.

It took six years to divorce Peter and settle our brutal custody battle in what my attorney Robert Cohen called "the court case of the decade," as TV crews flooded the Long Island courthouse where our trial played out for months, publicizing the most intimate details of my marriage for everyone to see and savor. Every time I was within a mile of the Suffolk County Family Court, photographers snapped my picture and reporters thrust microphones under my face, asking embarrassing, probing questions about Peter's "sexcapades," as the press put it, after the sordid details of his trysts with teenagers and his predilection for online porn became national news.

I never talked about Peter in the media, except for one time, on the *Today Show*, when I thought I had been asked on to promote a new, exciting project but was then ambushed by Matt Lauer, even though I had been unequivocal that I wasn't interested in airing dirty laundry—and I'm still not. Peter, for his part, was willing to speak with the media, which left the press abuzz with stories, a situation worsened by the cameras that lined the perimeter of my Hamptons home like privet hedges. For years, all I had to do was open up the paper or turn on the TV to see another accusation, mistruth, or scandalous tidbit about me or the situation. Our divorce was the subject of such hot tabloid gossip that the *New York Post* even created a "Peter Meter," with a photo of Peter's face over an illustrated gauge to indicate, based on how well he had performed that day in court, whether he was "cooked" or could "partay." (The meter never once drifted toward "partay.")

The public seemed to have a voracious appetite for the salacious details of our divorce, so much so that anytime I left my home, I felt a little self-conscious wondering whether the person pushing the grocery cart in the market next to me was reading all about it and believed the spiteful or untrue things being said about me. But I never once blamed the press—they were just doing their job—and I even went out of my way to show them compassion, bringing Popsicles and bottles of water to the reporters and camerapeople staked out at the end of my driveway on particularly hot summer days.

Still, it was challenging to overlook many of the things being said about me that were either patently misleading or blatantly false— like the idea that I had requested an open court so the press would be able to attend the trial when, in reality, New York State courts are always open, meaning it's the law, not anyone's personal choice. The idea too that Peter had had any role in buying, financing, or owning any of "our" houses, boats, and other high-priced items, all of which became public fodder in our divorce trial, was so infuriating that it took all my willpower not to clarify that, from the day that he and I were married at my Bridgehampton home, I had always paid for basically everything. (And I mean almost *everything*, to the point where, as I later learned, Peter's nickname for me in his office was "the cash cow.")

During my six years in family court, I also got an unsolicited education on how the system fails children when I saw firsthand how kids can be dragged through their parents' divorce for years on end like mine were. Divorcing someone who's betrayed you on any level should never take so long, cost so much, or be so soul-sucking. Many days, I wondered why anyone took wedding vows to honor and protect when there were no consequences for when they didn't honor, protect, or even extend basic civility. Also, what's the point of a prenup if it can't prevent a divorce from crawling along at snail's pace and affecting the kids on every level? Even today, I still can't believe how many hours of precious life I wasted giving depositions and litigating every silly detail of my life with Peter.

But I always try to find a silver lining, and one positive outcome of the publicity surrounding my divorce was that it helped other people grapple with their divorces and custody battles, which I realized after I received dozens of letters from women (and even men) telling me so. One of those letters was from author Tina Swithin, who had heard me say on the courtroom steps the one time I spoke out there, "Google 'divorcing a narcissist.'" These words, she told me, changed her life after she started the blog One Mom's Battle about her own struggles divorcing a narcissist, which, after hearing my story, she knew didn't apply to just "one" mom anymore. Later, she wrote the book *Divorcing a Narcissist: One Mom's Battle*, and for me, Swithin's blog and book are beacons of light, and I'd encourage anyone going through a bitter divorce or custody battle to read either.

WHILE I was dealing with the injustices of family court and the fictions and fabrications in the press, I also had to confront another ugly monster under the bed that hadn't been there during my other divorces: the internet. I had never been online before, but because everything with Peter was so publicized, sensationalized, and scandalized, our divorce attracted hundreds of online trolls, many of whom wrote lewd or lascivious things about me every chance they got. Suddenly, not only was I waking up to upsetting headlines, but I was also reading running commentary in the cybersphere on how I looked, how I compared sexually to Peter's teen trysts, and whether I was a MILF, a GILF, "fugly," or "the GOAT," all words I didn't know or want to learn. And while some comments were complimentary, I was horrified these conversations were even taking place about me in dark corners of the Web—in part because I knew that if my kids weren't reading them already, they probably would someday. I wanted my life back; more important, I wanted my *kids'* lives back.

But none of us got our lives back, not even after the divorce was settled in 2012, when I gained full custody of Jack and Sailor. For years after, Peter continued to drag me into and out of court over one thing or another.

When the universe wants to teach you "what doesn't kill you makes you stronger," sometimes it really likes to clonk you over the head, because during the divorce trials and tribulations, I endured other hardships, too.

One, which was more a scare than a hardship, involved Alexa Ray, who went through a devastating breakup with the first man she had ever loved and lived with, who also happened to be her band's bass player and manager. It was a tremendous heartbreak for a twenty-three-year-old, especially given that the relationship had cycled on again, off again for months. I knew she was in a lot of pain, and I was there for her, but I was still shocked when I got a call one snowy evening in December 2009 that she had been rushed to a hospital in the city for a suspected overdose. Distraught, I raced into Manhattan, calling Billy on the way to make sure he knew, as a thousand thoughts ran through my mind, including how it was even possible—I knew that Alexa Ray, while sensitive and romantic at heart, didn't have any self-harm tendencies and never drank, smoked, or took a single drug in her life, not even Advil, if she could help it.

When Billy and I were finally admitted to her room, I learned what had really happened: Alexa Ray had swallowed Traumeel, a homeopathic pain medicine, and while she had hoped it would soothe her heartache, she knew it would never kill her. Still, it was a cry for help, and after she was released that same night, she used the incident to speak out about the prevalence of heartbreak-related depression, which I was proud of her for doing.

WHILE CONSTANTLY worrying about my kids, all of them, I also couldn't put into perspective the suffering and agony I saw my parents endure. In 2012, shortly after my mom had her first stroke, my dad was diagnosed with Parkinson's disease and scoliosis, which left him wheelchair-bound and attached to permanent feeding tubes, just so he could eat. Then my mom started to have heart attacks in addition to the strokes. I was constantly on cross-country flights, taking a break only when I had to have emergency back surgery, the whole recovery time for which I spent on the phone with my divorce attorneys.

But then, my mom suffered another heart attack, and this time, the doctors told us that she needed emergency open-heart surgery. Immediately, I flew to California, and while I was waiting in the hospital, Greg picked up my dad, who had been released from the same hospital only days before, driving him back so we could all be by my mom's side.

Before she went in for surgery, I did something I'd never done before: I asked the internet for help, posting on Facebook that I needed a miracle for my mom and asking my friends to send light, love, good wishes, prayers, positive energy, vibes—whatever they were into—to her that morning. Afterward, the kindest words, wishes, and sentiments came pouring in like a tidal wave of support, so beautiful and uplifting that I couldn't wait to read them to my mom. As she listened in her hospital bed, moments before she was scheduled for surgery, I could see the words physically lift her, healing her with love and kindness and creating a prism of love and light around her that followed her as nurses pushed her through the closing doors of the OR.

At the same time, while I was in the waiting room, my dad and brother were about to turn into the entrance of the hospital when they got blocked by a delivery truck with the name "Milagro" written in giant, bold letters on its side. Greg looked at my dad and told him that *milagro* meant "miracle" in Spanish, which could only be a good sign.

When they finally made it into the hospital, at the same moment that Greg pushed my dad in his wheelchair into the waiting room, the OR doors swung open and out walked a doctor to talk to us about my mom. "There's no word to describe it other than 'miracle,'" the doctor said excitedly before explaining that the heart damage they'd detected earlier wasn't present in her pre-op exam. "Your mom just had a medical miracle."

The miracles kept happening, too, so much so that we started calling my mom "Miracle Marge," because she would suffer a stroke or a heart attack, then keep going at the same speed, with little to no lasting effects. At the same time, my parents still needed constant care, and eventually, I convinced them to move from Los Angeles to Sag Harbor, so I could oversee their medical needs directly, building them a beautiful house on the harbor where they could watch the boats go by right from their living room.

BUT IT wasn't easy taking care of my parents and three kids *and* going through an ugly divorce *and* being beaten down by online trolls and the travesties of family court day after day after day. There were many times when I wondered if I would ever recover, but whenever I felt this, I stopped, looked inward, and counted my blessings, which was a long list that always started with Alexa Ray, Jack, and Sailor. Whether I was aware of it or not, I also tried to use the negativity and adversity in my life to propel myself forward and prove everyone wrong, because I was bigger, brighter, and stronger than any injustice or ugly comment made online or in the press. Like a catalytic converter, I wanted to transform the toxic fumes in my life into a fuel I could use to drive myself to new, exciting destinations—which is how I ended up soaring to one of the best places I'd ever been: Broadway.

One snowy day in early 2011, in the middle of my divorce and amid my parents' ever-worsening health scares, my agent, Brian Dubin, called. As usual, he had a stack of offers and emails he wanted to review with me: Was I interested in doing this cover for that magazine? Or what about a feature story? Or an advertisement for a certain company? Then, very nonchalantly, as though he were telling me what he had had for lunch that day, Brian said, "Oh, and *Chicago the Musical* wants to know if you'd consider playing Roxie or Velma, but I know you don't have the time for that, so I told them—"

"Wait a minute, wait a minute," I interrupted, excited by what I was hearing for the first time since I'd picked up the phone. "What did you say? *Chicago the Musical?*"

"Yes, but Broadway is obviously too time-consuming," he said.

"No, wait. They want *me?*" I asked incredulously, wondering what it would be like to have my time consumed by anything other than family court, infuriating press stories, and disheartening hospital visits. Years before, I had also seen Ann Reinking as Roxie in *Chicago* with my parents, and I had thought she was so cool and that it was the best Broadway show I'd ever seen. Plus, I liked how the musical portrayed women who could be strong and tough, yet still sexy

391

and beautiful—which, at that point in my life, seemed an exhilarating assurance, if not a downright liberating one.

Right then and there, I told Brian I wanted to try out for Roxie.

For the audition, I had to learn the song "Roxie"—"the name on everybody's lips"—which starts with one of the longest monologues in all of Broadway. I also had to prepare another song, which was an easy choice, because for years, I'd been doing my own version of "Tonight" from *West Side Story*, singing both Tony's and Maria's parts in a funny, operatic way that inevitably made everyone in the room laugh.

On the day of my audition, I got dolled up in my best vaudeville look, curling my hair and wearing a black turtleneck over tiny black shorts, fishnet stockings, six-inch Louboutins, and a fedora—I was part-*Chicago*, part-*Cabaret*, and all ham, especially for a vegetarian. The audition was exactly how I had imagined one would happen on Broadway, held in a rehearsal room with a piano in one corner and some show people holding coffee cups and sitting listlessly around folding tables. Right away, I launched into my own invented "showbiz-y" choreography while belting out my *West Side Story* duet, which, like a foregone conclusion, caused everyone to crack up. The show's producer, Barry Weissler, then walked into the room, along with Gregory Butler and Gary Chryst from the music video "Uptown Girl." They were there to show me how to do a few authentic Bob Fosse moves, and within minutes, I was singing my numbers to *Chicago*'s top casting VIPs while dancing new steps, all in six-inch heels.

"Well," said Barry, after I had finished and taken a little bow. "I'd be honored to have you join our show."

"And I'd be honored to be part of it," I said, with a wink and a smile.

I never imagined that that little exchange would amount to an official offer, but when my agent called me later that night, he confirmed, then reconfirmed at my insistence, that it had been just that.

While the chance to play Roxie was one of the most thrilling, exciting, and frightening opportunities completely outside my comfort zone I'd ever been offered, I wanted to speak with my parents and kids about it first. So, I hurried over to my parents' house in Sag Harbor, where they had watched with delight as I practiced my numbers over and over before the audition. When I asked my mom about the part, explaining I wouldn't be around as much if I took it, she said simply, "Oh, honey, you have to do it," while my dad, who had lost his ability to speak, signaled for his pen and paper and started scratching some words, which finally took shape: "Take it." He then pumped his fist in the air, and I burst into tears, knowing I had the most loving and generous parents in the world.

AFTER A month of rehearsal, it was finally showtime, and I was bursting with energy and excitement. On opening night, April 8, 2011, I was the first person in the cast to get to the playhouse, which soon became my routine—I adored being in the theater and everything about it. I loved opening the big metal stage door and, after coming in from the loud city streets, slipping inside the quiet playhouse, where I was ushered inside a magical and timeworn world I felt so fortunate to join. I'd walk over the frayed carpet down the darkly lit backstage halls, waving hello to the stage manager and the costume hands, until I reached my dressing room, which looked like something out of an old Hollywood movie, filled with bouquets of flowers and little handwritten cards from friends that I had tucked into the edges of my mirror. As the other cast members started to arrive, poking their heads into my dressing room to say hi and tell me to break a leg, I could hear and feel the theater beginning to come to life, the orchestra tuning their instruments, the actors warming up their own pipes, and the ushers busying about. I was mesmerized as I transformed myself into Roxie Hart, applying her big fake eyelashes, her bright red lipstick, and her little blond bob of a wig.

Before opening night, I peered through a thin break in the curtains to make sure my kids and parents had made it safely to the theater and had found their seats. While I easily spotted my kids, I couldn't see my parents, but then the stage manager told me that he'd helped bring my dad into the theater in his wheelchair, and I was elated that my entire family was there to see my big Broadway debut.

When I dashed out onstage and into the spotlight for the first time, I was stunned to hear the house immediately erupt into applause, cheers, and whistles. I didn't expect it, but I didn't let it distract me either as I proceeded to dance, sing, flirt, throw a temper tantrum, shoot my lover dead, and run from the stage right through the backstage labyrinth and up the ladder to where Roxie sings her first song—all which takes place in the first ten minutes of the show. When I delivered my epic monologue, I was overjoyed when the house laughed.

But the best part came at the end of the evening, when I took my bow and saw the entire audience for the first time all night—I had been far too focused to look out before—and there were my kids, on their feet, clapping fanatically and beaming at me with so much pride. Even Jack, who had been so nervous that he hadn't wanted to come, was bouncing out of his seat, looking around in awe at the other audience members giving the cast a standing ovation. I've never forgotten that moment, which was just what I needed at the time, after everything we'd been through as a family, and in that second, I felt triumphant, resilient, reborn.

During the curtain call, I also saw my dad, clapping as enthusiastically as he could from his chair, and while I didn't see my mom, I figured someone in the audience was blocking her, since she was so petite. But after the show, my dad broke the news that my mom didn't come because she had suffered another heart attack and had to be rushed to the hospital, insisting from the gurney (if not demanding, knowing my mom) that my dad go to the theater without her. So, my dad, the kids, and I all rushed off to the hospital, where we found Miracle Marge, as bubbly and optimistic as ever, flirting with the doctors as she always did and wanting to hear every last detail of my Broadway debut.

That's how my eleven-week run on Broadway started; how it continued was with sold-out shows nearly every night, and each time I stepped onstage to rounds of applause, I felt stronger, tougher, and more resilient. My run on Broadway also seemed to revive my parents, and they came to many shows, my mom now in a wheelchair too, and after most performances, some of the dancers carried her like a queen on a throne, lifting her whole chair up the backstage stairs and setting her down again in my dressing room, where she held court with a glass of champagne in one hand. And I always popped a bottle for the band, cast, and any friends and family who had come to see me. But no matter who was there, the show's crew always felt like family, and every time I was in the theater with them, it was like being inside a music box, the kind you had as a kid, with a tiny ballerina inside who twirled around to a tinkling little tune after you wound the key to watch her dance. I felt honored to be able to perform with that kind of talent onstage, and to this day, I remain indebted to all the *Chicago* cast and crew.

Before my first run was over, the directors asked if I would play Roxie Hart in London's West End, recognized as one of the most eminent live theater districts in the English-speaking world. I couldn't think of a dreamier destination, in part because my longtime assistant Paul had been a footman to the Queen for nine years, so I knew that I would be traveling with one of the most knowledgeable (and kindest) tour guides possible.

For the London run, I took a room at the historic Claridge's Hotel, and once onstage, I tried to bring every ounce of authentic *Chicago* sass to the United Kingdom, in addition to all that jazz (the title of one of the musical's iconic songs). It was thrilling to work on an entirely different stage with a whole new cast of characters—all new except for my Velma, Amra-Faye Wright, whom I adored and who had also come across the pond with me from New York. My kids, out of school on summer break, also flew over to watch me perform, spending a total of ten days in London, when Paul took us to see his old room inside Windsor Castle before we all chartered a boat together down the Thames.

The following winter, back in the United States, I got a call from Barry Weissler, who asked if I would come back to Broadway to play Roxie again, by popular demand. I was flattered beyond my wildest expectations, so I dusted off my dance shoes, put back on my red lipstick, and headed into the city to be Roxie Hart once more, trading my life for hers again by channeling all her grit and determination—and what, I was beginning to realize, had become *my* grit and determination.

When my second Broadway run was just as successful as the first, the directors invited me to headline the show's national tour, which made stops in San Diego, Los Angeles, Boston, and other cities across the country. Traveling around the United States to bring Broadway to new audiences on different stages was both challenging and exhilarating, leaving me with the understanding that I could be as tough as Roxie Hart anywhere I went and anytime I wanted.

During our first stop, in San Diego, I received one of the highest compliments I ever had when an elderly man who'd worked in theater his entire life told me I reminded him of Marilyn Monroe, with whom he'd worked closely as a young man.

During our second stop, in Los Angeles, a dozen classmates of mine from grade school came to see the show—a full-circle moment for me. It was also an honor and a real treat to be onstage in front of Hollywood stars in the historic Pantages Theatre, where I had attended the Academy Awards with my mom and dad when I was nine, sitting right behind Audrey Hepburn and getting led back to my seat by Cary Grant after I got lost trying to find the ladies' room.

Days later, while I was still on tour, I got a call from my mom.

"Honey," she said, her voice raspy and pained. "It's your dad—he's dying. He's not going to make it through the night. You need to come home now."

Within minutes, I was on a plane to the airport in East Hampton, where I rushed to my dad's side at their home on the harbor. When I got there, I found my mom leaning anxiously over him and holding his hand, so I sat on the other side of my dad's bed, taking his other hand, and there the two of us stayed for hours, holding his hands and holding vigil as we talked, cried, laughed, and filled the room with as much love as we could.

When my dad took his last breath, on July 14, 2012, Bastille Day, we were still holding hands. But my mom kept talking to him, and after a while, I covered her hand that held his with mine and looked at her with soft, wet eyes.

"Mom," I said gently, "I think Dad has passed away."

"Oh, honey," she said, looking back at me as her eyes widened. "I don't think I can live without him. I'm so sorry—I know I can't. I hope you understand."

"I know, Mom," I said, tears now streaming down my face. "I understand. But you've got all of us, and we're going to surround you with love."

In that moment, a rainbow suddenly appeared in the kitchen, spreading across the back wall where no glass, crystal, or ray of reflecting light could have created it. It wasn't possible, physically or atmospherically, but there it was nonetheless, and in an instant, my mom and I both knew exactly what—or who—that rainbow was. Since then, I always say, "Hello, Dad, I love you," to every rainbow I see.

After my dad died, we all made sure to surround my mom with as much love as possible. But the same evening, when she came for dinner, she had a stroke, and this time, she didn't bounce back, like she usually did. I think she really wanted to go be with the love of her life. It took her three months to get there, but on the ninth day of the ninth month, at nine in the morning, she died, making her last exit as unforgettable as the entrances she made all throughout life.

If my life has ever seemed lucky or magical, it's only because I've made it that way, and that's a gift I thank my parents for every day. They taught me self-determination, independence, gratitude, how to see beauty in everyone and everything, and how to never stop dreaming, reaching, living, and loving.

And if my dad were still alive today, he would say, *Christie, baby, you write your own script.*

MY SCRIPT isn't done—not yet. I'm still writing it, Dad, and I have no plans to slow down anytime soon.

So, put the needle back on the record, turn up the volume, and cue the encore. The best is yet to come.

Acknowledgments

Wow, writing a memoir is a really big deal, and I never could have done it without the help of some really great and talented people.

Actually, I would have never done it at all without the encouragement of Lisa Sharkey, which came in the form of a gorgeously written letter spelling out a number of reasons why I should write my memoir. Far be it from me to argue with such an articulate missive. So, my first heartfelt thanks goes to you, Lisa, for inspiring and convincing me that I have a story worth telling.

I kept detailed journals my whole life, but writing a memoir is a whole other story! I knew that I would need some help if it was ever going to get done, so I enlisted the help of a great writer, but despite his incredible talents, it didn't sound like me . . . so, take two! Although now I was behind schedule and the pressure was on . . .

Enter the brainy beauty Sarah Toland. As it ends up, we have a lot in common, like our love of the wild seas and rugged mountains, so we were off and running. She got my stories immediately and she loved them, to the point where she even started dreaming them. And she gave them polish and a luster that still sounded like me. Instead of one head, I now had two—and you know that two heads are always better than one! Thank you, Sarah, for helping me capture the magic.

Acknowledgments

Now that we've finished this book, let's get to work on our "sister act"! Cue the hot honey rag!

Fabulously talented and lovely people seem to be as ubiquitous as books at HarperCollins, and I had two of the coolest, editor Maddie Pillari and interior designer Bonni Leon-Berman, helping me. With their talent, professionalism, and cheerful, upbeat demeanor, I could always hear a smile on the other end of the line. I also want to thank David Weiner in legal for spending hours on the phone with us (and seemingly enjoying every moment), in addition to the other folks at HarperCollins, including Lexie von Zedlitz, Robin Bilardello, Heather Drucker, Katie O'Callaghan, Frieda Duggan, and Michael Siebert.

To my legendary agents, Dan Strone and Brian Dubin, thank you for always leading me to the right people at the right time for the past forty-some years. Can you believe this is our third book together? That speaks volumes about our great team effort. Another integral team member is press agent Claire Mercuri, who's ever-ready through thick and thin to put out any fires and pop corks in celebration! Here's to more corks than fires! I also want to thank my former-assistant, now-friend Kate Carlucci for her can-do positive energy and bright smile. Finally, I must give credit to Claire Romine, with emphasis on *credit*, because she worked tirelessly to get all the credits for the photos in this book. Her calm demeanor kept me sane.

A million thanks to my divorce lawyer, Bob Cohen (who called me a "bad picker"), for getting me untangled when I did pick the wrong people.

To my friends who are family—Mindy Moak, Jill Rappaport, Lisa Greenberg, Paul Mesher, and Michael Atmore—and to my three kids, Alexa Ray, Jack Paris, and Sailor Lee, and also Alexa Ray's fiancé, Ryan Gleason: Thank you all for cheering me on. Your unyielding

Acknowledgments

support and exuberant enthusiasm for the snippets I read from the book and the hours-long conference calls going over life lessons with my sisterhood were all I needed to keep writing. Thank you all from the bottom of my heart—I love you all so much.

A special shout-out to living legend Joni Mitchell, whose music has always resonated throughout my soul.

Thank you, too, to a special someone who has been an integral part of my life for decades. You gave me one of my greatest gifts, my daughter Alexa Ray—and the title for this book! Thank you, Billy Joel.

And now that the book is finished, let's all celebrate with a bottle of white, a bottle of red, or perhaps a bottle of Bellissima rosé instead! Cheers, santé, and here's to love!

XO, Christie

Photo Credits

About the Author

CHRISTIE BRINKLEY is a model, actress, entrepreneur, illustrator, photographer, humanitarian, bestselling author, Smile Train ambassador, activist in children's environmental health and wellness, creator and owner of Bellissima wines and prosecco and the clothing line TWRHLL, and proud mom of three amazing kids. In her five decades in the modeling industry, she has been photographed on six continents, in more than thirty countries, and has appeared on more than five hundred magazine covers worldwide. She lives in the Hamptons.